T0095308

THE

FACES

BEHIND THE BASES

Brief biographies of those for whom our military bases were named.

iUniverse, Inc.
New York   Bloomington

The Faces Behind the Bases
Brief Biographies of Those for Whom Our
Military Bases were Named

Copyright © 2009. Mark W. Royston

All rights reserved. No part of this book may be used or reproduced by any means, graphic, electronic, or mechanical, including photocopying, recording, taping or by any information storage retrieval system without the written permission of the publisher except in the case of brief quotations embodied in critical articles and reviews. iUniverse books may be ordered through booksellers or by contacting:

iUniverse
1663 Liberty Drive
Bloomington, IN 47403
www.iuniverse.com
1-800-Authors (1-800-288-4677)

Because of the dynamic nature of the Internet, any Web addresses or links contained in this book may have changed since publication and may no longer be valid. The views expressed in this work are solely those of the author and do not necessarily reflect the views of the publisher, and the publisher hereby disclaims any responsibility for them.
Printed in the United States of America

ISBN: 978-1-4401-3712-9 (sc)
ISBN: 978-1-4401-3713-6 (e-book)

iUniverse rev. date: 5/14/2009

THE FACES BEHIND THE BASES

Ever wonder who they were and why they were picked to be honored? Some were obvious political appointments. Some were ranking officers who were from the area of the location of the base. The great majority were officers, many of flag rank. Most died for their country. Only a few were enlisted men.

Some military bases are named for their location, but most Army, Air Force and some Marine and Navy bases are named for individuals. It is these individuals to which this book is directed.

The bases are alphabetized in the way they are listed in the Military Indexes and by type of service for ease in satisfying your curiosity about a particular base. Each has its own story. Sometimes the information is scarce; others abound in detail. Many are names that you immediately recognize; others a surprise, in that the base has a familiar name but the one for whom the base is named is not the person you thought.

There are only a few details included about the base itself and since there are many bases, most of that information is cryptic.

If the reader desires more detailed information, please check out the particular web sites for all the details available.

FOREWORD

Curiosity is a strange animal. It starts with a "How can" or a "What if" and pretty soon your day is occupied by satisfying this most basic of instincts.

For some it is "I wonder how this works?" The net result may be an entirely new product which can revolutionize an industry. Or, in the case of the author's household, curiosity meant always that there was no ball point pen in the house that was not stripped down to its bare essentials because of the curiosity of one three year old.

The author's curiosity always centered around names. Driving through a new neighborhood or along the Interstate always brought the same question, "I wonder why that exit or street has that particular name."

The names of military bases have long held this same question, "I wonder how they got their name." The Internet provides an easy way to do the basic research and when it was decided to compile such a book, it was to the Internet that the author turned.

The curiosity has been pretty well satisfied but something more was found. The biographies of the persons for whom the bases were named, when looked at in total, provides a history of this great nation. From Fort Knox and Fort Lee, to Grissom and Onizuka Air Force Bases; the entire span of our country's life lies exposed. When one searches for just a particular base, the information may appear disjointed, but reading them all opens the history book.

It is hoped you enjoy reading the author's efforts as much as he did the writing. And thanks again for the Internet.

Cover

The cover is the flag flying over the Grissom Air Reserve Base and was taken by Daniel G. Wolf, Firefighter Lieutenant at Grissom ARB. The cover graphics are by Sarah Apke.

ACKNOWLEDGEMENTS

Most of the information contained in this book was obtained from Web Sites on the Internet. For each individual a number of web sites were researched and the result is a combination of the information found on these sites. The author thanks all of the Internet providers and Web Sites for their diligence which makes possible the compilation of this information by a stay at home researcher.

The author has taken the liberty of adding the Service Academies as most of their buildings were named after heroes who were responsible for that academy's prominence. Pardon the special attention to that of the Naval Academy as the author has a special interest in that institution.

Special thanks to the widows of two classmates who were generous with their memories of their husbands' exploits.

Thanks go also to The U.S. Coast Guard's Historian's Office and in particular Robert M. Browning, Jr., Historian.

Each base shows Source Numbers at its conclusion. Please refer to the closing pages of the book for an identification of these Numbers.

Proofreading and subtle pushes toward improvements, as always, were done by Doris, the author's wife.

Sources

Sources are mostly from the Internet and the generic internet address is listed. The reader is encouraged to log onto the web site and look for more details on the person of interest as well as other persons who might be listed.

Appendices

There are two appendices listed at the conclusion of the book.

Appendix "A" shows the bases listed by type of base with the base name then alphabetized. This can give the reader a quick glance at the name of the person for whom the base was named.

Appendix "B" lists all the persons and bases by the date the person was born. This gives the reader a chance to look at the book from a chronological history.

Dedication

The persons listed and for whom the bases are named become the representatives of all those who served and those who lost their lives to defend our country.

This book is dedicated to those who never had a base or hall named after them, but who served and in many, many instances gave their lives. Since it is impossible to name those millions, the author has selected four to represent them. Those four are Father John Washington, Rabbi Alexander Goode, and Reverends Clark Polling and George Fox. These Chaplains were all aboard the USAT Dorchester serving the spiritual needs of the soldiers who were being transported to fight the enemy.

A German torpedo hit the ship and within minutes it began to sink. The soldiers made their way on deck and began to assemble and put on the scattered life preservers as best they could find them.

The four Chaplains tried to calm the personnel and help them into life rafts. In less than thirty minutes the ship was on its way down and many of the soldiers had no life preservers. The four Chaplains removed their own vests and gave them to the last of the troops.

Two hundred and thirty were rescued out of the nine hundred and two aboard. As they were being plucked from the frigid waters they could see the four Chaplains, Washington, Goode, Polling and Fox standing on the deck with their arms linked together, singing hymns as the ship disappeared under the sea.

It is to them, as representatives of the untold millions of service men and women, that this book is dedicated.

United States Army Bases

Fort A. P. Hill

Fort A.P. Hill is located in Caroline County, Virginia and it was established as a site for maneuvers and heavy weapons training in 1941.

It was named for Confederate General Ambrose Powell Hill. He took command of one of Lee's three Corps in 1863 and was killed during the siege of Petersburg some two years later. He was nearing the age of forty at the time. One week later Lee surrendered at Appomattox Courthouse.

A. P. Hill was born in Culpeper, Virginia and graduated from the U.S. Military Academy at West Point with the Class of 1847. He served in the Mexican-American War and the Seminole Wars. He resigned his commission in March of 1861 and as the Civil War began he was appointed colonel in the 13th Virginia Regiment. He fought in the First Battle of Bull Run and was promoted to Brigadier General. He was a distinguished commander during many battles of the Civil War including Gettysburg.

(Source: 77, 266)

Camp Atterbury

Mount Pisgah & Kansas, Indiana

This was a Basic Training Camp for some 270,000 men during WWII. It also served as an internment camp for Italian and German prisoners of war. This base was named for Brigadier General William Wallace Atterbury.

General Atterbury was born on January 31, 1866 in New Albany, Indiana, the youngest of twelve children. He went to Yale University, graduating in 1886. He began work at the Pennsylvania Railroad and became famous for his service to the railroad during a workers' strike of 1894. He became vice-president of various divisions in 1909-1911.

He was elected President of the American Railway Association in 1916. He was called to Europe during the First World War to be in charge of the railroad system to serve the military. Much of the success of the troop movements in Europe was credited to his quick grasp of the system of the railroads in the various countries.

After the war he returned to the Pennsylvania Railroad and was made President in 1925. He was active in Republican politics. A simple man, he was proud of that trait. He died on September 20, 1935 in Bryn Mawr, Pennsylvania.

(Source: 226, 263, 264, 265)

Fort Belvoir

Fort Belvoir is located in Alexandria, Virginia just south of Washington, DC. While it can be considered to be named after a location, the historical site of Belvoir is worth mentioning.

Belvoir was the home of Lord Fairfax who had a land grant encompassing millions of acres in Northern Virginia. The grant included all the land from where the Rappanock River flows into the Potomac River to the headwaters of both rivers. The headwaters of the Rappanock were easy to establish since it began its journey in the Blue Ridge Mountains. The Potomac, on the other hand, wound its way through a cut in the Blue Ridge and started in the Alleghenies to the west. Young George Washington acted as surveyor for Lord Fairfax as he tried to add to the acreage of his land grant.

The manor house at Belvoir was destroyed by Fairfax County "Patriots" after the Revolutionary War.

(Source: 77)

Fort Benjamin Harrison

This fort is located near Indianapolis, Indiana and was founded in 1908.

It was named for President Benjamin Harrison whose hometown was Indianapolis. Benjamin Harrison was the 23rd President and served one term from 1889 to 1893. It was during his term that federal spending reached one billion dollars. He was born in North

Bend, Ohio on August 20, 1833 and died on March 13, 1901 in Indianapolis. He was twice married, a lawyer and a Presbyterian.

He was a grandson of President William Henry Harrison. He attended Miami University at Oxford, Indiana. He served in the Union Army during the Civil War and was appointed a colonel in the Indiana Volunteer Infantry Regiment. He became the President of the United States by winning a large majority of the Electoral College votes while losing the popular vote count by over 100,000 votes. During his administration the battle over tariffs was fought. The Treasury had a surplus and many thought the reduction of tariffs would make the country grow stronger. William McKinley and Senator Nelson Aldrich (grandfather of Nelson Rockefeller) were advocates of higher tariffs. Out of this battle came a payment of two cents per pound to sugar growers for their crops in return for lower tariffs on imported sugar.

Benjamin Harrison signed into law the Sherman Anti-trust Act to protect trade and commerce. It was the first federal law of its kind. By the end of his administration the surplus had vanished and he was defeated in his bid for reelection, losing to Grover Cleveland.

During his administration six states were admitted to the Union; North Dakota, South Dakota, Montana, Washington, Idaho and Wyoming.

(Source: 77)

Fort Benning

Fort Benning is located in Georgia and was established as Camp Benning in October, 1918 with its first mission to train troops for World War I. It was temporarily closed after the War but was expanded by the Civilian Conservation Corps as one of their work making jobs.

It was active in World War II as the home of the 555th Parachute Infantry Battalion.

Fort Benning was named for Confederate General Henry L. Benning who was a native of Columbus, Georgia. Benning was born on April 2, 1814 and died July 10, 1875 in Columbus, Georgia. He was a lawyer and a judge before the war and returned to that profession afterwards. He attended Franklin College (now the University of Georgia) and graduated in 1834. He was opposed to desegregation. He was a member of the Georgia Supreme Court and argued that the state supreme court was not bound by the U.S. Supreme Court on the matters involving the Constitution.

His political zeal became a problem when he became an officer in the Confederate Army as he questioned the right of the Army to do certain things, such as conscript persons. His early battle decisions were questionable but at the end he was known as the "Rock" for his battle qualities. He was wounded in the Battle of the Wilderness and was kept from action for many months. He returned in time to be a part of the Siege of Petersburg and was heartbroken when Lee surrendered at Appomattox Courthouse.

He returned to law practice after the war after finding that his house and all his savings had been lost during the war. He was stricken with apoplexy some ten years later and died in 1875. He is buried in Longwood Cemetery in Columbus, Georgia.

(Source: 77)

Camp Blanding / Fort Blanding

Camp Blanding is located near Stark, Florida. It serves the National Guardsmen, the Active Army and Reserves from all over the nation. It is named for Lieutenant General Albert H. Blanding.

Albert H. Blanding was born in Lyons, Iowa on November 9, 1876 but moved to Florida when he was two. He attended East Florida Seminary and graduated in 1894. In 1899 he joined the Florida National Guard and commissioned a captain. In 1916 he led the Second Florida Infantry against Pancho Villa. In 1917 he was activated to serve in World War I and he commanded the 53rd Brigade, 27th Division. For his service he was awarded the Distinguished Service Cross. Blanding served Florida and the Nation in many capacities, staying on active duty in the Florida

National Guard. One of his duties was the appointment as Chief, National Guard Bureau. He retired in 1940 with an honorary rank of Lieutenant General. He died on December 26, 1970.

(Source: 77, 105, 176, 253)

Fort Bliss

Fort Bliss is located in El Paso, Texas with a size as large as Rhode Island. It was built in 1849 and for a period was controlled by the Confederacy. One of its previous commanders was General of the Armies John "Black Jack" Pershing. It is the largest tract of unrestricted air space in the United States, containing some 1.1 million acres.

Fort Bliss is named for Lt. Col. William Wallace Smith Bliss, a son-in-law of Zachary Taylor. He was also Taylor's Adjutant General during the Mexican-American War and later his secretary.

William Wallace Smith Bliss was born in Whitehall, New York on August 17, 1815 and died August 5, 1853. His father was Captain John Bliss who had graduated from West Point with the Class of 1811. William Bliss entered West Point in 1829 when he was fourteen, graduating in 1833 before he was eighteen. He was noted for his mathematical ability and after serving at a post in Alabama, he returned to the Military Academy as an Assistant Professor of Mathematics.

He served in various capacities in the Army including Chief of Staff to the Commanding General of the Florida War. He fought in the Battle of Palo Alto and Buena Vista during the Mexican War and was promoted to Lieutenant-Colonel for meritorious and gallant service. During his service time he was under General Zachary Taylor. He was fluent in thirteen languages and was known as the best linguist in America.

In 1848 he married the youngest daughter of Zachary Taylor and when Taylor became President, Bliss became his private secretary. Since Taylor's wife took little interest in the White House, the duty fell to the wife of Bliss. Taylor died in 1850 followed by his wife in 1852. Bliss died of Yellow Fever in 1853.

In 1854 the fort at El Paso became Fort Bliss even though Bliss had never visited the base. He was buried in New Orleans but when the cemetery was moved in 1955 his remains were reinterred at Fort Bliss.

(Source: 77)

Fort Bragg

Fort Bragg is located in North Carolina near Fayetteville. It was established in 1918 near the end of World War I. It began as Camp Bragg and was named a fort in 1922. It was named after Confederate Army General Braxton Bragg.

Braxton Bragg was from North Carolina having been born in 1817. He graduated from West Point with the Class of 1837 and was known as a strict disciplinarian. He fought in the Seminole Wars as well as the Mexican-American War. His use of artillery tactics revolutionized the methods of artillery movement.

His Civil War activities included being a colonel and a major general in the Louisiana Militia, Commanding Department of Alabama and West Florida, Commanding Army of Pensacola, and Commanding Army of Tennessee. He was in charge of many other southwest Confederate activities, ending up as permanent commander in the west.

After the war he was Alabama's Chief Engineer and died while walking with a friend in Galveston, Texas on September 27, 1876. He was buried in Mobile, Alabama.

(Source: 77, 57)

Fort Campbell

Fort Campbell is located near both Hopkinsville, Kentucky and Clarksville, Tennessee. After early confusion as to the delivery of the mail it was officially designated as Camp Campbell, Kentucky. It was opened on November 15, 1941 and for most of the war was the training camp for many of the armored divisions. In April of 1950 it was officially designated as a permanent base and given the name of Fort Campbell. It was named in honor of the last Whig Governor of Tennessee, Brigadier General William Bowen Campbell.

(Source: 77)

Fort Carson

This base was established in 1942 at Colorado Springs, Colorado and was named after the Army scout, General Christopher "Kit" Carson. It started as Camp Carson and received full stature in 1954 and was renamed Fort Carson.

Kit Carson was born December 24, 1809 and died May 23 1868. He was best known for his exploits as a frontier scout. He was born in Madison County, Kentucky and his family was close friends with the Boone Family. He moved to Franklin, Missouri at an early age and settled on land near the sons of Daniel Boone. After his father's death when Kit was seven, he was forced to drop out of school and go to work. After a time he was apprenticed to a saddle maker and while working he would hear tales of travelers from the West.

At sixteen he signed on with a caravan heading west. In Taos, New Mexico he began to learn the skills of the trapper, becoming fluent in Spanish as well as Indian languages. He married an Arapahoe and had a daughter when he was around twenty four. He followed the fur trapping until 1837. His wife had died and he married a second Indian wife who left him as her tribe migrated to other spots. The beaver trapping waned as the styles changed and the demand changed from beaver to silk hats. By 1842 he met and married into

8

the family of a prominent Taos family. He converted to Catholicism and raised eight children.

He became a guide for General Fremont. The first expedition was a success and resulted in a wave of caravans heading west.

His second scouting expedition was to map the Oregon Trail. A second objective was to locate the fabled Buenaventura River which was supposed to run from the Great Lakes to the Pacific Ocean. It was Carson who showed it to be only a fable. This second expedition, which included near starvation in the Sierra Nevada, led to another report to Congress. Because of these reports, Fremont and Carson were becoming famous.

Carson became involved in the Mexican-American War in California and he was appointed as a lieutenant. Carson was the person assigned the duty of reporting to President Polk the occupation of California by Americans. Throughout the war his legend continued to grow.

During the Civil War, Carson was active on the Union side rising to the rank of Colonel. He later fought in the Indian Wars. For his bravery he was awarded the brevet rank of Brigadier-General. After the Civil War and the Indian Wars were concluded he took up ranching. He died of an aneurysm on May 23, 1868 and was buried in Taos, New Mexico.

(Source: 77)

Fort Chaffee

Fort Chaffee is located near Fort Smith, Arkansas and is used as a training center for the National Guard and the Reserve Corps. It was built in 1941 and was closed in 1997 but was kept as a Reserve Training Component.

It was named for the son of Major General Adna R. Chaffee who was born April 14, 1842 and died November 1, 1914. Chaffee, the senior, was born in Orwell, Ohio and enlisted in the Union Army at the outbreak of the Civil War as a Private. He fought in the Battle of Antietam and was promoted to Sergeant. He was commissioned in 1863 and was promoted to First Lieutenant in 1865. For meritorious service he was brevetted a Captain. He took part in the Indian Wars and later played a key role in crushing the Boxer Rebellion.

Adna R. Chaffee, Jr. was born in Junction City, Kansas on September 23, 1884. He graduated from the United States Military Academy with the Class of 1906. He fought in World War I, first as a Major then as a Colonel. In the 1920's he helped develop the armored concept of the Cavalry and predicted that mechanized forces would be the dominant factor in the next war.

General Chaffee took command of the 7th Cavalry Regiment in 1938. He died of cancer on August 22, 1941.

(Source: 77, 105, 266)

Fort Crook

Fort Crook was located near Bellevue, Nebraska. Before that, there was a base near Glenburn, California that began in 1857 and was named for George Crook, who as a lieutenant, recovered there from wounds received. In 1890 there was a post established near Bellevue, Nebraska that was also named for General George Crook. It is now a part of Offutt Air Force Base.

George Crook was born on September 8, 1828 in Taylorsville, Ohio. He received an appointment to the United States Military Academy and graduated with the Class of 1852. His early military career was as an Indian fighter in California and Oregon. It was during these battles that he was severely wounded and made his recovery at the base that was named for him in Glenburn, California.

In 1861 he returned east and was made Colonel of the 36th Ohio Volunteer Infantry. He fought in many battles during the Civil War in Virginia. He served under General Sheridan in battles throughout the Shenandoah Valley.

After the war he returned to his duties as an Indian fighter, battling the Sioux and the Apache. In 1888 he became Commander of the Division of Missouri and was there until his death. He died on March 21, 1890 and was buried in Arlington National Cemetery.

(Source: 77, 273)

Fort Detrick

This fort is located in Frederick, Maryland and is an Army Medical Command installation. It owes its name to a small airport located on its base. The airport was named by the Maryland National Guard for Squadron Surgeon Major Frederick L. Detrick who served in World War I and died in 1931.

Frederick Louis Detrick was born on April 21, 1889 in Frederick County, Maryland where his ancestors had lived since before the Revolutionary War. He was a graduate of the Rockefeller Institute and interned at Bellevue Hospital in New York City. He entered the military in 1918 and was commissioned a lieutenant in the Medical Reserve Corps.

Detrick served in Europe from March, 1918 as a battlefield physician during major battles such as St. Mihiel and Meuse/Argonne. He returned to Baltimore and opened a private practice. He was on the staff of Johns Hopkins University Hospital.

He rejoined the military and served with the Maryland National Guard. In 1931 he died after suffering three heart attacks. At this time the Maryland National Guard named their air base in Frederick after Detrick who was the one most respected by them.

(Source: 68, 77, 267)

Fort Devens

Camp Devens was established in 1917 in Massachusetts near Harvard and Ayer and was closed in 1996.

It was name for General Charles A. Devens and was built on land occupied by a military garrison in 1860. General Devens was a

Brevet Major General in the Civil War and who served as Attorney General for President Rutherford B. Hayes who was President from 1877 to 1881. Originally the base had been slated to be named for Major Simon Willard who was known for his trade with the American Indian but who was not a regular army officer.

General Devens was born on April 14, 1820 in Charleston, Massachusetts and graduated from Harvard in 1838. His degree was a doctor of laws and he followed a public career that included being a U.S. Marshall and a solicitor for the City of Worchester. In 1861 he entered the Army and fought in the Battles of Fredericksburg, Chancellorsville and Cold Harbor.

After the war he returned to public service in Massachusetts serving as a judge. He became Attorney General in 1877. He died on January 7, 1891.

(Source: 20, 268, 260)

Fort Dix

Fort Dix is located in Burlington County, New Jersey. Its construction began in 1917 and was named after Major General John Adams Dix.

John Adams Dix was born in Boscawen, New Hampshire on July 24, 1798. His father was Timothy Dix, a lieutenant colonel in the United States Army. His early education was at private academies, including Phillips Exeter Academy. When the War of 1812 broke, he was only fourteen but obtained a commission in the Army. He served as an Ensign in the Battle of Niagara. His father was killed in a battle in 1813. Dix remained in the Army while trying to help support his siblings and step-mother. He rose to the rank of Major and while still in the Army, studied law. In 1828 he resigned from the military to manage a part of his father-in-law's holdings. He became involved in the politics of New York and by 1833 he was Secretary of State of New York.

In 1850 he was appointed to the unexpired term of United States Senator Silas Wright. His strong anti-slavery sentiment gained him the enmity of Southern Democrats and an opportunity to become Secretary of State of the United States was lost. In 1849 he retired from politics and became president of two railroads. In 1861 he returned to the political scene and was appointed Post Master of New York. For a short period he was the United States Secretary of Treasury. During this time he issued the command for which he is remembered. Sending a telegram to New Orleans just before the onset of the Civil War, he warned anyone who might be considering taking over the Revenue Cutter stationed there, "If anyone attempts to haul down the American flag, shoot him on the spot."

He was replaced as Secretary of Treasury when Abraham Lincoln became President but was given the rank of Major General. As such he became the ranking volunteer General during the war. He was too old for active service but was put in charge of certain headquarters of the Military Departments. He was known for his prompt action in quelling riots that broke out in New York City during the War. In 1872 he was elected Governor of New York and during his one term he fought the corruption of Tammany Hall. He died on April 25, 1879 in New York City.

(Source: 39, 77, 290, 291)

Fort Douglas

This fort is located in Utah and was established in 1862 for the purpose of guarding the Overland Mail Route. It was named in honor of Illinois Senator Stephen A. Douglas. It began as a Camp and was named a Fort in 1878.

Stephen A. Douglas was born in Brandon, Vermont on April 23, 1813. He moved to Illinois and became active in the Democratic Party. He served in the House of Representatives from 1843 to 1847 when he was elected to the US Senate.

Though only five feet tall, he was known for his fiery orations. At the age of twenty eight he became judge of the Illinois Supreme Court. When elected to the Senate he was on the Committee on Territories and this brought him into the slavery question. When territories became states the choice had to be made as to whether they would be admitted as a slave state or a free state. He sponsored the Kansas-Nebraska Act which repealed the Missouri Compromise. A part of this act was to allow the territory to decide its slavery issue after being admitted to the Union. As a result the state of Kansas was in turmoil.

Abraham Lincoln was one of the anti-slavery leaders and he ran against Douglas for the Senate in 1858, basing his campaign on the Kansas-Nebraska Act. During one of the now famous Lincoln-Douglas debates, Lincoln enraged the South for his argument that the territories could exclude slavery by unfriendly legislation.

Douglas missed being the Democratic nominee for President because of the "Bleeding Kansas" condition and later broke with President Buchanan over the slavery issue. He defeated Lincoln for the senate but the debates brought Lincoln to the Nation's attention. The election of 1860 went to Lincoln as the Southern Democrats refused to support Douglas and instead supported John C. Breckinridge.

Douglas worked to oppose secession and pledged his support to Lincoln. Douglas died of Typhoid fever in Chicago on June 6, 1861.

(Source: 270, 271)

Fort Drum

Fort Drum is located in the Thousand Islands region of New York State. It has been used as an Army training base since 1908. The son of Ulysses S. Grant, General Frederick Dent Grant came to this area which was rich in military history, and located a permanent base to train soldiers. It was first called Pine Camp but became Camp Drum in 1951, named for Lt. General Hugh A. Drum who had commanded the First Army during World War II. It was designated as Fort Drum in 1974.

Hugh Aloysius Drum was born on September 19, 1879 and died on October 3, 1951. Born in Fort Brady, Michigan, he graduated from Boston College in 1898 and joined the U.S. Army. He was assistant Chief of Staff to General John J. Pershing and in 1918 was promoted to colonel and became the Chief of Staff of the First Army, American Expeditionary Forces.

Later he served as Director of Training at Fort Leavenworth, Kansas. He fought a publicized battle with General Billy Mitchell over the future of the Army Air Corps. He lobbied against its division from the Army into its own service. He served in the Pacific and there ran into another ambitious officer, George S. Patton, Jr. In 1939 he was passed over as Chief of Staff. General George S. Marshall became the Chief of Staff in his place. He was promoted to Lt. General and retired from service in 1943. From 1944 until his death he was President of Empire State Inc.

(Source: 77, 105)

Fort Eustis

This fort is located in Newport News, Virginia on what was known as Mulberry Island. It once was the home of John Rolfe, husband of Pocahontas. The camp was founded in 1918 and was the named for Brevet Brigadier General Abraham Eustis. It became a training school for the Transportation School. Before that it served as a federal prison used to house bootleggers during Prohibition. Today it is the home of the Transportation Regiment.

Abraham Eustis was born on March 26, 1786 and died on June 27, 1843. He was born in Petersburg, Virginia and was educated at Harvard College and Bowdoin College. He entered the Army in 1808 and fought in the War of 1812 and the Seminole Wars. In 1830 he was named Commander of Fort Monroe which guards the entrance to Hampton Roads, Virginia. In 1838 he became commander of Fort Butler which was a military post built to control the forced evacuation of the Cherokee Indian.

In 1918 an observation school was established in Newport News, Virginia and it was named Fort Eustis. He died June 27,

1843 in Portland, Maine and was buried in Mount Auburn Cemetery in Cambridge, Massachusetts.

(Source: 26, 77, 157)

Fitzsimons Army Hospital

This base is located in Aurora, Colorado and was founded in 1918 during World War I to treat the many casualties from chemical weapons in Europe. It is famous for its treatment of military and government celebrities, including Dwight Eisenhower. John Kerry was born at the Fitzsimons facility.

The base was named in 1920 for Lieutenant William T Fitzsimons.

William T Fitzsimons is considered the first American officer killed during the First World War. He was killed in a German Air raid on a base hospital in France on September 4, 1917 along with three enlisted men.

He graduated from St. Mary's College in 1906. As a young physician from Kansas City, he went to Europe with the Harvard University Units. He was dressing wounds of British Army Officers when he was killed by a shell dropped by a German bomber.

(Source: 77, 272)

Fort George G. Meade

Fort Meade is located in Maryland and is named for General George G. Meade. It was built in 1917 and trained more than 400,000 soldiers during the First World War. Major Peter F. Meade, nephew of General George G. Meade, was in command of the remount station during the war. In 1928 it was re-designated Fort Leonard Wood, but regained its original name when Pennsylvania congressmen held up an appropriations bill.

General George Gordon Meade was born in Cadiz, Spain on

December 31, 1815 while his father served as a naval agent for the U.S. Government. The father died in Spain and the family returned to the United States. George G. Meade entered the United States Military Academy and graduated with the Class of 1835. He fought in the Seminole Wars and resigned his commission to work as a civil engineer for a railroad. He married Margaretta Sergeant, the daughter of John Sergeant who was Henry Clay's running mate in the presidential election in 1832.

He reentered the Army in 1842 as a second lieutenant. He served in the Mexican-American War and was promoted to first lieutenant for gallantry during the Battle of Monterrey. After the war he was involved in lighthouse design and construction and was responsible for the design of a hydraulic lamp that was adopted by the Lighthouse Board.

When the Civil War broke out he was a captain and was promoted to Brigadier General of Volunteers. He was assigned command of the Second Brigade of the Pennsylvania Volunteers and worked to build the defenses around the Capitol.

He was wounded in the Battle of Glendale but partially recovered his strength by the Second Battle of Bull Run. He was given command of the Third Division, Army of the Potomac. He fought in the Battle of South Mountain, winning the acclaim of General George Hooker. He was wounded again in the Battle of Antietam as he took over for the wounded Hooker. He fought through many of the battles of the Civil War, including Fredericksburg, Chancellorsville and Gettysburg. It was his decision to stay and fight the Battle of Gettysburg after conferring with many of his staff officers. When Lee began his retreat back to Virginia, Meade's Army followed but exhaustion kept them from delivering a more severe blow to Lee's Army. He was promoted to Major General in August of 1864. His army was a part of the siege of Petersburg and Richmond. This lasted until April of 1865 when Lee surrendered at Appomattox Courthouse. Though severely ill he mounted his horse and rode to announce the surrender to his troops.

At the end of the war he was placed in command of military districts on the east coast. He died in 1872 after pneumonia set in caused by a flare up of the old wounds suffered during the war.

(Source: 26, 77)

Fort Gillem

Fort Gillem is located in Forest Park, Georgia. The fort began in 1941 when the Atlanta General Depot was moved to this location. Fort Gillem was named for Lieutenant General Alvan C. Gillem II, who was born in Nogales, Arizona in 1917. He enlisted in the Army in 1935 and received a congressional appointment to the United States Military Academy, graduating in 1940. He is the son of Lieutenant General Alvan C. Gillem, Jr. and the grandson of Colonel Alvan Gillem.

After graduation he entered pilot training and was given his wings in 1942. He served as a flight instructor for two years and in April 1943 he went overseas as a staff officer of the Mediterranean Allied Air Forces. He flew both the British Spitfire and the American P-51 and was credited with destroying three enemy aircraft.

After the war he was a part of the original group that set up the Strategic Air Command. From there he went to the CIA and later became Deputy Commander of the 31st Fighter Wing at Turner Air Force Base in Georgia. In 1951 he became Commander of the 108th Fighter Bomber Wing. Later in 1951 he went to England as Commander of the Royal Air Force Station Upper Heyford, a part of the SAC's 7th Division. Returning to the United States, he held commands and was promoted to Brigadier General in 1961. In July 1963 he was promoted to Major General. He held various commands in the Strategic Air Command including Director of Operations.

(Source: 25, 26)

Fort Gordon

Fort Gordon is located in four counties in Georgia and is the home of the United States Army Signal Corps. It was built in 1941 and was named for Major General John B. Gordon, CSA. It began as a camp and was designated a fort in 1956.

John B. Gordon was born in 1832 on a plantation in Upson

County, Georgia and died in 1904. He attended the University of Georgia and even though he held the highest grade point in his class he dropped out before graduation. He was the manager of his father's coal mine when the Civil War broke out.

With no military background he entered the Southern cause as captain of a company of mountain men. In four years he became known for his military skill and at the end was the commander of one-half of Lee's army. He was only thirty-three years old when he led his army to the surrender at Appomattox Courthouse, Virginia.

Much of his success came from his boldness and his ability to inspire his soldiers. He was wounded five times at the Battle of Antietam. He fought at Gettysburg, the Wilderness Campaign and the Spotsylvania Courthouse. He was weak as an administrator but more than made up for it with his tactical skills.

After the war he returned to Georgia and was one of the foes of Reconstruction. It was accepted that he was the leader of the Ku Klux Klan. He was elected to the U.S. Senate in 1872 and was one of the sponsors of the Compromise of 1877 which gave the election to Rutherford Hayes in exchange for the removal of Federal troops from Georgia. He was Governor of Georgia and for a quarter century he was dominant in Georgia politics. He was very active in veteran affairs and even though when he left political life it was tainted by a scandal concerning the appointment of his successor as senator, he was considered the "Living embodiment of the Confederacy."

(Source: 77, 103)

Fort Hamilton

Fort Hamilton was the first built in Ohio in 1791 in Indian Territory and is now the location of the city of Hamilton, Ohio.

(Source: 103)

Fort Hamilton

Brooklyn, New York

This fort was built to defend New York and was named after Alexander Hamilton, the first Secretary of Treasury. Alexander Hamilton was born in the British West Indies, out of wedlock, the son of Rachel Lavien and James A. Hamilton in 1755 (or 1757). Because of his lack of legal parentage he was not allowed to attend the church school. As a result he received private tutoring and became a student of the family library of books. Hamilton worked as a clerk at an import-export company after he was abandoned by his father and shortly thereafter the death of his mother.

In 1772 he was able to make his way to New Jersey where he attended a grammar school and later King's College (now Columbia University). His first political writings were against the writings of a Church of England clergyman who defended the Tory cause. While he was on the side of the revolutionaries, he defended those on the other side from mob vengeance.

As the Revolutionary War began he joined a New York volunteer militia. He studied tactics and military history and made successful attacks on British batteries. He asked for and became an aide to General Washington and rose to the position where he was allowed to issue orders over his own signature.

He wanted a command post and was finally given command of a New York light infantry division. He was heavily responsible for the surrender of Cornwallis at the Battle of Yorktown. At the end of the war he was frustrated with the weakness of the Articles of Confederation and proposed a stronger central government, especially one with the ability to tax. Many soldiers and service providers were not paid for their efforts and he supported their efforts to receive payment. He surrendered his commission and became a representative from New York to the Congress of the Confederation.

As a way to a more centralized government, Hamilton proposed that the Articles of Confederation be revised. This led to the call for a constitutional convention. He drafted a constitution based on the convention debates. While it was never presented, most of its features found their way into the Constitution. He, along with John Jay and James Madison, wrote some 85 essays defending the proposed constitution. These came to be known as the Federalist Papers.

In 1789 he became the first Secretary of the Treasury and served until 1795. Active and very vocal in politics, he made many enemies. He considered himself more than just the Secretary. He lobbied for a strong central banking system and helped establish the U.S. Mint.

One of the first sources of tax funds was an excise tax on whiskey. This caused the Whiskey Rebellion led by whiskey manufacturers in Western Pennsylvania. A strong showing by military forces squelched the rebellion and showed the power of a strong central government.

Known for his temper, over the years Hamilton had challenged others to duels. In the end he had a duel with Aaron Burr, the Vice President of the United States. The duel was fought along the west bank of the Hudson River near the same spot where Hamilton's oldest son had lost his life in a duel.

It has been argued that Hamilton deliberately missed the first shot of the duel. Burr's shot did not miss and Hamilton died from its effect the following day.

(Source: 26, 77)

Fort Hood

Fort Hood is located in Texas between Waco and Austin.

It was named for General John Bell Hood, CSA. The base was selected in 1942 for its wide open spaces to satisfy the need to test tank destroyers. It reached a strength of 95,000 troops in late 1943. It also housed some 4000 prisoners of war.

General John Bell Hood was known for his bravery and aggressiveness. He was successful in lower commands but less so as he was given larger units.

Hood was born in Owingsville, Kentucky. He was appointed to the United States Military Academy and graduated with the Class of 1853. He ranked low in his class and was beset with disciplinary problems. He was commissioned a second lieutenant and served in California. Later he served under Colonel Robert E. Lee in Texas and there received his first wound of many, an arrow through his left hand.

He resigned his U.S. Army commission at the onset of the Civil War, choosing to serve in a Texas Unit, as Kentucky was slow to enter the war. In September of 1861 he was promoted to Colonel and given command of the 4th Texas Infantry.

This Texas Brigade became a part of the Army of Northern Virginia. In the Battle of Gaines Mill, his troops broke through the Union lines, the most successful performance in the Seven Days battle. In the Second Battle of Bull Run, he nearly destroyed the Union Army but became involved in a dispute over his use of captured ambulances. He was arrested because of this dispute and had it not been for the personal intervention of Lee he would have been ordered to leave the Army. During the Maryland Campaign his Texas forces yelled for his return and Lee restored Hood to his command.

He was wounded severely at the Battle of Gettysburg, losing the use of an arm. After recuperation he rejoined his men and fought at the Battle of Chickamauga. Here he again was wounded and his right leg was amputated just below the hip. It was assumed that this was a fatal wound and the doctor sent the severed limb along with the patient so they could be buried together. Again he survived and was promoted to Lieutenant General in September of 1863.

He ended up fighting against Sherman as he advanced toward Atlanta, conducting campaigns that were characteristic of his aggressive nature. None were successful in breaking the Siege of Atlanta. In the end he evacuated the City of Atlanta, burning as many military supplies as possible. After a number of unsuccessful attempts to defeat the Union forces in the Tennessee area he retreated toward Mississippi and then at the end of the war surrendered his Texas troops. He was paroled in Natchez, Mississippi on May 31, 1865.

After the war he became a cotton broker and also president of an insurance business. In 1868 he married and fathered eleven children in ten years including three sets of twins. His insurance business was ruined during a yellow fever plague in 1878-79. He, his wife and oldest child were all killed by this plague within days of each other. The ten orphans were adopted by families in five states including New York.

(Source: 77)

Fort Hunter Liggett

This fort is located in southern Monterey County, California and is used as a training facility. The land was purchased from William Randolph Hearst in 1940. There was a hotel on the base that was used by Hearst as a hunting lodge. It was named for General Hunter Liggett.

Hunter Liggett was born in Reading, Pennsylvania on March 21, 1857 and died on December 30, 1935. He graduated from the United States Military Academy in 1879. His first service took him to the Montana and Dakota territories. He then served in the Spanish American War and the Philippine American War. In 1917 he was selected as Commander of the 41st Division in France. He directed the final phase of the Meuse-Argonne Offensive after participating in the Second Battle of the Marne.

He died in San Francisco in 1935 and is buried at the San Francisco National Cemetery.

(Source: 77)

Fort Irwin

Fort Irwin is located in the Mojave Desert near Barstow, California. The area is rich in history from the earliest days of the Indians, the Spanish travelers, the Gold Rush and the borax boom at Death Valley. It began as a military installation in 1940 as the Mojave Anti-Aircraft Range. In 1942 it was renamed to honor Major General

George Leroy Irwin by President Franklin Roosevelt. Toward the end of the war it was deactivated and was not returned to service until 1951 and named the Armored Combat Training Area. It became a permanent installation in 1961 and renamed Fort Irwin.

Deactivated again in 1971, in 1973 it became a part of the National Guard training facilities. In 1979 it was selected to be the site for the National Training Center.

George Leroy Irwin was the son of Brigadier General John Dowling Irwin, Medical Corps, U.S. Army. John Dowling Irwin served during the Civil War and was given credit for setting up the first tent field hospital which became an Army standard. George Leroy Irwin graduated from the United States Military Academy and served as a Brigadier General during World War I, commanding the 57th Field Artillery Brigade.

(Source: 25, 77, 167)

Fort Jackson

Fort Jackson is located in South Carolina and is the largest Initial Entry Training Center in the U.S. Army. It began in 1917 and contains more than 52,000 acres. It was named for Andrew Jackson, the seventh president of the United States.

Andrew Jackson was born in 1767 and received little formal education. He self-studied law and became an attorney in Tennessee. In a duel he killed a man who said improper things about his wife. He was elected to the House of Representatives from Tennessee and then as a Senator. His fame came from his heroic actions as a major general who fought and defeated the British at the Battle of New Orleans.

In 1824 he had gained sufficient popular vote to be elected President of the United States, but with the Electoral College System it was thrown into the House of Representatives. Adams was elected and throughout Adams tenure, Jackson became a thorn who insisted that he, Jackson, was the people's choice. He defeated Adams in 1828. In his first annual message to Congress, he suggested the elimination of the Electoral College. A strong adherent of democratic principles he wanted to decentralize the government. He suggested that the Washington jobs should be sufficiently simple so as to be handled by the common man.

Out of the polarization caused by his position came two political parties, the old Republican Party, now called the Democratic Party and the Whigs. Known Whig leaders of that time included Henry Clay and Daniel Webster. Political cartoonists of the day referred to him as King Andrew as he used the power of the veto to get his way. A part of this centered around the "Second Bank of the United States" which was a private corporation but was considered to be a government monopoly. It had sufficient political power to fight Jackson as they considered him an enemy to their future.

After he left Washington, he continued in politics, supporting the candidacy of Van Buren. He died at Hermitage, his home in Tennessee, on June 8, 1845.

(Source: 77, 215, 255, 274)

Jefferson Barracks Military Post

This post was located at Lemay, Missouri and was active from 1826 until 1946. In 1827 it was named after Thomas Jefferson. It was used as a base to fight Indian wars and was used as major post during the Mexican-American War. During the Civil War it was used as a military hospital for both sides of the war. In 1912 it was the site of the first parachute jump. It was a training center during World War I and as a major reception center during World War II. It was deactivated in 1946.

Thomas Jefferson was the third president of the United States. He was born in Shadwell, Virginia in 1743 and died on July 4, 1826 at age 83. He spent his early youth wandering the hill country of the Blue Ridge Mountains in an area which would later become his Monticello home. He graduated from William and Mary College. He was the principal author of the Declaration of Independence. He favored states' rights and limited federal government. It was during his administration that the Lewis and Clark expedition took place led by his personal secretary, Meriwether Lewis. Before serving as President he was Vice-president under John Adams. He was also the First Secretary of State and was the second Governor of the State of Virginia.

(Source: 77)

Fort Knox

Fort Knox is the home of the Army Armor Center and is located near Louisville, Kentucky.

It was named after Henry Knox, the Continental Army's Chief of Artillery during the Revolutionary War and the country's first Secretary of War. First fortifications at the location were constructed at the beginning of the Civil War with both sides fighting for its strategic location.

Henry Knox was a bookseller from Boston. He was born July 25, 1750 and died on October 25, 1806 in Maine. His father was a ship's captain who died when Henry Knox was nine years old. Knox left school at twelve and worked in a bookstore to support his mother. He opened his own bookstore and was self taught. He had an early interest in military tactics. He married the daughter of British loyalists. Her parents left Boston with the British Army and she spent the Revolutionary War alone.

Knox had been an early supporter of the Independence cause and served at the Battle of Bunker Hill. He impressed Washington with his knowledge. During the Siege of Boston it was at his suggestion that the cannons captured at Fort Ticonderoga be brought to take part in the battle. Washington commissioned him a colonel and asked him to lead an expedition to bring the cannons from Fort Ticonderoga. With the cannons in place the British Navy was forced to withdraw.

During the battle of Trenton, New Jersey, Knox was in charge of Washington's crossing the Delaware. For this logistical success, including the movement of the troops to New Jersey and their return, he was promoted to Brigadier General. He was responsible for the establishment of the Springfield Armory in 1777.

After Washington retired from military service after the War, Knox was the senior officer of the Continental Army. He was made Secretary of War in 1785 and remained at that post until 1789. During his tour as Secretary of War, the regular Navy was established.

He left government service in 1795 and moved to Thomaston, Maine, becoming a cattle grower, ship builder and brick maker. He died of a punctured intestine received from eating a chicken bone.

(Source: 26, 77)

Fort Lee, New Jersey

This area, now a city, was the location of fortifications when George Washington used the area as a defense of New York. It was named for General Charles Lee. The George Washington Bridge originates in Manhattan and terminates on the New Jersey side in Fort Lee.

Charles Lee was born in England, son of a British general. He entered the British Army and in time was sent to America in 1754 to fight in the French and Indian War. He married the daughter of a Mohawk Indian chief. At the end of the war he returned to England and fought in Poland. He became sympathetic to the American cause and moved to the Virginia colony in 1773.

When the Revolutionary War began he volunteered his services, expecting to be named the head of the Continental Army. Washington was picked over him and while not given the official position, he was considered the second in command. He received various commands during the war including Commander of the Canadian Department and Commander of the Southern Department.

He is best remembered for the Battle of Monmouth, not for winning it, but for his animosity toward Washington which came to a boil during this battle. Ordered to attack, he in turn ordered a retreat marching into Washington's advancing troops as he did. There was some question as to which was the right battle maneuver but Lee was court-martialed. He resorted to verbal attacks on Washington and his popularity waned. He resigned from the Army in 1780.

There was some question as to his loyalty as there were plans in his handwriting which were given to the British for military operations against the Americans. This may have been because of his fear of being tried as a deserter of the British Army as he had entered the American Army some days before he resigned from the British Army.

(Source: 77)

Fort Lee, Virginia

Fort Lee, Virginia became a mobilization camp a few days after a state of war was declared with Germany in World War I. It was built rapidly and when it was completed it could house over 60,000 men. In 1917 it was announced that the camp would be named for General Robert E. Lee, CSA. After the war it was taken over by the Commonwealth of Virginia and parts were incorporated into a National Military Park. In 1940 a new Camp Lee was built on the original site. By 1941 the Quartermaster Training Center began operations.

Robert E. Lee, son of General "Light Horse Harry" Lee, was born in Westmoreland County, Virginia on the Stratford Hall Plantation. His ancestry was from the earliest settlers in Virginia. On his maternal side he descended from "King" Carter who was a large land holder in the Shenandoah Valley and for whom the Carter Hall Plantation, near Millwood, Virginia was named.

Robert E. Lee graduated from West Point in 1829 having the distinction of not receiving a demerit during his four years there. He was the head of his class in artillery and tactics at graduation. Overall, he was second in his class. He was commissioned into the Corps of Engineers and spent his early military career building bases and surveying. A part of his time was spent laying out the state line between Ohio and Michigan. He also supervised the modernization of the barge traffic on the Mississippi including the blasting of a channel through the rapids at Keokuk, Iowa so as to allow barge traffic to the upper reaches of the Mississippi.

He married Mary Anne Randolph Custis, the great granddaughter of Martha Washington. He had seven children, five of whom never married. In 1852 he became Superintendent of the United States Military Academy. In 1859 he led a force of Marines to capture John Brown after his raid on the U.S. Arsenal at Harpers Ferry, Virginia (Now West Virginia). In 1861 he took the painful step of resigning his commission from the U.S. Army to be a part of his native Virginia's Army. His war time exploits are well known and at its end he returned to Richmond as a paroled prisoner of war. He refused all offers to exploit his status for monetary gain. He became the President of Washington College (now Washington and Lee University) in Lexington, Virginia. He died on October 12, 1870 and was buried at Lexington.

(Source: 57, 77)

Fort Leonard Wood

Fort Leonard Wood is located in Pulaski County, Missouri.

It was named for General Leonard Wood who was awarded the Medal of Honor. Leonard Wood was born in Winchester, Massachusetts. He attended Pierce College and Harvard Medical School, earning his Medical Degree in 1884. He took a position as a contract physician and served in Arizona. He was awarded the Medal of Honor for carrying dispatches 100 miles through hostile territory and then commanding a military detachment whose officers had been lost.

In 1893 he was stationed at Atlanta, Georgia. He enrolled at Georgia Tech and became the school's first football coach and also as a player, its team captain. He was the personal physician to Presidents Grover Cleveland and William McKinley. At the outbreak of the Spanish-American War he joined with Teddy Roosevelt to form the Rough Riders and commanded it during the

Battle of Las Guasimas. He stayed in Cuba after the war and was named Military Governor of Santiago. In 1902 he was sent to the Philippines as Commander of the Philippine Division. During this time he was in charge of campaigns against Muslim rebels including the Moro Crater massacre.

In 1910 he was named Army Chief of Staff under President Taft and is the only medical officer to hold that position. He began a number of programs including the Reserve Officers Training Corps (ROTC) and the Preparedness Movement for Universal Military Training. He was an unsuccessful candidate for the Republican presidential nomination in 1920. One of the reasons for his losing the nomination was his strong anti-communist sentiments.

Wood died in Boston after undergoing brain surgery. He had undergone brain surgery some twenty years before and his success was hailed for the progress it made in neurosurgery. He is buried in Arlington National Cemetery.

(Source: 77)

Fort Lesley J. McNair

This fort is located in Maryland near Washington, DC. It has been an Army post for over 200 years, having been established in 1791. It was originally called Greenleaf Point as it was located where the Anacostia River joins the Potomac. It was renamed in 1948 to honor Lieutenant General Lesley J. McNair who was killed in Normandy, France on July 25, 1944.

Lesley J. McNair was born in Verndale, Minnesota. He graduated with the Class of 1904 from West Point, standing 11th in his class of 124. He served in the Artillery forces and later was sent to France in 1913 to observe French artillery. He saw service under General John J. Pershing in the Pancho Villa Expedition. When the First World War was declared he went to France to serve with the 1st Infantry Division. By 1918 he was promoted to Brigadier General, the youngest general officer at the time.

Between wars he reverted back to Major as a permanent rank and taught at a number of posts. He was promoted to Colonel in 1935 and to Brigadier General in 1937. In June of 1942 he was promoted to Commanding General of the Army Ground Forces. He received the Purple Heart from wounds in the North Africa Campaign. He was killed by friendly fire on July 25th by a pre-attack bombardment of the Eighth Air Force. His son, Colonel Douglas McNair was killed by sniper fire just two weeks later on Guam.

(Source: 77)

Fort Lewis

Fort Lewis is located in the state of Washington. It consists of about 87,000 acres and is one of the premier military bases in the country. It is located in Pierce County and is notable for its citizens who bonded themselves to purchase the land to donate to the federal government in 1917. The base is named for Meriwether Lewis of the Lewis and Clark expedition.

Meriwether Lewis was born in Albemarle County, Virginia on August 18, 1774 to Colonel William Lewis and Lucy Meriwether. His father died at an early age and his mother remarried to Captain John Marks. He grew up in Georgia and was mostly taught at local schools by ministers. He was sent back to Virginia for further education with one tutor being Matthew Maury, an uncle of Matthew Fontaine Maury. The Maury relationship extended to the family of Thomas Jefferson where Jefferson was taught by Maury's father.

To complete the Lewis and Clark picture, George Rogers Clark graduated from Liberty Hall, now Washington and Lee University and joined the Army. He was a part of the detachment sent to put down the Whiskey Rebellion. In 1801 he was appointed as an aide to President Thomas Jefferson. When Jefferson decided to explore a route west to the Pacific he chose Meriwether Lewis as its leader. Lewis asked that William Clark be appointed co-leader as he had served with Clark in the Army and knew of his abilities. From 1803 to 1809 Lewis and Clark explored a route to the Pacific using the Clearwater, Snake and Columbia Rivers as the route.

but repurchased in 1885. During the First World War, it housed German naval prisoners of war. It is scheduled for closure in 2011.

General James Birdseye McPherson was born near Clyde, Ohio and graduated from the United States Military Academy with the Class of 1853. He was first in his class, a class that included several noted Civil War officers. He performed civil engineering duties after graduation including being the superintending engineer for the construction of the defenses of Alcatraz Island at San Francisco.

At the beginning of the Civil War he transferred East ending up at Saint Louis, Missouri. He was the Chief Engineer of Brigadier General Ulysses S. Grant's Army during the capture of Forts Henry and Donelson. By 1862 he was promoted to major general and given command of a part of Grant's Army of Tennessee. In 1864 he was given command of the entire Army of Tennessee. He was killed during the Battle for Atlanta.

(Source: 77)

Fort Monroe

Fort Monroe is located near Hampton, Virginia and traces its history back to 1819. Even before that, it was a natural defense point to deter any unwanted vessels from entering the Chesapeake Bay area. The fort was in the Confederacy geography during the Civil War but it remained in Union hands throughout the war. While the base has been selected to be closed in 2011, it has been a base which has served the Nation throughout its long and storied history. It was named for James Monroe, the fifth President of the United States.

James Monroe was born on April 28, 1758 in Westmoreland County, Virginia. He attended the College of William and Mary. He dropped out of college to become a part of the colonists wishing to fight for independence from England. He later studied law under Thomas Jefferson.

During the Revolutionary War he fought in the Battle of Trenton, was wounded and spent three months recovering. He served in the Continental Congress. He was elected United States Senator in

1790 and after one term was sent to France as Minister. In 1799 he was elected Governor of Virginia. He returned to France in 1803 and helped Robert Livingston negotiate the Louisiana Purchase. He served as Minister to England and helped lay out a treaty to replace the Jay Treaty. It was labeled as unsatisfactory as it did not settle the main dispute of seamen impressments that later was to bring the two nations to war again. In 1811 he became Secretary of State and then Secretary of War.

In 1816 he ran for President and succeeded James Madison as the Fifth President of the United States. He continued as President through two terms and the Monroe Doctrine was promulgated during his terms in office. This was a warning to Europe that the Americas would be free of any further colonization. It also stated that America would be a neutral nation in any wars fought between European nations.

During his presidency, five states were admitted to the Union; Mississippi, Illinois, Alabama, Maine, and Missouri.

Monroe died on July 4, 1831, thus becoming the third president to die on the anniversary of the birth of our nation. He was first buried in New York but later reinterred to the President's Circle in the Hollywood Cemetery in Richmond, Virginia.

(Source: 77, 255, 292,293)

Fort Myer

Fort Myer is located in Virginia and is named after Albert James Myer. He was born in Newburgh, New York on September 20, 1828. This birth date may be a year off as 1829 shows up on a monument and tombstone.

He entered Geneva College when he was thirteen. He received his medical degree from Buffalo Medical College in 1851.

He was interested in science and in particular, the electrochemical telegraph. He worked as a telegrapher during his college years.

He was interested in modernizing the communication system used by the military and spent much time pursuing that objective.

He went into private practice in Florida but in a few years obtained a commission as assistant surgeon in the regular army. During this time he also concentrated on signaling and devised the codes used by the Army during the Civil War.

His code used a simple signal flag for day time use and a kerosene lantern or torch at night. His system was distinctly different from semaphore signaling. In 1858 the Army showed interest in his system and field tests were conducted that same year. The board appointed by the Army to examine this new system was chaired by Lt. Col. Robert E. Lee. In 1860 he was authorized to form the new Army Signal Corps but it was not until 1863 that it truly became an entity.

Myer also recognized the value of electrical telegraphy and a field telegraph train was introduced to use a device called the Beardslee telegraph, which proved to be less than dependable but which was easier to learn than the tapping system used to transmit the Morse Code. He was removed from his post by Secretary of War Edwin Stanton, when he tried to discard the Beardslee telegraph and bring in trained telegraphers.

Sent West in exile, he continued his interest in signaling and devised a code for sending messages. In 1866 he was reinstated as Commander of the Signal Corps and was later promoted to Brigadier General on June 16, 1880, two months before his death.

(Source: 77, 275)

Fort Ord

Fort Ord is located in California and is well known to the many soldiers who passed through its gates. It has been deactivated and a part is now a campus for California State University, Monterey Bay.

In 1940 it was named for Major General Edward Otho Cresap Ord who was born on October 18, 1818, in Cumberland, Maryland. Coming from military families (His father was an officer in the Navy and afterwards an Army officer during the War of 1812. His mother was the daughter of Colonel Daniel Cresap, an officer in the American Revolution.), he gained an appointment to the U.S. Military Academy and graduated with the Class of 1839. He was known for his mathematical skills. After service in the Florida Everglades he served on garrison duty in the East. In 1847 he was sent to California along with two classmates, William W. Halleck and William Tecumseh Sherman, arriving in 1847. He was soon put in charge of the Monterey Garrison. During this time he surveyed Sacramento and mapped the new City of Los Angeles. Later he was engaged in the Coast Survey.

He continued his frontier duties and in 1859 he was sent to Artillery School at Fort Monroe, Virginia. While there he participated in the suppression of the John Brown insurrection. He returned to Frontier duty in Washington and California. In 1861 he was given command in the Army of the Potomac to defend the Capitol. Shortly afterward he was ordered to lead a fight against General J.E.B. Stuart at Dranesville, Virginia. In December he was transferred to the Western Theater and was severely wounded at Hatchie, Mississippi. He recovered and took part in the Siege of Vicksburg. Later he was to hold commands in Louisiana and the Shenandoah Valley in Virginia.

He again was wounded at the Battle of Fort Harrison, Virginia and was out of action until January 1865. After the war he returned to duty in the West and retired in December 1880 at the age of 62. After retirement he became involved in number of civilian projects including the building of a railroad in Mexico. It was here that he contracted yellow fever which took his life in Havana, Cuba on July 22, 1883. He was interred at Arlington National Cemetery.

(Source: 154)

Fort Pickett

Fort Pickett is located near Blackstone, Virginia and is a National Guard Installation. Its beginnings were as a Civilian Conservation Corps base and in 1941 the land was being prepared for buildings.

There was a runway sufficient to land C-47 transports. Besides its training use in World War II, it also served as a prisoner of war camp. In 1997 it was turned over to the Virginia National Guard. It was named for Major General George E. Pickett, CSA.

George E. Pickett was born in Richmond, Virginia on January 28, 1825, the oldest of eight children. He went west to study law but earned an appointment to the U.S. Military Academy being appointed by Illinois Congressman John Stuart, a partner of Abraham Lincoln. At the Academy he was known as the class clown, graduating last in his class in the Class of 1846.

He married Sally Harrison Steward Minge, a descendent of Benjamin Harrison, a signer of the Declaration of Independence. She died in childbirth, following an Indian raid, in Fort Gates, Texas. In 1856 he commanded the construction of Fort Bellingham in Washington. At the outset of the Civil War he resigned his U.S. Army commission and joined the Confederacy. He was made first a colonel then a brigadier general. He fought under General Longstreet in the Seven Days Campaign. Wounded at Gaines' Mill he commanded a division at Fredericksburg.

It was at Gettysburg that his name was attached to history. The name "Pickett's Charge" was given to the charge against the Federal lines. He did not carry the day and his troops were forced to retire. After the war he was an insurance salesman in Richmond, Virginia. He died in Norfolk, Virginia on July 30, 1875.

(Source: 57, 77, 276)

Fort Polk

Fort Polk is located near Leesville, Louisiana in 1941. It was named for the Right Reverend Leonidas Polk, the first Episcopal Bishop of the Diocese of Louisiana and a Confederate War General. The post was closed after World War II, but reopened for the Korean conflict. It was then closed again. In 1961 it was activated as a permanent base and became an infantry training center.

Leonidas Polk was born on April 10, 1806 in Raleigh, North

Carolina and died June 14, 1864. He was a planter in Maury County, Tennessee and a third cousin of President James K. Polk. He graduated from West Point with the Class of 1827. During his senior year he joined the Episcopal Church and upon graduation he resigned his commission and was ordained a deacon in 1830. In 1841 he was appointed Bishop of Louisiana. He founded the University of the South at Sewanee, Tennessee.

When the Civil War broke out he joined the Southern cause at the urging of Jefferson Davis. He was given the rank of Major General and fought in the Battles of Shiloh, Perryville, Stones River, Chickamauga, and the Atlanta Campaign. He was killed by cannon fire on June 18, 1864 in Cobb County, Georgia.

(Source: 77, 178)

Fort Ritchie

Fort Richie is located along the Pennsylvania-Maryland border. It was founded in the 1890's and closed in 1998.

The base was named for Maryland Governor Albert Cabell Ritchie, who was born in Richmond, Virginia on August 29, 1876. His family moved to Baltimore shortly after his birth and he attended Maryland schools. He graduated from Johns Hopkins University in 1896 and received his law degree in 1898 from the University of Maryland School of Law. In 1903 he was appointed Assistant City Solicitor of Baltimore. He made his name fighting the gas and electric utilities for producing inferior quality products. His rise up the political ladder included being the Attorney General of Maryland where he served until 1919. He was known for economizing the state government by having the state law department take over the legal activities of most of the Maryland state departments.

In 1918 he took a leave of absence to serve on the War Industries Board. Returning to Maryland he ran for governor and defeated his Republican rival by the slimmest of margins. He became known for redistributing the wealth from the richer counties to the poorer

After the war he became an industrial leader in Birmingham and given the honorary title of "General."

(Source: 77)

Fort Sam Houston

Fort Sam Houston is located in San Antonio, Texas and is named for the first President of the Republic of Texas, Sam Houston. Fort Sam Houston is the home of Army Medicine and is the training center for combat medics. It is the largest of its kind in the world and annually trains more than 25,000 students. It was founded in 1876.

Sam Houston was born on March 2, 1793 and died on July 26, 1863. He was born in Rockbridge County in the Shenandoah Valley of Virginia. He was one of nine children and at an early age moved to Tennessee after his father died.

He ran away from home and for a period lived with a Cherokee Tribe. Adopted into their Nation he was given the nickname of "The Raven." At the age of nineteen he founded a one-room school which in 1812 was the first school in Tennessee. Shortly thereafter he enlisted to fight the British in the War of 1812. Though wounded by an Indian arrow, he remained in the Army until 1818. He was elected to the Tennessee House of Representatives and served from 1824 to 1827. At that time he ran and was elected governor of the state. He resigned in 1828. He was known as a hard drinker and after an unsuccessful marriage he lost the backing of Andrew Jackson. In 1836 he moved to Mexican Texas and became involved with politics there. His volunteer army fought Mexican General Santa Anna. After the loss of the Alamo, Houston attacked and defeated Santa Anna. The result was the Treaty of Velasco where Texas was granted its independence.

He was twice elected President of the Republic of Texas, first from 1836-38, and as the third President of the Republic of Texas from 1841-44. After Texas became a state he was elected the seventh Governor of Texas in 1859. The City of Houston, Texas is named for him. He is the only person to serve as governor of two different states, Tennessee and Texas. He died in Huntsville, Texas on July 26, 1863 from pneumonia.

(Source: 77)

Schofield Barracks

Schofield Barracks is located in Oahu, Hawaii. The camp got its start around 1905 to provide protection to the Navy ships while in port. In 1909 it was named Schofield Barracks to honor Lieutenant General John McAllister Schofield.

John Schofield was born on September 29, 1831 in Gerry, New York. He graduated from the United States Military Academy with the Class of 1853 and commissioned into the Artillery. He taught at West Point and at Washington University. At the onset of the Civil War he served as Brigadier General of the Missouri Volunteers and Militia. He served throughout the war in command positions and was awarded the Medal of Honor for heroism. After the war he continued to command and in 1868-69 he served as Secretary of War. In 1869 he was appointed Major General and commanded the Department of the Missouri.

In 1872 he was sent to the Hawaiian Islands and was the one who recommended that Pearl Harbor be established as a military base. From 1876-1881 he was Superintendent of the Military Academy. In 1891 he became Commanding General of the United States Army. In 1895 he retired from active service and died on March 4, 1906 in St. Augustine, Florida. He was buried at Arlington National Cemetery.

(Source: 25, 59, 77, 238)

Fort Sheridan

Fort Sheridan is located in Illinois and was established though the efforts of the Commercial Club of Chicago who saw the need for a military garrison in the 1870-80's. During the Spanish American War it became a mobilization, training and administrative center. Continuing into the Second World War it processed over 500,000 personnel. It was closed in 1993 but the Army Reserve continues to use about 90 acres.

The base was named for Philip Henry Sheridan who was born on March 6, 1831 and who died on August 5, 1888. He was born in Albany, New York to Irish immigrants. He received an appointment to the U.S. Military Academy from a congressman who frequented the store where he clerked. While at the Academy he was suspended for a year for fighting with a classmate. He graduated in 1853 and was assigned to service in Texas. He then went on to California and later spent much time as a part of a survey party mapping the Willamette Valley.

At the onset of the Civil War he was appointed Chief Commissary Officer of the Army of Southwest Missouri. Later he met superior officers who were impressed enough to appoint him Colonel of the Third Michigan Cavalry. His actions at the Battle of Booneville won him his promotion to Brigadier General. He was known for his aggressiveness in battle and was responsible for a number of Union victories because of this trait. His aggressiveness brought him into displeasure later in the war and some battles that were lost were ascribed to his being willing to engage at any cost.

In the latter part of the war he was picked to ravage the agricultural land in the Shenandoah Valley. This he did throughout the northern part of the Valley. His biggest deterrent was the raids by Mosby's Rangers into his camps. The locals remembered and were unforgiving of his hanging of some of Mosby's troops, calling them guerillas. Mosby retaliated and the war from then on was fought along more accepted lines. Later he was responsible for the capture of twenty percent of Lee's remaining troops at the Battle of Sayler's Creek. He was made commander of the Military District of the Southwest with orders to defeat the remaining forces of the Confederacy in Texas. His speed in assembling a force of 50,000 men caused the country of France to abandon its plans for conquest in the Southwest.

After the War he was involved in the Reconstruction of the

South and was known for his lack of tact and feelings for those who became involved in politics. He finally was sent west to deal with Indian uprisings and he used the same scorched earth policies that were successful in the Shenandoah Valley to drive the Indians back onto their reservations. In 1869 he was sent to Europe to report on the Franco-Prussian War and was present when Napoleon III surrendered to the Germans.

He returned to the United States and was present during the Great Chicago Fire. The City was placed under martial law with Sheridan in charge. In 1883 he succeeded William T. Sherman as Commanding General of the United States Army. He became enamored with the beauty of Yellowstone and was responsible for bringing it to the attention of President Chester A. Arthur. It was made a National Park and the 1st Cavalry ran the Park until 1916. He died from heart trouble in Nonquitt, Massachusetts and was buried at Arlington National Cemetery. Later on when his widow who was some twenty years younger than Sheridan, was asked why she didn't remarry, reportedly said "I would rather be the widow of Phil Sheridan than the wife of any man living."

There are many things and places named after Sheridan, including the M551 Sheridan Tank.

(Source: 77)

Fort Sill

This fort is located in Oklahoma and was staked out by Major General Phillip H. Sheridan on January 8, 1869. Sheridan's winter campaign into Indian country included such frontier scouts as "Buffalo Bill" Cody, "Wild Bill" Hickok, Ben Clark and Jack Stilwell. The Buffalo Soldiers were a part of the first soldiers encamped there and built many of the buildings. Sheridan named it in honor of a West Point classmate Brigadier General Joshua W. Sill who was killed during the Civil War.

Joshua Woodrow Sill was born in Chillicothe, Ohio on December 6, 1831. His father was an attorney and taught Sill much of his education. Sill obtained an appointment to West Point and graduated third out of 52 cadets in the Class of 1853. His first assignments were at ordnance posts and in 1855 he returned to West Point as an instructor.

He resigned his commission in January of 1861 but offered his services to the Governor of Ohio at the onset of the Civil War. He was commissioned Colonel of the 33rd Ohio Volunteers and went into Eastern Kentucky with that regiment.

He took part in the bloodiest battle of the Civil War (when measured by percentage of casualties), the Battle of Stone Mountain, Tennessee. He was killed on the first day of battle by a sniper. He was buried in a battlefield cemetery nearby but later his body was reinterred at the Grandview Cemetery in Chillicothe, Ohio.

(Source: 26, 77)

Fort Stewart

Located in the Counties of Liberty and Bryan, Georgia, it has 280,000 acres making it the largest base in the Eastern United States. It was built in June of 1941 and was used during World War II. It was deactivated at the end of the war but reactivated in 1950. It is named in honor of General Daniel Stewart who was a native of Liberty County, Georgia and who fought with Francis Marion during the Revolutionary War.

Daniel Stewart was a Brigadier General in the Georgia Militia. He fought in both the Revolutionary War and the War of 1812. He was born on December 20, 1761 on a plantation in which is now Liberty County, Georgia. His mother died when he was five years old. His father died at the onset of the Revolutionary War and he enlisted in the Georgia Militia and fought under the command of Colonel John Baker as they attempted to oust the British from Florida.

In 1778 he was captured by the British and confined aboard a prisoner-of-war ship in Charleston Harbor. He escaped and hid in

South Carolina where he met his first wife. She died in childbirth a year later. He was promoted to Colonel and served as Commander of the Minutemen of Georgia.

After the war he returned to Liberty County and married a second time. He continued in the militia and fought in the Creek Indian Wars. He also became involved in politics, serving as sheriff and state senator. His second wife died in 1807 with two children being born from this union. He married a third time in 1810 and had two daughters from this marriage.

In 1809 he was promoted to the rank of Brigadier General and commanded a Cavalry brigade during the War of 1812. He died on May 27, 1829. He was the great-grandfather of Theodore Roosevelt.

(Source: 77, 87, 105, 103)

Camp Wallace

Camp Wallace was located in Galveston County, Texas. It originally was used as a training center for World War II anti-aircraft units. In 1944 it was transferred to the Navy to be used as a boot camp and distribution center. It was closed in 1944. One of its World War II trainees was Howard "Howie" Beach who won the Silver Star for bravery in Europe.

Camp Wallace was named after Colonel Elmer J. Wallace of the 69th Coast Artillery and who was killed in the Meuse-Argonne offensive in 1918.

(Source: 177, 229)

United States
Air Force
Bases
&
Army
Air
Bases

Andrews Air Force Base

Andrew Air Force Base is located in Maryland near Washington, DC and is the home of Air Force One, the official airplane of the President of the United States. It was originally known as Camp Springs Army Air Base but was renamed in 1945 to honor Frank Maxwell Andrews. Frank Maxwell Andrews was born in Nashville, Tennessee on February 3, 1884 and died on May 3, 1943. He was the great-great-nephew of two Tennessee Governors, John C. Brown and Neill S. Brown. He graduated from the U.S. Military Academy with the Class of 1906. When he graduated, the U.S. Army was smaller than that of Bulgaria.

In 1914 he married the daughter of Major General Henry Tureman Allen. His request to transfer to the fledgling Army Air Corps was held up but as the country entered the First World War he was transferred to the Aviation Section of the Signal Corps. In 1918 he earned his aviators wings at the age of 34. He never saw duty overseas during the War but was assigned to command various air fields around the country. After the War he succeeded General Billy Mitchell as the air officer assigned to the Army Occupation of Germany.

In 1923 he assumed command of Kelly Field, Texas. In 1928 he attended the Army Air Corps Tactical School at Langley Field. Promoted to Lt. Colonel, he was the Chief of the Army Air Corps Training and Operations Division. He then commanded the 1st Pursuit Group at Selfridge Field, Michigan.

He was an advocate of the four engine B-17 Bomber when others saw the need for a larger number of two engine bombers, such as the Douglas B-18. His theory was proven correct by the need for the four engine long range bomber in World War II. Politics played a part in this and his zeal for the larger bomber resulted in his being demoted and sent to a remote air base. His friend, General Omar Bradley, was named Chief of Staff in 1939 and Andrews was one of his first selections for senior staff. As Assistant Chief of Staff he was responsible for the readiness of the entire Army. In 1940 he commanded the Army's Panama Air Force and in 1941 became the Commander of the Caribbean Defense Command. In 1942 for three months he was in command of the United States Forces in the Middle East.

In 1943 as a Lt. General, he was given command of all the United States Forces in the European Theater of War. On May 3, 1943 a B-24 aircraft carrying Andrews and fourteen others crashed trying to land at the Royal Air Force base in Kaldadarnes, Iceland. There was only one survivor, the tail gunner.

Andrews was buried at Arlington National Cemetery. It was said that if he survived he would have most likely been named the Supreme Allied Commander for the Invasion of Europe.

(Source: 77)

Arnold Air Force Base

Arnold Air Force Base was named after General Henry H. "Hap" Arnold, Commanding General of the U.S. Army Air Forces during WWII.

Henry Harley "Hap" Arnold was born on June 25, 1886 in Gladwyne, Pennsylvania. He went to Lower Merion High School in Ardmore, Pennsylvania. He took a competitive exam to enter West Point and received the appointment after the person ahead of him was not allowed to enter because of being married. He graduated with the Class of 1907. He ended up being commissioned into the Infantry, rather than his choice of Cavalry, as he stood in the lower half of his class.

While on assignment in the Philippines he volunteered to help Captain Arthur Cowan of the Signal Corps map the Island of Leyte. Afterwards Cowan returned to the United States and chose Arnold as one of two persons to receive pilot training. It took two years before the transfer to the Signal Corps became a reality and he was sent to Dayton, Ohio where he was instructed to fly by the Wright Brothers. He became the second rated pilot in the Army Air Corps. In September, 1911 he became the first pilot to carry mail. He had many near fatal crashes and ended up with a phobia of flying. He returned to the Philippines and there became a close friend of George Catlett Marshall.

On his return to the United States he was offered the rank of Captain by Major William T. Mitchell, if he would return to the Signal Corps. He was asked to go to the Panama Canal to find a suitable place for an air field. While on his way there the United States declared war on Germany. He asked for overseas duty but the need for qualified officers at headquarters overrode his request. In June of 1917 he was promoted to Major and two months later to Colonel, becoming the youngest full colonel in the Army.

He fought to get a large appropriations bill for the Air Service through Congress. This was a failure but the experience would stand him in good stead in later years. After the war he was ordered to demobilize the air unit. He fought for its preservation. At Rockwell Field he met many of the officers who would later become his aides. During this time the battle raged between the Army and the advocates of air service. Arnold was banished to a western post and there he met Major General James Fechet who intervened to have Arnold's exile ended. By 1929 he became executive officer of the Air Material Division and on November 27, 1931 the Commander of March Field, California. One of his assignments was to heal the rifts that occurred between the base and the citizens of nearby Riverside. He accomplished this though relief efforts and having his personnel join in the local service clubs.

In 1935 he took command of the First Wing of the newly created Air Corps. By 1935 he had become Assistant Chief of the Air Corps. His boss, General Westover, was killed in a plane crash and Arnold became Chief of the Air Corps. Arnold fought for an expansion of the Air Corps into a unit equal to the Army ground units.

In June of 1941 the United States Army Air Forces was created and Arnold was chosen to be Commander. He became a member of the Joint Chiefs of Staff. It was through his leadership that the growth of the Army Air Corps during World War II made it an air fighting force unequalled in the world.

During the war he suffered numerous heart attacks, some of which were not reported as he might be taken from his duties as "the Chief." He worked long hours, particularly trying to solve the problems associated with the B-29 Super Fortress.

In 1945 he founded Project RAND which became a think tank called the RAND Corporation. He retired in 1946 to a small ranch in California. On May 7, 1949 he was honored to be named also the General of the Air Force, making him the only five star general in two military services. He died on January 15, 1950 and is buried at Arlington National Cemetery.

(Source: 77)

Bakalar Air Force Base

Bakalar Air Force Base was first named Atterbury Air Base for its nearness to Camp Atterbury to its North. On November 13, 1954 it was renamed Bakalar Air Force Base after Lieutenant John Edmund Bakalar. The base had been closed after World War II but was reopened in 1949. In 1969 it was deactivated and deeded to the City of Columbus, Ohio.

John Edmund Bakalar was born on August 29, 1920 in Hammond, Indiana. He joined the Army Air Corps on January 26, 1942. He was a part of the 354th fighter Group and flew P-51 airplanes. He was killed on September 1, 1944 in France.

His decorations included the Distinguished Service Cross, Purple Heart, the Air Medal with six Oak Leaf Clusters, the World War Victory Medal, American Campaign Medal, European-African-Middle Eastern Campaign Medal with three bronze Service Stars, Distinguished Unit Citation, Aviation Badge "Pilot" and the Sharpshooter Badge.

(Source: 33, 35)

Barksdale Air Force Base

Barksdale Air Force Base is located near Shreveport, Louisiana and was opened in 1933. It is the home of the 2nd Bomb Wing which includes three B-52 Squadrons. It was named for Lieutenant

Eugene Hoy Barksdale, U.S. Army Air Corps.

Eugene Hoy Barksdale was born on November 5, 1897 in Goshen Springs, Arkansas. He attended Mississippi State College for three years before entering Officers Training Camp. While still a private, he volunteered for the aviation section and went through flight training with the Royal Air Force and was assigned to their 41st Squadron in 1918. In 1919 he was assigned to Mitchel Field, Long Island, New York.

He received his pilot's training in England and was commissioned there. Flying with the Royal Air Force he was in the Somme and Amiens Offensives. He was credited with shooting down three enemy aircraft in aerial combat and destroying five others on the ground.

On August 11, 1926, Lt. Barksdale lost his life while testing a Douglas O-2 Observation plane. He was buried at Arlington National Cemetery.

(Source: 36, 77)

Beale Air Force Base

Beale Air Force Base is located near Marysville, California and was established in 1943. The U-2 and the RQ-4 Global Hawk fly out of Beale Air Force Base. The base was named for Edward Fitzgerald Beale. Before becoming an air base, it was used as a training base for the 13th Armored Division. During World War II it contained 60,000 personnel as well as housing German Prisoners of War. In 1948 it became Beale Air Force Base and was used to train bombardier-navigators in radar techniques. By 1958 the first runway was operational.

Edward Fitzgerald Beale was born in Washington, DC on February 4, 1822, the son of a paymaster in the Navy who had received the Congressional Medal of Honor during the War of 1812. His mother was Emily, the daughter of Commodore Thomas Truxun of the U.S. Navy. He was a student at Georgetown University when he was appointed to the Naval School at Philadelphia where he graduated in 1842. (The U.S. Naval Academy was founded in 1843.)

In 1845 he sailed for California on a frigate under the command of Commodore Robert F. Stockton. He was sent back to Washington with important documents and on his arrival was promoted to Sailing Master. By the time he was able to return to California, hostilities with Mexico had begun and he was sent to Monterey to serve with the land forces. He joined General Stephen W. Kearney's column and fought in the Battle of San Pasqual. When their force was surrounded, he, Kit Carson and his Delaware Indian servant slipped through the enemy lines and found reinforcements in San Diego. Two months later, he was sent east with dispatches. He made six more trips across country, one of which was in disguise, carrying gold to show proof of its presence in California. He resigned from the Navy in 1851 and became manager of the lands acquired by W.H. Aspinwall and Commodore Stockton.

In 1853 he was appointed Superintendent of Indian Affairs for California and Nevada by President Fillmore. On his way back to California he surveyed a route across Colorado and Utah for the first Transcontinental Railroad. He was appointed a Brigadier General in the California Militia so as to have more authority in dealing with the Indians. In 1861 he was appointed Surveyor General of California and Nevada. There is a passage through the mountains near Newhall, California which was known as the Beale Cut that made the passage of the railroad easier through that area.

In 1857 he was appointed surveyor to build a road from Fort Defiance, New Mexico to the Colorado River. Later he extended it to Fort Smith, Arkansas. In 1854 Beale established Fort Tejon, located south of Bakersfield, California. When the fort was abandoned in 1864, Beale purchased the Mexican land grants which now comprise the 270,000 acre Tejon Ranch.

He lived alternately between the Tejon Ranch and the Decatur House in Washington, D.C. except for a period of four years when he was Ambassador to Austria-Hungary.

He died at the Decatur House in 1893.

(Source: 77)

Bellows Air Force Station (Bellows Field)

Bellows Field is located on Oahu, Hawaii and was one of the air fields attacked at Pearl Harbor.

It is named for Lieutenant Franklin Barney Bellows who was a pilot during World War I. Bellows was born in Evanston, Indiana on July 9, 1896. He went to local schools and graduated from Northwestern University. He joined the Army just one month short of his graduation but was at the graduation ceremonies in his military uniform. He received his commission in the Coast Artillery but soon joined the Air Service. By February he had received his wings while still retaining his position in the Coast Artillery.

On September 13, 1918 he flew a low level reconnaissance mission and was wounded by anti-aircraft and machine gun fire. While the plane was able to return to its base, Lieutenant Bellows had been killed by the enemy fire. He was buried in the American Cemetery at Sebastopol and awarded the Distinguished Service Cross posthumously by order of General Pershing.

(Source: 77, 111, 238)

Bergstrom Air Force Base

This base was opened in1942 and was located near Austin, Texas. It was used in World War II as a troop carrier training base and later became a Strategic Air Command Base. Now it is the Austin-Bergstrom International Airport serving Austin, Texas. It was named for John August Earl Bergstrom who was the first person from Austin killed in World War II. He was killed during the Japanese attack on Clark Field in the Philippines, the day after Pearl Harbor while serving as an administrative officer of the 19th Bombardment Group.

John August Earl Bergstrom was born on August 25, 1907 and was a part of a well known Swedish family in Austin, Texas. After his death the Army Air Base was renamed in his honor at the urging of Congressman Lyndon B. Johnson. On December 7, 2002 he was posthumously awarded the Purple Heart which is displayed at the Airport bearing his name.

(Source: 11, 34, 54, 77, 201)

Bolling Air Force Base

Bolling Field was opened in July of 1918 in Washington, DC. It was named for Colonel Raynal C. Bolling, the highest ranking Army Air Corps officer killed in World War I. It was used to test new aviation equipment as well as to provide aerial defense for the Capitol. It served as the beginning point for the first air mail service from Washington to New York in 1918.

In 1927 the "Spirit of St. Louis" was returned to this country and reassembled at Bolling Field. From there Lindbergh, Wiley Post and Carl Spaatz used it to fly goodwill flights to Mexico and South America. Other early flight pioneers used it to begin or end historic flights. The last fixed wing flight out of Bolling Field was in 1962 because of the congestion at National Airport (now Ronald Reagan Airport).

Ranal Bolling was born in Hot Springs, Arkansas on September 1, 1887. He attended Penn Charter School and graduated from Harvard in 1900 and its law school in 1902. He was in the legal department at the U.S. Steel Corp and by 1907 he was Assistant General Solicitor, becoming the Solicitor General in 1913. The sinking of the Lusitania triggered his desire to be a part of what he knew would become a world war. He organized a motorized machine gun company which consisted of a sixty man unit, driving vehicles upon which were mounted machine guns. He was commissioned a first lieutenant in the New York National Guard and became known for his advocacy of air power. He was promoted to the rank of Captain in the Army Signal Corps where he continued his fight for the fledgling Army Air Corps.

He became a part of the American Expeditionary Forces and was killed in France by a German ambush during the Second Somme

Offensive. He was awarded the Cross of the Legion of Honor and the Distinguished Service Medal.

(Source: 7, 66, 77, 80, 121)

Brookley Field Air Force Base

Brookley Field, now Mobile Airport was named for Captain Wendell H. Brookley. Wendell Brookley attended college in Nebraska and joined the Signal Corps in 1917. After he graduated from flight training he served as an instructor. He went to the Philippines in 1919 and then was assigned to Fort Sill, Oklahoma. He went from there to testing airplanes at what is now Wright-Patterson Air Force Base. In 1924 he placed second in the Pulitzer Trophy Event at Dayton.

In 1934 he was piloting a Douglas biplane that had been updated with a new propeller and a radial engine. The propeller disintegrated and while his companion jumped in time, Brookley was too late and he perished in the crash when his parachute failed to open. He is buried at Arlington National Cemetery.

(Source: 25, 209)

Brooks Air Force Base

Brooks Field was established at the beginning of World War I and is located near San Antonio, Texas. It was named for Cadet Sidney Johnson Brooks, Jr. Brooks was born on May 21, 1895 in San Antonio. He worked as a reporter but joined the Army when World War I began. He had finished ground training and only needed to land at San Antonio after a flight to earn his wings. As he flew over the City, the nose of the plane went down and it crashed at the edge of the air field. Some said it was because an immunization shot and that he had passed out as he approached the air field. The Kelly Field No. 5 was renamed in his honor.

(Source: 74, 77, 163, 229)

Buckley Air Force Base

Buckley Air Force base is located in Aurora, Colorado and its mission is to provide global surveillance to combatant commanders. It was founded in the early years of World War II when it was received as a gift from the City of Denver.

It is named for Lt. John Harold Buckley who was killed on September 17, 1918 while on a strafing mission. He was a native of Longmont, Colorado.

(Source: 41, 77, 81, 89, 233)

Cannon Air Force Base

This Air Force base is located near Clovis in Curry County, New Mexico. It began as a civilian facility and later was the Clovis Municipal Airport. In 1943 it was assigned to the military and became Clovis Army Air Field. It became a SAC base in 1946. In 1957 it was renamed Cannon Air Force Base in honor of General John K. Cannon who was a former Commander of the Tactical Air Command.

John Kenneth Cannon was born March 2, 1892 in Salt Lake City, Utah Territory. He graduated from Utah Agricultural College in 1914 and was commissioned a Second Lieutenant in 1917. He took pilot training at Kelly Field in 1921 and became director of flying at Kelly in 1922. He progressed through the ranks serving at various facilities. He was promoted to Colonel in 1941. He was sent to Mitchel Field, New York as Chief of Staff of the First Air Force. He was promoted to Brigadier General in 1942. He commanded the 12th Air Support Command during the invasion of French Morocco. Later he was in command of the Tactical Air Command, the Air Training Command and the 94th Pursuit Squadron. In 1948 he was given command of U.S. Air Forces in Europe and in 1951 command of the Tactical Air Command at Langley Air Force Base. He retired in 1954 and died on January 12, 1955.

He was awarded four Distinguished Service Medals, Legion of

Merit, Bronze Star, and the Air Medal as well as receiving decorations from Great Britain, Morocco, Yugoslavia, Poland, Italy and France.

(Source: 77)

Carswell Air Force Base

Carswell Air Force Base is located in Fort Worth, Texas. It was originally known as Tarrant Field Airdrome. In 1946 it became a SAC base and was designated as a candidate for closure in 1990 with all heavy bombers transferred to Barksdale Air Force Base. It later became a U.S. Naval Air Station and was designated the Naval Air Station Fort Worth Joint Reserve Base. It was named for Major Horace S. Carswell, a Fort Worth native.

Horace Seaver Carswell, Jr. was born in Fort Worth on July 18, 1916. He attended the local high school, North Side High, where he was known as a standout athlete. He attended Texas A & M for one year and then Texas Christian where he graduated in August, 1939. He married Virginia Ede from a ranching family in San Angelo.

In 1940 he became a flying cadet and was commissioned as a second lieutenant. His many medals earned during World War II included the Air Metal, the Purple Heart, the Distinguished Flying Cross, the Distinguished Service Cross and the highest award that can be given a military man, the Medal of Honor.

The Medal of Honor came from his heroic action over the South China Sea where he was flying a B-24 Bomber. In an attack on a Japanese convoy two engines were shot out and the third failed as he tried to return to his base. After ordering his crew to bail out he found that his bombardier's parachute was damaged to the extent that he wasn't able to follow the other crewmen. Carswell and the co-pilot elected to stay with the plane and try a crash landing. The aircraft crashed into a mountain and he and the co-pilot were killed.

(Source: 77, 151, 216, 229)

Castle Air Force Base

(Now Castle Airport)

Castle Air Force Base is located near Atwater, California in Merced County. It began as the Air Corps Basic Flying School in 1941 as a training base for pilots and aircrew. It became a part of the Strategic Air Command (SAC) in 1946. It was put on minimum activity for a short period and reactivated in May, 1947. The B-36 became a part of the base operations in1948 and was renamed Castle Air Force Base. It was named for General Frederick Walker Castle, a member of the Air Corps during World War II.

Frederick Walker Castle was born on October 14, 1908 at Fort McKinley in the Philippines. He was the son of Benjamin Castle, a graduate of the U.S. Military Academy, Class of 1907. He attended Boonton High School in Mountain Lakes, New Jersey and also the Storm King Military Academy. He joined the New Jersey Air National Guard in preparation for entry into West Point, graduating with the Class of 1930. He earned his wings in October of 1931 at Kelly Field. In 1934 he resigned from the military and took a job at Allied Chemical and Dye Corporation. He later joined Sperry Gyroscope as assistant to their president. He worked in developing both the electrically powered gun turrets and the Norden Bombsight.

He was recalled to duty in January of 1942 and was assigned the duty of organizing bases and depots for the new 8th Air Force. By January 1943 he was promoted to full colonel and made Air Chief of Supply for the Eighth Air Force.

He wanted a combat command and 1943 he was given command of the 94th Bomb wing. Losses of the bombers over Europe were so severe that he was one of the two staff members that were assigned combat commands. In April 1944 he was given Command of the 4th Combat Wing Group and shortly thereafter was promoted to Brigadier General. On a mission at the beginning of the Battle of the Bulge, he assigned himself to lead a wing. During the mission their plane was hit and Castle took over the controls while ordering the abandonment of the airplane. They could perhaps have survived if they had jettisoned their bomb load. This would have imperiled the friendly troops on the ground. Eight of the crew members parachuted, with five surviving the crash. He had ordered the pilot to abandon also but when the fuel tank exploded the pilot was in the nose putting on his parachute. He and the pilot were still aboard when the plane crashed. For his bravery he was posthumously given the Medal of Honor.

Besides the Congressional Medal of Honor, he was awarded the Silver Star, Legion of Merit, four Distinguished Flying Crosses and five Air Medals. He was buried in the American Cemetery at Henri Chappelle, Belgium.

(Source: 15, 77, 160, 167)

Chanute Air Force Base

The Chanute Air Force Base is located in Rantoul, Illinois. It was founded in 1917 at this location because of its nearness to the War Department's ground school located at the University of Illinois at Urbana. During World War II it served as a training ground for new recruits who were entering the Air Corps. Many of the "Tuskegee Airmen" received their initial training here. It was named for Octave Chanute, a civil and railroad engineer and an early aviation pioneer. It was closed in 1993 and now houses the Octave Chanute Aerospace Museum.

Octave Chanute was born in France on February 18, 1832. During his career he designed the Chicago Stock Yards and the Kansas City Stockyards. He designed and built the Hannibal Bridge at Kansas City, the first to cross the Missouri River. Other bridges to his credit were the Illinois River rail bridge and the Genesee River Gorge rail bridge in New York. He invented a pressure system for treating railroad ties and telephone poles with creosote to give them extended life. He also invented the date nail, a method of stamping the head of a nail with a date so as to record the date of any wooden item put into service.

He became interested in aviation after a trip to Europe and in his systematic way became the first to record the early years of flight. While too old to fly himself he was instrumental in designing early improvements in aircraft construction including the method of tying together the multiple stacked wings. He is credited with the bi-wing design as well as the tri-wing design. He encouraged and publicized the Wright Brothers in their efforts. His friendship with the Wright Brothers was strained as he wanted to freely share any knowledge learned about flying while the Brothers wanted to protect their invention. He died in 1910 and Wilber Wright was one of those delivering a eulogy.

(Source: 77)

Dannelly Field
(Montgomery Airport)

Dannelly Field, now known as the Montgomery Airport, serves the area of Montgomery, Alabama. It was opened in 1929 and in 1940 it was chosen to serve as a pilot training facility. It was named for Ensign Clarence Moore Dannelly, Jr., a Navy pilot who was the first casualty from Montgomery in World War II. In 1946 the city took possession of the facility.

(Source: 77)

Davis-Monthan Air Force Base

The Davis-Monthan Air Force base is located in Tucson, Arizona. It started as a military base in 1925. It was named for Lts. Samuel H. Davis and Oscar Monthan who were World War I pilots and who attended the same high school. They died in separate aircraft accidents. The base is responsible for the storage of surplus aircraft.

Lieutenant Davis was killed in a crash of a Curtis JN 6 HG in Arcadia, Florida.

Oscar Monthan was born in England in 1885 and moved to Arizona in 1900. In 1917 he enlisted in the Army Air Corps and received his wings in 1918. He became the Chief Engineer at Rockwell

Field in San Diego in 1920 and was involved in the study of the latest aviation advances. He was killed in a training mission while flying a Martin B-2 bomber on March 27, 1924.

(Source: 70, 223, 278, 279)

Davison Army Air Field

Davison Army Air Field is located at Fort Belvoir, Virginia, a short distance south of Washington, DC. It was named for Brigadier General Donald A. Davison. The air field serves the Army, Navy, Marines and Air Force as well as some private aircraft.

Davison was born at San Carlos, Arizona on October 26, 1892, the son of Lt. Col. Lorenzo Paul Davison. He graduated from the United States Military Academy with the Class of 1915. In 1943 Davison was given command of Twelfth Air Force Engineers. He served in Italy supporting the Air Corps raids against Axis targets in the area. Being a well known aviation engineer, he was sent to India to supervise construction of B-29 bases and died while on duty there. He is buried at Arlington National Cemetery.

(Source: 25, 105, 197)

Dobbins Air Reserve Base

This base is located in Marietta, Georgia. It started in 1940 as Rickenbacker Field. After the Air Force was split from the Army after the War, the airfield became Marietta Air Force Base. It was renamed Dobbins Air Force Base in 1950 in honor of Captain Charles M. Dobbins of Marietta, a World War II transport pilot.

Captain Dobbins' died near Sicily on 11 July 1943 when U.S. Navy gunners who had earlier suffered a Luftwaffe attack mistakenly downed his C-47. He was flying his third mission of the day, dropping paratroopers.

(Source: 77, 104)

Dover Air Force Base

This base is listed only because it so well known for its handling of military personnel killed in both peace and wartime. It is named for its location at the City of Dover, Delaware. It is home to the largest military mortuary in the Department of Defense. It also is the home of the C-5 Galaxy which is flown by the 436th Airlift wing.

(Source: 77)

Dyess Air Force Base

Dyess Air Force Base is located near the city of Abilene, Texas and began as Tye Army Air Field in 1942. It is named for Lt. Col. William Edwin Dyess who was a native of Albany, Texas.

He was the son of Judge Richard and Hallie Graham Dyess. He took his first airplane ride on a barn storming plane in 1920. He graduated from Albany High and John Tarleton College in Stephenville, Texas.

He joined the Army Air Corps and earned his wings at Randolph Field, Texas. At the time of Pearl Harbor he was stationed in the Philippines where he and a small group of airmen flying the P-40 Aircraft, fought the Japanese.

He was captured by the Japanese on Bataan in April of 1942 and was a part of the Bataan Death March. He was able to escape and was picked up by a submarine in July of 1943. After his return he was one of those testifying of the atrocities of the Japanese as they tortured and mistreated their prisoners.

During retraining in December of 1943 his P-38 caught fire near Burbank. Instead of bailing out he chose to stay with the plane and steered it to a crash in a vacant field. Tye Field was renamed in his honor in 1956. He was awarded two Distinguished Service Crosses, two Silver Stars, the Legion of Merit, two Distinguished Flying Crosses and the Soldiers Medal.

(Source: 60, 77, 166, 224)

Eaker Air Force Base

This Air Force base was closed in 1992 and became the City of Blytheville, Arkansas International Airport. It is still used by the military for flight training maneuvers. It was named in honor of Lieutenant General Ira C. Eaker who was the first commander of the 8th Air Force during World War II.

Ira Clarence Eaker was born on April 13, 1896 in Field Creek, Texas, the son of a Texas tenant farmer. He attended Southeastern State Teachers College in Durant, Arkansas and joined the Army in 1917. Though he was an enlisted man he was able to attend the officer's training program and was commissioned a second lieutenant in 1917. He received his pilot's wings in 1918.

In 1930 he became the first pilot to fly coast to coast entirely with instruments. Along with Billy Mitchell, Jimmy Doolittle, and Hap Arnold, he led the fight for the establishment of air power.

In the early part of World War II he was sent to England as second in command of what was to be the Eighth Air Force. His training was in fighter aircraft but he led a bombing force that numbered some 2400 heavy bombers. He personally led many of the bombing raids including the first strike against the German occupation forces in France. After the war he worked in the aerospace industry, including being the vice-president of Douglas Aircraft for many years. He died on August 6, 1987 at the age of 91and is buried at Arlington National Cemetery.

He was awarded the Silver Star, Distinguished Flying Cross, and a special gold medal from Congress in 1979.

(Source: 11, 25, 77)

Edwards Air Force Base

Edwards Air Force Base is located in the Antelope Valley near Rosemont, California. It was originally named Muroc Army Air Field. It is the home of the United States Air Force Test Pilot School and was so chosen because of its proximity to a dry lake bed so that emergency landings could be made. It serves as an alternative landing site for our returning space craft. It was renamed Edwards Air Force Base to honor Glen Edwards who died in a test flight of a Northrop YB-49 aircraft. It began its life as a bombing range site in 1933. The first flight to break the sound barrier was at Edwards by Chuck Yeager in the Bell X1. Muroc, as a name, came from the name of early homesteaders in the area, Ralph, Clifford and Ellie Corum. Finding the name "Corum" already assigned as a post office name, the name was reversed so that a new post office could be assigned.

Glen Edwards was born on March 5, 1918 in Medicine Hat, Alberta, Canada. In 1931, his parents moved to California. He graduated with a degree in chemical engineering from the University of California at Berkeley and enlisted in the U.S. Army. He went through flight training and was assigned to a bombardment squadron. He served in North Africa as a flight commander. For his daring low level bomb runs he was awarded four Distinguished Flying Crosses and six Air Medals.

In May of 1945 he graduated from the Flight Performance School and began a career as a test pilot. While assigned to Wright Field, Ohio, much time was spent testing aircraft at Muroc. He was instrumental in testing many of the transitional planes from prop to jet, including the "Flying Wing."

He was sent to Princeton to study aeronautical science and with his masters degree in aeronautical engineering became the vanguard of those who would take us into space. In June of 1948 he was flying as a test crew in the Northrop YB-49, an all jet version of the flying wing, when it broke apart. He and five others died in the crash. In 1949 Muroc Air Force Base was renamed Edwards in honor of this true test pilot.

(Source: 50, 77)

Eglin Air Force Base

Eglin Air Force Base is located near Valparaiso, Florida and is the center for the development, acquisition, testing and deployment of all air-delivered weapons. It began as Valparaiso Bombing and Gunnery Base in 1935and became Eglin Field in 1937. It was named for Lt. Col. Frederick Irving Eglin who was born in 1897. He was responsible for the early training of World War I pilots. He was killed in 1937 when his pursuit plane crashed on a flight from Langley, Virginia to Maxwell Field, Alabama.

The base has ten air fields, each named after Air Force flyers who were killed in plane crashes.

They are listed here along with the biography given by the Eglin Air Force Base Guide.

Field One: named for Major Walter J. Wagner who died in a plane crash on October 10, 1943. He was a former commanding officer for the First Proving Ground at Eglin Air Force Base.

Field Two: Named after Lt. Col. George E. Pierce, who died in a plane crash on October 19, 1942. He was a former commanding officer of the First Proving Ground Torpedo Squadron.

Field Three: Named for First Lieutenant Robert L. Duke, who died in an aircraft crash on December 29, 1943. He was assigned as an assistant to the Army Air Forces Proving Ground Command at Eglin Air Force Base.

Field Four: Named for Second Lieutenant Garland O. Peel, Jr., who died in an air crash on January 2, 1942. He was a gunnery school instructor at Eglin Air Force Base.

Field Five: Named for Captain Anthony D. Piccolo who died in an aircraft accident on October 6, 1942. He was the Commanding Officer of the 386th Single Engine Gunnery Training Squadron at Eglin Air Force Base.

Field Six: Named for First Lieutenant Andrew Biancur, who died in an aircraft accident on January 8, 1944. He was a test pilot with the Medium Bombardment Section of the First Proving Ground at Eglin Air Force Base.

Field Seven: Named for Colonel Robin E. Epler, who died in an aircraft crash on January 28, 1944. He was Deputy Commander (Technical) of the Army Air Force Proving ground at Eglin Air Force Base.

Field Eight: Named for Second Lieutenant Richard E. Baldsiefen, who died in an aircraft crash on March 4, 1942. He was a gunnery school instructor at Eglin Air Force Base.

Field Nine: Named for First Lieutenant Donald W. Hurlburt, who died in an aircraft crash on October 2, 1943. He was a member of a fighter section in the First Proving Ground at Eglin Air Force Base. It was here that Jimmy Doolittle practiced taking off on a short runway prior to their flying off of an aircraft carrier to bomb Tokyo.

Field Ten: Named for Captain Barclay H. Dillon, who died in an aircraft crash on October 2, 1943. He was a member of a fighter section of the First Proving Ground at Eglin Air Force Base.

(Source: 70, 77, 232)

Eielson Air Force Base

Eielson Air Force Base is located near Fairbanks, Alaska and is named for Carl Ben Eielson who was born in 1897 in Hatton, North Dakota. He was an aviator, bush pilot and an explorer. In 1917 shortly after America's entry into World War I he joined the Air Service. In 1918 he became a part of the newly formed aviation section of the Signal Corps. After the War and after an initial beginning as a barn-stormer, he entered law school in what is now Georgetown University in Washington, D.C. He was talked into going to Alaska to teach school. There he continued flying and was the first to carry mail from Fairbanks to McGrath, a distance of three hundred miles. He cut the mail delivery time from twenty days to four hours.

He was the first air explorer of the Arctic as he and an Australian explorer flew across the Arctic Ocean in 1928. The flight was some 2200 miles and took twenty hours. They were searching for an island that might exist between Alaska and the North Pole.

Eielson was killed in a flight in 1929 as he attempted to rescue passengers from a cargo vessel trapped in the ice. A number of schools and landmarks have also been named for him.

(Source: 77, 84, 85)

Ellington Field

Ellington Field is located near Houston, Texas and was established in 1917. It is now being used by the military, commercial, government, and general aviation groups. It was named for Lt. Eric Lamar Ellington who was killed in a plane crash near San Diego on November 24, 1913.

Eric Lamar Ellington was born in Clayton, North Carolina on May 15, 1889. Interested in the military from an early age, he gained an appointment to the United States Naval Academy. Weighing only 100 pounds, he fought successfully to remain at Annapolis and graduated seventh in his class in 1909. He went to sea as a Midshipman in Training and was commissioned as an Ensign on June 5, 1911.

Desiring to become a part of aviation, he resigned his Navy Commission and went into the Army and was assigned to the First Aero Squadron at Texas City, Texas and San Diego, California.

On the last day of his life he took another officer up for flight instruction. The Wright "C" aircraft malfunctioned and both officers were killed in the crash.

(Source: 49, 74, 77, 94, 253)

Ellsworth Air Force Base

Ellsworth Air Force Base is located near Rapid City, South Dakota. It began as the Rapid City Army Air Base as a training site for B-17 Flying Fortress bombers in 1942. In July of 1949 it became the home of the B-36 Peacemaker. In 1953, one of its aircraft crashed in Newfoundland on a routine flight from Europe. In 1953 the base was renamed Ellsworth Air Force base in honor of Brigadier General Richard E. Ellsworth, who was one of the twenty three man crew who perished in that crash.

Richard E. Ellsworth was born in Erie, Pennsylvania and entered the U.S. Military Academy in 1931. Upon graduation he went through flight training at Randolph and Kelly Fields. He studied meteorology at Cal Tech and by the beginning of World War II he had been promoted to Lieutenant Colonel. After a tour of duty in Alaska he was assigned to the South Pacific where he flew more than 400 combat missions. His awards from World War II included the Legion of Merit, two Distinguished Flying Crosses, three Air Medals and the Chinese Air Force Wings.

Later he was Chief of Operations and Training for the Air Weather Service. He commanded the 308 Reconnaissance Group. By September 1952 he had been promoted to Brigadier General.

On March 18, 1953 he was co-piloting an American Convair on a 25 hour simulated combat mission flying from the Azores to Rapid City, South Dakota. The flight plans included low level flying with the radar guidance turned off. The plane went off course during bad weather and crashed into a hill near Newfoundland. He was killed along with twenty two others.

(Source: 11, 77)

Elmendorf Air Force Base

Elmendorf Air Force Base, Alaska is named for Hugh Merle Elmendorf who was a captain in the United States Army Air Service. It was said that he never visited Alaska or was assigned there. He was born in Ithaca, New York on January 3, 1895, son of William C. Elmendorf, the mayor of the city. He attended local schools and graduated from Cornell University with a Mechanical Engineering Degree.

As he graduated, the First World War was beginning and he joined the infantry and served as an instructor. He transferred to the Army Air Service in 1921. He earned his wings and served at a number of bases. In 1927 he received serious injuries as his plane which was landing collided with a plane that was taking off. He suffered a broken back but returned to flying in time to help establish an altitude record of 30, 000 feet, surpassing the old record of 10,000 feet. He was an excellent gunner and won the national competition at Langley Field in 1927.

On July 13, 1933 he and another pilot were flying a Y1P prototype aircraft when Elmendorf suddenly slumped over and died. He was buried at Arlington National Cemetery.

(Source: 25, 77, 120)

England Air Force Base

England Air Force Base was located near Alexandria, Louisiana and was opened in 1942. It was put on inactive status in 1946 but reactivated in 1952. It is now the Alexandria International Airport.

The base was named for Lt. Col. John B. England, a pilot who flew combat in both World War II and Korea. During World War II he flew 108 missions and is credited with shooting down 19 enemy planes. He flew P-51 fighters and was a leading ace. He also flew combat missions during the Korean War. He was killed in a crash of a Sabre Jet in France as he sought to miss a barracks area in dense fog.

(Source: 77, 167, 228)

Fairchild Air Force Base

This base is located in Spokane County, Washington and was established in 1942. It was made possible through the money donated by the residents of Spokane as they bought some 1400 acres and gave it to the government to be used as a base. It was called the Spokane Army Air Depot and until 1946 served as a repair base for damaged aircraft. In 1950 it was named in honor of Air Force Vice Chief of Staff, General Muir S. Fairchild, a native of Bellingham, Washington.

Muir Stephen Fairchild began his Army service in 1916 when he joined the Washington National Guard as a sergeant. He shortly became a flying cadet and earned his wings in time to fly bombing missions in World War I. After the war he served at various Army

Air Fields including Langley Field, Virginia, McCook Field, Ohio, and Michel Field, New York. He was a part of the Good Will Tour to South America and for this was awarded the Distinguished Flying Cross.

By 1939 he had risen to be Director of Air Tactics and Strategy. In March of 1942 he was assigned the duty of Director of Military Requirements. Later he was a member of the Joint Strategic Survey Committee of the Joint Chiefs of Staff.

After the war he was named Commandant of the Air University at Maxwell Field. In 1948 he became Vice Chief of Staff at Fort Myer, Virginia. He died while on active duty on March 17, 1950.

(Source: 77)

Forbes Air Force Base

Forbes Air Force Base had its beginnings shortly after Pearl Harbor. It grew to be a major training center for B-29 Bombers during World War II and served as a SAC base in post war years. It was deactivated in 1973 and is now a part of the City of Topeka, Kansas.

It was named for Major Daniel S. Forbes, an Air Force test pilot. He was born on June 6, 1920 in Carbondale, Kansas. He attended Wichita University and Kansas State University before joining the Army in 1941. He was a pioneer in photoreconnaissance as he flew combat mission in North Africa. He flew B-29 planes in the Pacific Theater. He was killed in a test flight of the Northrop Flying Wing on June 5, 1948 along with all of the crew. Among the crew was the co-pilot Captain Glen Edwards, for which the Edwards Air Force Base is named.

(Source: 77, 216)

Joe Foss Field

(Sioux Falls Regional Airport)

Joe Foss Field is located near Sioux Falls, South Dakota and is the home base of the South Dakota Air National Guard.

It was named for Marine Corps flying ace Joseph Jacob Foss who was the recipient of the Medal of Honor in 1943. Joe Foss was born near Sioux Falls, South Dakota on April 17, 1915. When he was 12, he saw Charles Lindbergh on tour with the "Spirit of St. Louis." By 1940 he had a pilot certificate and a degree from the University of South Dakota. He joined the Marines and after pilot training was commissioned a Second Lieutenant in the U.S. Marine Corps. During World War II he flew Wildcats and was the leader of a flight of eight that became known as Foss's Flying Circus. By the time he left Guadalcanal his "Flying Circus" had shot down 72 Japanese aircraft with 26 credited to him. He and Gregory "Pappy" Boyington vied for most planes shot down by a Marine during the war. The Medal of Honor given him in 1943 was in recognition for his bravery during this operation, one which helped secure the victory by America in the Solomon Islands.

After the war he left the service and started a flying school as well as being a car salesman. He helped start the South Dakota Air National Guard. Active in many areas, he helped start the American Football League and was instrumental in the establishment of the Super Bowl.

In 1955 he became the 20th Governor of the State of South Dakota. He died on New Year's Day, 2003 and was buried at the Arlington National Cemetery.

(Source: 77, 234)

George Air Force Base

George Air Force base is located near Victorville, California and was constructed in 1942 as a flight training school. It first was called the Victorville Army Flying School, and then renamed the Victorville

Army Air field. It became the Victorville Air Force Base in 1948. In June of 1950 it was named for Brigadier General Harold H. George.

Harold H. George was born in 1892 and graduated from high school in Niagara Falls, New York. He joined the New York National Guard and in 1917 finished his flying training at Mineola, Long Island, New York. He was commissioned a first lieutenant and sent to Kelly Field, Texas. In 1917 he went to France as Commanding Officer of the 201st Aero Squadron.

He instructed other pilots and took courses in pursuit and gunnery training. He qualified as an ace by shooting down five enemy aircraft and received the Distinguished Flying Cross for his heroic actions.

During the twenties he served at various bases and in 1938 graduated from the Air Corps Tactical School as well as the Command and General Staff School. In 1941 he was promoted to Brigadier General and was sent to the Philippines to command all air units as a part of General Douglas MacArthur's staff. He was awarded the Distinguished Service Cross for his action in defending the entrance to Manila Bay. He was taken from Corregidor on PT Boat 32 commanded by Lt. (jg.) Schumacher, at the time General MacArthur was rescued by PT Boat 41, commanded by Lt. John Bulkeley. There were two other PT Boats in the squadron removing other ranking personnel to Darwin /Port Moresby, Australia.

General George lost his life in an aircraft accident near Darwin on April 29, 1942.

(Source: 11, 77, 236)

Goodfellow Air Force Base

This base is located in San Angelo. Texas and was named after First Lieutenant John J. Goodfellow, Jr. Goodfellow was killed in World War I while conducting aerial reconnaissance behind enemy lines. The base was established in 1941 and was used to train pilots to fly medium bombers during the war.

John J. Goodfellow, Jr. was born May 17, 1891 in Fort Worth, Texas. He moved to San Angelo in 1907 and graduated from high school there. He attended the University of Texas where he, along with 200 other students, volunteered for service on May 5, 1917. He attended officers' training school and transferred to aviation training.

In February 1918 he was commissioned and sent to France. He was assigned to the 24th Aero Squadron and made almost daily flights over enemy lines. He was killed in action on September 17, 1918. In his obituary he was remembered for his high school athleticism and for his musical talent. At the University of Texas he had been studying Electrical Engineering.

(Source: 77, 200)

Griffiss Air Force Base

Griffiss Air Force Base is located in Rome, New York and was first known as the Rome Air Depot. It was founded in 1941 and in 1948 it was renamed for Lt. Col. Townsend E. Griffiss. In 1995 the base was deactivated and returned to civilian ownership. It is known as the site of the Woodstock concert in 1999.

Townsend E. Griffiss was born in Buffalo, New York on April 4, 1900. He graduated from the U.S. Military Academy with the Class of 1922. He earned his wings at Brooks and Kelly Fields. He was killed on February 15, 1942 over England when his aircraft, which was returning from a flight to Russia, was shot down by the R.A.F. by mistake. At the time he was designing ferry routes between England and Russia. He was a Lieutenant Colonel and was the first American airman killed in the European Theater of War.

(Source: 77, 107, 191, 216)

Grissom Air Reserve Base

First known as Grissom Air Force Base, it is located near Peru, Indiana. It is named after Lt. Col. Virgil I. "Gus" Grissom. It was once called the Bunker Hill Air Force Base and before that the Bunker Hill Naval Air station. It began in 1942 and operated through World War II. It was closed after the war and was returned to farm land. It was reopened in 1954 as the Bunker Hill Air Force Base. In 1994 it became a Reserve Command Facility. There were both Navy and Marine Corps reserve groups there in 2001 and 2002. In 1968 it was officially renamed after Gus Grissom, a Purdue University graduate who was a part of the space program.

Gus Grissom was born on April 3, 1926 in Mitchell, Indiana. In 1944 he joined the Air Force, wanting to become a pilot. The war ended before he was able to accomplish this and he returned to civilian life and entered Purdue University and graduated with a degree in Mechanical Engineering. He rejoined the Air Force and became a pilot in time to see combat in Korea. He flew 100 combat missions and was awarded the Air Medal and Distinguished Flying Cross.

He logged 4600 flying hours, 3500 in jet aircraft. He was a captain when selected for astronaut training and was the pilot of the Mercury-Redstone 4. He survived near drowning after splashdown when the exit hatch blew off prematurely. In 1964 he was named Command Pilot of the Project Gemini mission and thus became the first astronaut to return to space. He was killed along with astronauts Ed White and Roger B. Chaffee in the Apollo 1 fire at Cape Canaveral on January 27, 1967.

Many in the Space program said that if Grissom were alive he would have been the choice to have been the first man to step foot on the moon.

He was awarded the Congressional Space Medal of Honor.

(Source: 25, 77, 83, 129, 135)

Gunter Air Force Base

Gunter Air Force Base is located in Montgomery, Alabama and began as the Montgomery Municipal Airport but was renamed Gunter Field after the Mayor William Gunter. It was chosen as a flying training school in 1940. It was commonly called Gunter Field while the Mayor was still alive, to his protestations. The mayor died in late 1940 and in 1941 it was officially named for him. Gunter Field is a part of the Maxwell Air Force Base.

(Source: 14, 38, 77)

Hamilton Air Force Base

Hamilton Air Force Base was located in Marin County, California. It began in 1929 and was known as Air Corps Station, San Rafael. As it grew it was renamed for First Lieutenant Lloyd Andrew Hamilton, a decorated pioneer airman from Marin County. It was decommissioned in 1974.

First Lieutenant Hamilton was killed during World War I as he flew with the 17th Aero Squadron. He was awarded the Distinguished Service Cross for heroism at Varssonaore, Belgium as he flew a low level bombing attack. Thirteen days later he was killed in action near Lagnecourt, France.

(Source: 154, 212)

Hanscom Air Force Base

Hanscom Air Force Base is located near Boston, Massachusetts and is the headquarters of the Electronic Systems Center. It is named for Laurence G. Hanscom who was a pilot and an aviation enthusiast. He was a reporter for the Worchester Telegram-Gazette. He died in a plane crash on in February 1941, in an accident at Saugus, Maine.

During this time he had been vigorously lobbying for an airport at the site of what is now Hanscom Air Force Base. He was the founder of the Massachusetts Civil Air Reserve.

(Source: 77, 216)

Hickam Air Force Base

Hickam Air Force Base is located on Oahu, Hawaii and was originally known as Hickam Field. It was one of the primary targets of the Japanese when they launched their attack on Pearl Harbor on December 7, 1941. It was dedicated on May 31, 1935 and named for Lieutenant Colonel Horace Meek Hickam.

Horace Meek Hickam was born on August 14, 1885 in Spencer, Indiana. Unlike his father and two brothers who were lawyers, Hickam showed an interest in aviation and the military. While in high school he formed a cadet corps. He went to the University of Indiana for one year, then on to the United States Military Academy where he graduated with the Class of 1908. While at the Academy he was active in athletics including football, track and gymnastics. His first duty after graduation was with the Cavalry and in 1911 he volunteered for aviation training. At this time aspiring aviators still had to fulfill their regular assignments and train to be pilots in their spare time.

He served in the Philippines and upon returning to the United States he fought against Pancho Villa's forces, earning a Silver Star for his heroics. In 1917 he joined the Signal Corps and reported for flight training. By 1918 he was commanding Dorr Field and Carlstrom Field. After World War I he was one of the vocal proponents for a separate Air Corps arguing that the airplane should not be considered just an arm of the ground forces. In 1932 he was given command of the Third Attack Group at Fort Crockett in Galveston, Texas. In 1934 President Roosevelt gave the Air Service the duty of carrying the air mail after the cancellation of contracts with the commercial airlines. He gave the Central Zone operations to Lt. Colonel Hickam.

When this service terminated he returned to duties as Commander of the Third Attack Group. He was killed on November 5, 1934 while practicing night landings on an unlighted air strip at Fort Crockett. He was buried at the Arlington National Cemetery.

(Source: 77, 285)

Hill Air Force Base

Hill Air Force Base is located near Ogden, Utah and is the home of the Air Force Material Command. The base was named in the honor of Major Ployer Peter Hill in 1939.

Major Hill was born in Newburyport, Massachusetts on October 24, 1894. He graduated from Brown University in 1916 with a Bachelor of Science in Civil Engineering. In 1917 he enlisted in the Aviation Section of the Army Signal Reserve Corps. He received a commission as a second lieutenant in the Army and served as an instructor. He saw duty in Washington, DC, the American Army of Occupation in Germany and at Fort Bliss, El Paso, Texas. He served as Commanding Officer of the 6th Photo Section in Manila.

In 1932 he served as a test pilot at Wright Field in Dayton, Ohio. On October 30, 1935 he died as a result of the crash of a Boeing experimental aircraft and was buried at his birthplace, Newburyport, Massachusetts.

The experimental aircraft was the forerunner of the B-17 Flying Fortress. After the crash it was determined that the airplane was too complicated to fly and the contract was given to another company. There were those who thought the B-17 was the superior aircraft and the reason for its crash, though determined to be "pilot error" could be resolved by creating a check-off sheet that the crew used at the beginning of each flight. Thus, this was the beginning of the now standard check-off list used before all flights, no matter how simple.

(Source: 77, 140, 225, 286)

Holloman Air Force Base

This base is located near Alamogordo, New Mexico and was established in 1942. It was named for Colonel George Holloman a pioneer in early rocket and pilot-less aircraft. Colonel George Holloman was killed in the crash of a B-17 bomber on March 19, 1946 on a flight over Taiwan.

(Source: 77, 89, 102, 286)

Howard Air Force Base

Howard Air Force Base is located in Panama. It was decommissioned in 2000 and turned over to the Republic of Panama. It is now being used to house call centers for technology companies. General "Hap" Arnold went to the area in 1939 to select a site for an airbase. He also suggested its name, that of Howard Field, in honor of Major Charles H. Howard who had served in the Canal Zone in 1926-29. Howard had been a part of Arnold's crew when he made a flight to Alaska in 1934. Major Howard died in a plane crash on October 1, 1936.

(Source: 77, 105)

Keesler Air Force Base

This base is located in Biloxi, Mississippi and is used as an advanced training base, as well as a medical center. It began in 1941 and remains in use. It was named in honor of Second Lieutenant Samuel Reeves Keesler, Jr. who was a native of Mississippi and who was killed in action in France during World War I. It is known as the training ground for the Tuskegee Airmen. It became a radar training center in 1947. In 1956 it became a training site for the Atlas missile.

Samuel Reeves Keesler, Jr. was born on April 11, 1896 in

Greenwood, Mississippi. He entered the Army in May of 1917 and was commissioned that same year. He sailed for France after receiving training as an aerial observer at Fort Sill, Oklahoma. While flying a reconnaissance mission on October 8, 1918, he and his pilot were attacked by four enemy fighters. They shot down one of the attackers but in the end they lost control of their own damaged plane. He was wounded six times as he continued to fire his machine gun at the enemy. He survived the crash landing but the enemy continued to strafe them. The two were captured but died from their wounds as they were unable to receive immediate medical attention. Keesler was awarded the Distinguished Service Cross for his gallantry.

(Source: 77, 167)

Kelly Air Force Base

Kelly Air Force Base is located in San Antonio, Texas. At present it supports a part of the Air Force Reserve Command. The base was founded in 1916 and was originally called the South San Antonio Aviation Camp. It was named in honor of Lt. George E.M. Kelly who crashed while landing at Fort Sam Houston in 1911. During the First World War it was training aviation mechanics, graduating them at the rate of 2000 a month. Most of the World War I aviators were trained at Kelly Field. After the war most of the military pilots were trained here including the names of many who became famous for their achievements in World War II. During this war it continued its training mission and worked on all the major types of aircraft in use throughout the war.

Lt. Kelly was the first U.S. military pilot to lose his life while flying a military aircraft. He crashed on May 1, 1911 at Fort Sam Houston when a front strut collapsed. To avoid hitting an Infantry encampment, he veered away and was killed in the crash. He is buried in the San Antonio National Cemetery, San Antonio, Texas.

George Kelly was a native of England and joined the U.S. Army in 1904.

(Source: 46, 77, 88, 216)

Key Field

Key Field is located at Meridian, Mississippi and was named for the brothers, Al and Fred Key. In 1935 they took off in an effort to break the world record for sustained flight. They developed refueling methods to prove that air to air refueling could work. They stayed aloft for 27 days flying 52,300 miles at 80 MPH. The record still stands for sub space flying. They served in World War II and flew the B-17 Flying Fortress.

They were "barnstormers" in the 1920's and became managers of the municipal airport at Meridian. The depression came and there was the danger of the airport being closed. They searched for ideas that would draw publicity to their airport and came up with breaking the flight endurance record. With no experience, they, along with a local mechanic, modified an aircraft to increase its fuel capacity and devised a method of refueling the airplane in flight. They came up with a fuel nozzle that was spill free and its valve would only open when it was actuated by a probe in the receiving fuel line. The design was so novel that it continues to this day and is the type used in refueling aircraft in flight.

The aircraft had to be modified so that the pilots could get to its extremities to do maintenance. A catwalk was devised so that one of the brothers could do maintenance while the other brother flew the plane.

On their third attempt in June of 1935 they set the record of 653 continuous hours in the sky, flying some 52,000 miles over a 27 day period. They consumed some 6000 gallons of fuel and 300 gallons of motor oil as they fought the elements to stay aloft. This flight was in a Curtis-Robbins aircraft named "Ole Miss" after the University with that nickname. The airplane is now displayed in the National Air and Space Museum in Washington, D C.

(Source: 3, 77, 282)

Kincheloe Air Force Base

Kincheloe Air Force Base was located near Sault Ste. Marie, Michigan, originally to protect the Soo Canal. It started as the Kinross Auxiliary Air Field and construction was started in 1943. It was used for commercial service after the war but was reactivated in 1952. In 1959 it was renamed after Captain Iven C Kincheloe, Jr. who was a Korean War Ace and an Air Force Test Pilot.

Iven Kincheloe was born in Detroit, Michigan on July 2, 1928. He attended Purdue University and majored in Aeronautical Engineering. He graduated in 1949 and was commissioned into the Air Force. He began his Air Force life as a test pilot at Edwards Air Force Base but then was transferred to Korea. He flew 30 missions in F-80's and 101 missions in F-106's. He downed ten enemy planes and was awarded the Silver Star. He was also given three Distinguished Flying Crosses and four Air Medals.

After the war he returned to test piloting and flew the X-2 plane to a record altitude of 126,000 feet, being the first human to fly over 100,000 feet. He lost his life in a flight over Edwards in an F-104 jet on July 26, 1958. He is buried at Arlington National Cemetery.

(Source: 9, 25, 77)

Kingsley Field

This base was located near the City of Klamath Falls, Oregon and originally was a U.S. Naval Air Station beginning in 1942. It was deactivated in 1946 and subsequently was selected by the U.S. Air Force to be the home of an all weather intercept squadron. The base is named after Lieutenant David R. Kingsley, an Oregon native, who was killed in action during a bombing mission over the oil fields in Ploesti, Rumania. The base was closed as an Air Force base in 1978. It is the home of the 173rd Fighter Wing of the Oregon Air National Guard.

David Kingsley was one of nine children, five boys and four girls. He was next to the oldest. His father died in an automobile accident when David was ten. From then on, he was an indispensible help with the raising of the children. His family was members of St. Michael's Church and David attended St. Michael's School. When David was 18 his older brother joined the Navy. David took over the chores of running the family as his mother was diagnosed with cancer. Three years later she died when David was 21. When World War II started in December, his brother Tom was stationed on the USS Phoenix at Pearl Harbor. The following April, David quit his fire fighting job and joined the Army Air Force. He wanted to be a pilot but ended up as a bombardier-navigator. In July of 1943 he received his commission and was assigned to Lieutenant Edwin Anderson's B-17 crew.

They flew many missions including a sixty day period that totaled twenty missions. Ploesti, Rumania became a target of many raids because of its many oil refineries. While heavily defended, flight after flight of B-17's and B-24's sought it as a target. It was known as the "Widow Maker" because of the heavy losses. Lt. Anderson and his crew were finally given their own B-17 rather than having to fly one of the pool bombers. It was christened the "Sand Man" and they flew a number of missions using that plane. On the fateful day of June 23, 1944 the plane had mechanical problems and the crew was switched to another B-17 with the name given it by another crew, "Opissonya." They were late taking off and this plane also suffered a mechanical problem of a blown oil line. After canvassing the potential results, the crew decided to fly on with three engines. They were hit by anti-aircraft fire which damaged the plane severely. They were able to drop their bombs on target and turned back toward home. Losing air speed and altitude they attracted the enemy fighter planes which not only further damaged the aircraft but wounded some of the crew. The tail gunner had to leave his position and crawl toward the mid-section where Lt. Kingsley attempted to staunch the flow of blood. Other wounded came forward to be treated by Kingsley as the pilot fought to fly the plane with now almost nonexistent controls. Finally all hope of saving the aircraft was gone and the order to bailout was given.

As Lt. Kingsley prepared the wounded tail gunner for jumping, he saw that his parachute rigging had been damaged. Without hesitating David Kingsley took off his own parachute and strapped it on the other crewman. All of the nine crewmen parachuted to safety except David Kingsley who died in the crash of the B-17. Thus David fulfilled his mother's encouragement to her children, "Love each other, take care of each other, and take care of anyone in need."

For this he was awarded the Congressional Medal of Honor.

(Source: 2, 123, 283)

Kirtland Air Force Base

Kirtland Air Force Base is located in Albuquerque, New Mexico and is the third largest installation in the Air Force Material Command. It was named for Colonel Roy C. Kirtland in 1942 at the request of General "Hap" Arnold. He learned to fly in 1911 in a Wright Brothers airplane. During World War I he commanded a regiment of mechanics. Recalled to duty in 1941 he was the oldest military pilot in the U.S. Army Air Corps. He died of a heart attack at age 65 that same year.

Roy Kirkland was born at Fort Benton, Montana on May 14, 1874. He enlisted in the Army in 1898 and earned his commission in the Infantry in 1901. He transferred to the Air Service and became commander of the U.S. Aviation School at College Park, Maryland. It was he who recommended "Hap" Arnold to be selected for flight training. In 1912 he was the first to fire a machine gun from an aircraft after Isaac M. Lewis petitioned the aviation service to test his Lewis gun.

He was one of the first military pilots, holding Certificate # 46. He returned to the Infantry in 1915 and was in command of the Third Regiment in France during World War I. He also served as Inspector of Aviation in England.

After the war he was a flight instructor and in 1930 became Commandant of Langley Field, Virginia. He retired in 1938 but was called back into service in 1941.

(Source: 74, 77, 136)

K.I. Sawyer Air Force Base

This is a decommissioned U.S. Air Force base in Marquette County, Michigan. It was built in 1944 and closed in 1995. It was named for Kenneth Ingalls Sawyer, a Marquette County Road Commissioner who had originally proposed the airport to be built there. It was a part of the Air Defense Command and the Strategic Air Command became a tenant in 1960. A portion of the base is now the Sawyer International Airport.

He served as Engineer-superintendent for 27 years of the Marquette County Commission. He is believed to be the first to mark the centerline on any rural highway in America. He served as President of the Upper Peninsula Road Builders Association for eight years. He was born in 1884 and died in 1944.

(Source: 77, 126, 153)

Lackland Air Force Base

Lackland Air Force Base is located near San Antonio, Texas. It was named for Brigadier General Frank Lackland in 1948. Originally a part of Kelly Field, it began in 1941. A year later it became a separate facility and at that time was given the name of the San Antonio Aviation Cadet Center. It became a part of the Department of Defense's Base Realignment and Closure Program in 2005.

Frank D. Lackland was born in Fauquier County, Virginia in 1885. He joined the Army in 1911 and served in the Infantry. Previous to that he served six years in the Washington, DC National Guard. During the First World War he transferred to the Signal Corps and served as Executive Officer at Kelly Field. He was the Commanding Officer of the First Wing at March Field. He died on April 28, 1943 at Walter Reed Hospital at the age of 58. Lackland had proposed that an aviation facility and cadet training center be built on the site of what is now Lackland Air Force Base.

(Source: 16, 43. 77, 105)

Langley Air Force Base

Located just north of Hampton, Virginia, Langley Air Force Base is the home of the United States Air Force 1st Fighter Wing and the 480th Intelligence Wing. It was named for Samuel Pierpont Langley. The base had its beginnings in 1917 and was designated Langley Field.

Langley was born on August 22, 1834 in Roxbury, Massachusetts. He graduated from Boston Latin School. He was an assistant at the Harvard College Observatory and the Chair of Mathematics at the United States Naval Academy. In 1867 he became the director of the Allegheny Observatory and a professor of astronomy at what is now the University of Pittsburgh. He was the third Secretary of the Smithsonian Institution and was the founder of the Smithsonian Astrophysical Observatory. He was the inventor of the bolometer which was an instrument to measure minute differences of radiant energy from a source by the changes in its electrical resistance. This procedure was used to first measure the greenhouse effect by other scientists in 1890.

Langley was racing with the Wright Brothers to be the first to fly a heavier-than-air aircraft. His models flew but he was unsuccessful in his first attempts at piloted flight. His unpiloted flight from a catapult which flew about a half mile is considered the first sustained flight by a heavier-than-air craft. His attempts at piloted flight in 1903 were unsuccessful and he was ridiculed by the press. Langley died on February 27, 1906 in Aiken, South Carolina.

(Source: 77, 131, 134)

Laughlin Air Force Base

Laughlin Air Force Base is located just east of Del Rio, Texas and is the largest training base of the United States Air Force. It was originally named the Laughlin Army Air Field in the honor of Jack T. Laughlin who was Del Rio's first World War II causality when he was shot down while navigating a B-17 Flying Fortress over Java in

January of 1942. The base was closed in 1945 and reopened in May of 1952 as the Laughlin Air Force Base.

Jack T. Laughlin was born in Del Rio, Texas on September 14, 1914. He graduated from the University of Texas in 1938 with a degree in Business Administration. He joined the Army Air Corps in 1940 and earned his pilot's wings. His plane was shot down over the Makasser Strait, Indonesia.

(Source: 65, 77)

Lawson Army Air Field, Fort Benning, Georgia

This Army Air base is located to serve Fort Benning. It was constructed in 1930 as a balloon landing field.

Lawson Army Air Field was first named for Captain Walter Ralls Lawson, Sr. and then later for Major Ted W. Lawson. Both biographies are included.

Walter Ralls Larson was born on October 23, 1893 in Chattahoochee County, Georgia. He was a member of the Alabama National Guard when World War I started and he went overseas with the "Rainbow" Division. He entered the Air Service and served as Operations Officer and Aerial Observer. For his heroism he was awarded the Distinguished Service Cross. He was wounded during a reconnaissance flight but returned to fly even with his wounds. After the war he was an instructor. He was killed in an airplane accident on April 21, 1923 near Dayton, Ohio. General Billy Mitchell called Lawson the greatest bomber pilot there was. At the time of his death he commanded the Twentieth Bombardment Squadron. He was buried at Arlington National Cemetery as is his son Colonel Walter R. Lawson, Jr.

Major Ted W. Lawson was born on March 7, 1917 in Alameda, California. He joined the Army Air Corps in 1940 and received his wings on November 15, 1942. He became a B-25 bomber pilot and in 1942 he was selected to pilot one of the bombers in the squadron led by Jimmy Doolittle that bombed Tokyo. He flew an airplane nicknamed the "Ruptured Duck" and was one of the airplanes that ran out of fuel after finishing its bombing mission. During the ditching of the airplane in the East China Sea he received severe lacerations which required a leg amputation after he was able to return from the raid. After the ditching he and his crew were found by Chinese guerrillas and in a seven week period they were carried by many types of conveyances until they were picked up by an Army Air Force plane that flew them to India.

Later he cooperated with columnist Bob Considine to write a book about the raid called "Thirty Seconds Over Tokyo." The book was made into a movie that starred Van Johnson, Spencer Tracy, and Robert Mitchum. Major Larson died in Chico, California on January 19, 1992. His awards included the Distinguished Flying Cross, Purple Heart, Chinese Army, Navy and Air Corps Medal, Class A, First Grade.

(Source: 25, 77, 93, 105, 156)

Loring Air Force Base

This is a former Air Force base located in Aroostook County, Maine. It was named for Charles J. Loring, Jr., a Medal of Honor recipient. Loring was the first United States site specifically constructed for the storage, assembly and testing of atomic weapons and was originally called the Caribou Air Force Station. It was officially closed in September, 1994 after many disputes within the government.

Charles J. Loring, Jr. was born on October 2, 1918 in Portland, Maine. He fought in Europe during World War II and was shot down and taken prisoner after fifty five combat missions. Major Loring was sent to Korea in 1952 where he was killed after his plane was hit during an attack run. He deliberately crashed his plane into the guns that fired upon him.

He died on November 22, 1952 at the age of thirty four. He was one of four airmen to receive the Congressional Medal of Honor for his heroism in Korea. He entered the Air Force on March 16, 1942 and received his wings in December of 1942. After World War II he served at Victoria and Foster Fields, Texas. In May of 1952 he went to Korea as a part of 8th Fighter Bomber Group. He was flying an F-80 with three other pilots where he was to dive bomb enemy gun positions that were shooting at United States ground troops. His plane was damaged while going into the dive bombing run. He altered his course so as to hit the gun emplacements.

(Source: 25, 77, 123)

Lowry Air Force Base

Lowry Air Force Base is located in Aurora/Denver, Colorado. It was established in 1937. It was closed in 1994 but during World War II it served as training center for bomber crews. It was named for Second Lieutenant Francis Lowry whose plane was shot down during the First World War.

Francis Lowry was a Denver native who was born on December 1, 1894. While serving as an aerial observer, his plane was shot down by German antiaircraft fire on September 26, 1918 and he became the first Denver aviator killed in wartime. The weather at the time was bad for flying but he attempted a photo-reconnaissance mission to assist in the Meuse-Argonne Offensive. He was buried in France but then was reburied in a cemetery adjacent to Lowry Air Force Base.

(Source: 77, 257)

Luke Air Force Base

This base is located near Glendale, Arizona and presently trains pilots in the F-16 airplane. It was named in honor of Lieutenant Frank Luke, Jr., who was born in Phoenix.

Frank Luke was born on May 19, 1897. His family had emigrated from Germany. Frank Luke, Jr. was an active child showing a competitive spirit that included bare knuckle boxing. He enlisted in the Army on September 25, 1917 and received flight training in

Texas. He went to France and was known for his aggressive flying as he attacked observation balloons. He also was a flying ace, second to Eddie Rickenbacker in the number of flying victories. His last day alive was one in which he shot down three observation balloons but was hit by antiaircraft fire. He was able to land but was killed by soldiers. His body was found along with an empty pistol and seven dead enemy soldiers around him. He was awarded the Congressional Medal of Honor for his heroics. He was killed on September 29, 1918 when he was twenty one.

(Source: 12, 15, 77, 167)

MacDill Air Force Base

This base is located in Hillsborough County, Florida. It was formally given the status of a military base in 1939 and was dedicated as MacDill Field in 1941. It was named in honor of Colonel Leslie MacDill who had been killed in an aircraft crash in 1938. From this base flew the early antisubmarine aircraft whose duty was to eliminate the German U-Boat threat in the Atlantic. At the beginning of our entry into the war this duty was turned over to the Navy. It was used as training facility for those who were being sent overseas during the Second World War.

Leslie MacDill was born in Monmouth, Illinois on February 18, 1889. He was commissioned into the Coast Artillery in April of 1912. In 1914 he became a part of the Aviation Section, Signal Corps and was an early aviation pioneer. He was flying out of Bolling Field on November 9, 1938 when his airplane crashed shortly after takeoff.

(Source: 74, 77, 221)

Malmstrom Air Force Base

This base is located in Cascade County, Montana and is the home of the 341st Space Wing. The base was started in 1941 and was known as the East Base and later the Great Falls Air Force Base. After the war it was used to train pilots who were flying the Berlin Airlift. The base was renamed for Colonel Einar Axel Malmstrom who had served as Vice Wing Commander at the base. Colonel Malmstrom was killed in a plane crash on August 21, 1954. He had become such a friend of the local citizenry that they successfully petitioned to have the base renamed in his honor.

Einar Axel Malmstrom was born in Chicago, Illinois on July 14, 1907. He entered the military service on May 12, 1929 as a private in the Washington State National Guard and was commissioned a second lieutenant in 1931. During World War II he was in the European Theater Operations and was shot down on his 58th combat mission. He was taken prisoner of war and was awarded the Bronze Star for his duty as commander of the POW camp prisoners. He returned to the United States in May of 1945 and served at various air bases.

In 1954 he was transferred to Great Falls Air Force Base where he served as deputy wing commander. He was killed in an airplane crash near the base.

(Source: 77)

March Air Reserve Base

March Air Force Base is located near Riverside, California. It began as Alessandro Flying Training Field in February, 1918 and then was shortly thereafter named for Peyton C. March, Jr.

Peyton C. March, Jr. was born on December 31, 1896 at Fort Monroe where his father was stationed. He attended Lafayette College and in 1917 joined the United States Army. He was commissioned a Second Lieutenant in the Air Corps in 1918. He died after sustaining injuries in an airplane crash in Fort Worth, Texas on March 11, 1918. At that time his father was the Army Chief of Staff. March Field was named for him shortly after his death.

(Source: 77)

Mather Air Force Base

This base is located in Rancho Cordova, California and began as a part of the U.S. Army Signal Corps in1918 as a pilot training base with the name of Mills Field. It was renamed in honor of Second Lieutenant Carl Spencer Mather, who, as a pilot, lost his life in an air collision at Ellington Field, Texas in January, 1918. He had earned his pilot's license at age 16. Five days after he received his commission as a second lieutenant, he was killed in a training accident. His class was then sent to Mills Field and as a group petitioned the base be named in his honor. During World War II the base was used for navigation training. It was decommissioned in 1993. It is now the Sacramento Mather Airport.

(Source: 77, 154)

Maxwell Air Force Base

Maxwell Air Force Base is located at Montgomery, Alabama and is the headquarters of the Air University. It began as one of the first flying schools established by the Wright Brothers in 1910. The school was closed in May of 1910 after a short life. It served as a repair depot during World War I. It was named Maxwell Field in 1922 after Lieutenant William C. Maxwell, a native of Atmore, Alabama.

William Calvin Maxwell was born on November 9, 1892. He was an Army ROTC student at the University of Alabama who left to enter the Army in 1917 and served in the continental United States during the War. After the War he was transferred to the Philippines and on August 20, 1920 he lost his life in an airplane crash. He was headed for an emergency landing but found that a group of children were playing in his path. He turned to miss them and struck a flag pole, costing him his life.

(Source: 24, 77, 219)

McChord Air Force Base

This base is located in Pierce County, Washington and was land donated to the U.S. Government by the citizens of Pierce County in 1917. It started as Camp Lewis and later was Fort Lewis. In 1927 an airbase was established as a part of the base, again on land given by the Citizens of Pierce County. This airbase began as Tacoma Field but was renamed in 1940 as McChord Field to honor Colonel William C. McChord who was killed in an accident near Richmond, Virginia the year before. It became independent of Fort Lewis in 1948 with the creation of the U.S. Air Force. It was a part of the Alaskan Air Defense System and in 1968 became a part of the Military Airlift System.

William C. McChord was born on December 29, 1881 in Lebanon, Kentucky. He graduated from the United States Military Academy with the Class of 1907. In 1918 he received his flight training and was designated a Junior Military Aviator. He was assigned a number of duties during the twenties and spent time at the Panama Canal Zone. In 1938 he was assigned to duty at Washington, D.C. and after became Chief of the Training and Operations Division. He was killed while flying out of Bolling Field when his Northrop A-17 attack bomber had an engine malfunction.

(Source: 77, 149)

McClellan Air Force Base

McClellan Air Force Base was located northeast of Sacramento, California and was established in 1935. It was named in honor of Major Hezekiah McClellan, a pioneer in arctic aeronautical tests. The base operated as an air depot and was known as the Pacific Air Depot. In 1938 it was renamed the Sacramento Air Depot. During World War II most planes going to the Pacific were prepared at this base. Jimmy Doolittle's B-25 was armed here in 1942.

(Source: 77, 202)

McConnell Air Force Base

This base is located in Wichita, Kansas and is used to do air-to-air refueling. It began in 1924 as the Wichita Municipal Airport. In 1941 it was activated as a military air base and served throughout World War II. B-17s and B-29s were built at an adjacent Boeing plant. It was closed in 1946 and returned to civilian use until 1951. The base was named for Fred and Thomas McConnell who were Wichita natives. Both were World War II pilots. Fred was killed in a private plane crash in 1945. Thomas died in a bombing raid over Bougainville.

There were three McConnell brothers who entered the Army Air Corps the same day, Fred, Thomas and Edwin. They all became bomber co-pilots and served in the same squadron in the South Pacific. Thomas was killed on his third mission as his plane crashed into a mountain while returning to his base in Guadalcanal. The other two survived the war and Fred was killed in a private plane crash in 1945 as he flew from Cook field to Garden Plains Air Force Base. Edwin resigned from the service in August of 1945 and returned to college at the University of Colorado. He died in 1997 at the age of 76. The base had been originally named for the other two brothers but was rededicated in 1999 to include the name of Edwin.

(Source: 77, 190, 195, 258)

McEntire Air National Guard Station

This base is located near Columbia, South Carolina and is operated by the South Carolina Air National Guard. It was first named Congaree Air Base. It was renamed in honor of Brigadier General Barnie B. McEntire, Jr. General McEntire was the first Commander of the South Carolina Air National Guard and was killed in the crash of his F-104 into the Susquehanna River as he avoided crashing into the populated area of Harrisburg, Pennsylvania.

Barnie McEntire had an early love for aviation when he was

a teenager. He washed Piper Cubs at Columbia, South Carolina's Owen Field. He graduated from the University of South Carolina and entered pilot's training in 1939. Earning his wings in 1940 he went on to a military career lasting more than twenty years. During World War II he served as Chief Pilot of the North Atlantic Division of the Air Transport Command. In 1946 he was the organizer of the South Carolina Air National Guard. In 1959 he was given the rank of Brigadier General.

(Source: 105, 204)

McGuire Air Force Base

McGuire Air Force Base is located in Burlington County, New Jersey and began as Rudd Field in 1937. It was built to support nearby Fort Dix. It was named after Major Thomas B. McGuire, Jr. who was killed in action in January 1945. He was the second leading air ace in World War II and was posthumously awarded the Medal of Honor.

Thomas McGuire was born on August 1, 1920 in Ridgewood, New Jersey. He moved to Florida and graduated from Sebring High School in 1938. He left Georgia Tech in his third year to join the U.S. Army Air Corps. He finished his flight training at Randolph Field, Texas.

During the early part of the war he flew missions over the Aleutian Islands. In 1943 after finishing training in the P-38 Lightning he was sent to the South Pacific. Flying over New Guinea, in two days he shot down five Japanese Aircraft and was established as an "Ace." Later in October he shot down three of seven Zeros that were attacking a single American plane. His plane and he suffered damage from the other four Zeros. With his controls no longer functioning he bailed out only to have his parachute harness become entangled in the cockpit of the falling aircraft. He was able to disentangle his chute only 1000 feet above the water. He was rescued by a P.T. boat and spent six months in the hospital.

He returned to service and on December 25-26, and shot down at least seven Zeros over Luzon. He was killed on January 7, 1945 in a "dog fight" with a Japanese Zero when his plane stalled during a low level maneuver. He was awarded the Silver Star for his gallantry.

(Source: 9, 77)

General William Mitchell Airport

This is the name of the Milwaukee County Airport. It was named after Billy Mitchell as he was born nearby on December 29, 1879. His father was the only child of a millionaire banker and this may have played a part of the independent streak that Billy Mitchell showed during his military career. As a graduate of George Washington University, he entered the service and rapidly rose through the ranks to become the youngest person ever appointed to the General Staff.

Billy Mitchell was born in Nice, France. His father was a Wisconsin senator. He enlisted in the Army as a Private at the age of eighteen. Using his father's influence he gained a commission in the Army Signal Corps. As early as 1906 he predicted that future wars would be fought with air power. In 1908 he observed Orville Wright at a flying demonstration at Fort Myer, Virginia. By 1917 he was a lieutenant colonel and while in France he studied the leadership of Lord Hugh Trenchard. By the end of the war he commanded all American Air Forces in Europe. He had earned his pilot's license at his own expense at age 36 in 1916. His outspoken ways got him into trouble with superiors as he fought for the United States to concentrate on becoming an air power; arguing that superior air power would mean a lesser role for the land troops as well as the Navy. He argued that World War I was not the war to end all wars but that the country that amassed air power could control not only a continent but the entire world.

In 1921 he proposed the testing of air power by bombing surplus ships from World War I. One of the ships attempted to be sunk was the unsinkable German battleship Ostfriesland. The result was in favor of the air power with all ships targeted being sunk. The battle was joined between the advocates of air power and the Navy. Before it was through, Billy Mitchell said such incendiary things that in 1925 he was court marshaled and he resigned from the service. He continued his fight for air power but died at an early age on February 19, 1936. While he did not live to see the vindication of his efforts, the need for superior air power came to fruition in World War II. In 1942, President Roosevelt elevated him posthumously to major general and the B-25 bomber was called the "Mitchell" bomber, the only aircraft to be named after a person. He is buried at Forest Home Cemetery in Milwaukee.

(Source: 281)

Moody Air Force Base

Moody Air Force Base is located near Valdosta, Georgia and had its beginning in 1940 when a group of citizens from the area began to look for a way to help the expanding defense program. It was named for Major George Putnam Moody. It served as a training base for pilots for thousands of Air Corps pilots. It continued its training mission until 1975 when an air tactical fighter wing as assigned there.

Major George Moody was an aviation pioneer who was killed in 1941 while serving with Beech Aircraft in Wichita, Kansas. He was serving on an inspection board of a trainer type that was sent on to Moody to provide advance training to students.

(Source: 77)

Nellis Air Force Base

Nellis Air Force Base is located in Clarke County, Nevada and was named for William Harrell Nellis, a Las Vegas resident. He was killed in action as a P-47 pilot during the Battle of the Bulge.

William Harrell Nellis was born in Santa Rita, New Mexico on March 16, 1916. His family moved to Searchlight, Nevada when he was a child. He moved to Las Vegas to attend high school. By 1942 he had enlisted in the Reserve Corps and he became an aviation cadet on March 2, 1943. He went overseas in May of 1944 and was reassigned to the 513th Fighter squadron in May of 1944. He flew 70 aerial missions and was shot down three times. On December 27, 1944 he was hit by ground fire while on a strafing mission. He was too low to bail out and his remains were found among the wreckage the following April.

(Source: 77, 138, 174)

Norton Air force Base

Norton Air Force Base was located in San Bernardino, California. It was named for Captain Leland Francis Norton who was killed in action flying an A-20 Havoc in France in May of 1944. It was closed on 1995 as a part of the Department of Defense's base closure program. It was a part of the Air Lift Command and served the U.S. Army and U.S. Marine Corps airlift requirements.

Upon its closure it became the San Bernardino International Airport.

Captain Leland Norton was attacking an enemy position on his 16th combat mission when his plane was struck by anti-aircraft fire. He ordered his crew to bail out and Captain Norton went down with his plane.

(Source: 77)

Offutt Air Force Base

Located in Sarpy County, Nebraska, Offutt is the home of the Headquarters of the United States Strategic Command. It was named for First Lieutenant Jarvis Offutt, a Nebraska native who was killed while flying with the Royal Air Force in World War I. It began as a refueling stop for mail and transcontinental flights in 1921. In 1924 it was officially named Offutt Field.

During World War II, the Glenn L. Martin Company built bombers here, including the two bombers used to drop the atomic bombs.

Jarvis Jennes Offutt was born on October 26, 1894 in Omaha, Nebraska. He attended Omaha Central High School. He graduated from Yale University in 1917. At Yale he was a member of the Varsity Club, the Glee Club, and was a high hurdler on the track team. While still at Yale, he served as a company supply officer for the Yale Field Artillery. Later in 1916 he began flight training and was one of 300 persons trained by the Royal Canadian Flying Corps. In January 1917 he began to ferry airplanes from England to France. He was killed on August 13, 1918. It is unsure whether the death resulted from an accident or from enemy fire.

(Source: 77)

Onizuka Air Force Station

This station is located in Sunnyvale, California. It is used to control military satellites in an area that was once a part of Moffett Field. It was named in honor of Lt. Col. Ellison Onizuka, one of the astronauts who died in the Space Shuttle Challenger explosion on January 28, 1986. This station is scheduled for closure by 2011.

Ellison Shoji Onizuka was from Kealakekua, Kona, Hawaii. Growing up he was active in the 4-H Club and the Boy Scouts where he became an Eagle Scout. He graduated from Konawaena High School in 1964. He received his Bachelor's degree in Aerospace Engineering in 1969 and a Master's in the same field from the University of Colorado at Boulder, Colorado. At the University he completed four years of ROTC training. He entered the U.S. Air Force in January 1970 and became a test pilot. He was selected as an Astronaut in 1978. He took his first space flight in 1985 on the Space Shuttle Discovery.

He was aboard the Space Shuttle Challenger when it was destroyed seventy three seconds after liftoff from the Kennedy Space

Center along with six other crew members. He was buried at the National Memorial Cemetery of the Pacific in Honolulu, Hawaii.

(Source: 20, 77)

Otis Air National Guard Base

This base is located in the Cape Cod area of Barnstable County, Massachusetts and is home to the State Air National Guard. From 1955 to 1972 it was operated by the U.S. Air Force. Until 1973 it was the largest Aerospace Defense Command Base and the only air base named for a doctor. It was named for Lieutenant Frank "Jesse" Otis, a pilot, flight surgeon and well known as a surgeon at the Boston City Hospital.

Lieutenant Frank "Jesse" Otis was a Massachusetts National Guard pilot who was killed on January 11, 1937 when his observation aircraft crashed into the Illinois River near Hannepen, Illinois during a cross country training mission. In 1935 he was one of the first flight surgeons to attend the U. S. Air Corps School of Aviation Medicine.

(Source: 64, 77, 145)

Patrick Air Force Base

Patrick Air Force Base is located in Brevard County, Florida. It started in 1940 as the Naval Air Station Banana River but was taken over by the Air Force in 1948. In August of 1950 it was named in honor of Major General Mason Patrick. It is a part of the Air Force Missile Test Center.

Mason Mathews Patrick was born on December 13, 1863 in Lewisburg, West Virginia. He graduated second in his class from West Point with the Class of 1886. John J. Pershing was one of his classmates. He was involved in many Army assignments including teaching engineering at West Point from 1897 to 1891. He was the Chief Engineer of Cuban Pacification in 1907.

In 1917 he went to France as Chief Engineer of Lines of Communication. General Pershing found that the Air Service was rife with petty bickering and in a state of disarray. Matthew Patrick was known for his organizational talents and General Pershing called on him to take command of the Air Service in May 1918 as a Major General.

He returned to the United States in 1919 and resumed engineering duties. In 1922 he was again appointed the Chief of the Air Service and in 1925 sat in on the court marshal of General Billy Mitchell. At his urging and that of Mitchell, the Air Service was reorganized as the Air Corps. He retired in 1927 and later acted as Public Utilities Commissioner for the District of Columbia. He died on January 29, 1942 and is buried at Arlington National Cemetery.

(Source: 11, 77)

Perrin Field

Perrin Field is located near Sherman, Texas and was opened in 1941.

It was named for Lieutenant Colonel Elmer D. Perrin. Perrin was born in Boerne, Texas on April 7, 1896. He lived on a 400 acre farm with eight brothers and sisters. He attended Texas A&M before enlisting in the Army as a private. In 1918 he was accepted into the Air Service and he began his aviation career. He was a command pilot and spent his life strengthening the Air Corps. He was commanding officer of the 41st School Squadron. In 1939 he went to the Baltimore, Maryland area and was the Air Corps representative at the Glenn L. Martin Company.

On June 21, 1941 during the testing and accepting of a B-26 bomber he crashed, killing him and a civilian instructor, A.J. Bowman. Perrin Field was renamed from its original name of Grayson Field to Perrin Field in his honor.

(Source: 77, 188, 189)

Peterson Air Force Base

This base is located in El Paso County, Colorado at Colorado Springs. It was established in 1942 as the Colorado Springs Municipal Airport. In that same year it was renamed Peterson Field in honor of First Lieutenant Edward J. Peterson, an airman who lost his life in a crash at the base on August 8, 1942.

It was used to train bomber crews in 1943 and in 1944 it was changed to a fighter pilot training base. It was deactivated and reactivated a number of times. In 1951 it was reactivated and in 1976 became the Peterson Air Force Base.

(Source: 77)

Pope Air Force Base

Located in Cumberland County, North Carolina, this base provides transportation for the 87th Airborne Division of the U.S. Army at nearby Fort Bragg and was established in 1919. It was named for First Lieutenant Harley Halbert Pope who was killed in an aircraft crash on January 7, 1919. In the beginning it performed yeoman services as it photographed terrain for mapping, carried the mail and spotted for artillery fire. It operated as a troop carrier training site during World War II. It began paratroop training during this time.

Harley Halbert Pope, a native of New Bedford, Indiana, was the first officer assigned to Pope Field. On the day of his crash he and Sergeant W.W. Fleming were on a scouting mission looking for air mail routes. The plane ran out of fuel and crashed in the Cape Fear River. He was born on May 26, 1879 near Mitchell, Lawrence County, Indiana. He is buried in the Greenhill Cemetery, Bedford, Indiana.

(Source: 77, 88, 99, 143, 167, 173, 247)

Randolph Air Force Base

This base is located near San Antonio, Texas and serves as a training base. One of the few bases that used specific architecture in its original design, the base began as an idea by General Lahm who saw the need for a new base to institute ground training in the area. The field was dedicated in 1930 and was named for Captain William Millican Randolph who was killed on February 17, 1928 during takeoff from Gorman Field. At the time of his death he was serving on the committee to find a name for the new base. During World War II it served as a training base for instructors and graduated over 15,000 instructors.

Captain Randolph was a graduate of Texas A&M and a native of Austin, Texas. He is buried at Fort Sam Houston National Cemetery.

(Source: 77)

Reese Air Force Base

This base was located near Lubbock, Texas and began in 1941. During the war it trained pilots and was closed on December 31, 1945. It was reactivated in 1949 and continued its mission as a pilot training school. It was named for First Lieutenant Augustus Frank Reese, Jr., of nearby Shallowater, Texas, who was killed in action when his P-38 Lightning crashed after a strafing run near Cagliari, Sardinia. Lieutenant Reese graduated from Texas Technological College with a degree in Civil Engineering in 1939.

The base was a part of the Base Realignment and Closure Program and was closed in 1997.

(Source: 77, 218)

Richards-Gebaur Air Force Base.

This base was located in Belton, Missouri and was originally the Grandview Airport in 1941. It was built by the City of Kansas City. It was named in honor of John Francis Richards II, who was killed in World War I, and Arthur William Gebaur, Jr. who was killed in the Korean War. The base was deactivated in 1976 and it returned to general aviation.

John Francisco Richards II was born in Kansas City, Missouri on July 31, 1896. He was shot down during the Meuse-Argonne Offensive on September 18, 1918. He had graduated from Yale University in 1917. His grandfather founded the Richards and Conover Hardware Company in Kansas City.

Arthur William Gebaur, Jr. was born on February 22, 1919 in Kansas City, Missouri. He graduated from Northeast High School in 1936. He was missing in action on August 29, 1952 during the Korean War.

(Source: 20. 77)

Rickenbacker International Airport

This airport serves the City of Columbus, Ohio and is the headquarters of the Ohio Air National Guard 121st Air Refueling Wing. It was named for Eddie Rickenbacker who was born on October 8, 1890 and who died on July 27, 1973. He was an "Ace" during the First World War. He was a race car driver and a pioneer in air transportation. He was born in Columbus, Ohio and died in Zurich. He was born of German speaking Swiss parents and changed his name from the characteristic German to a more American spelling because of the anti-German sentiment popular in that day. He was self-educated as his formal education ceased with the death of his father. By 1910 he was racing cars and was known as the first to drive 60 miles per hour. He raced in the Indianapolis 500 four times with his highest finish being 10th.

At the onset of World War I he traveled to England and became

106

the vanguard of American forces who volunteered early. He fought to be able to fly though he had mechanical skills which were in demand so there was organized resistance to his being a pilot. Finally he was allowed to be a pilot and he began flying missions in unarmed aircraft alongside French pilots. He shot down his first enemy plane on April 29, 1918. By September 18, he was named commander of the squadron and shot down two more planes, making the total 26. In 1931 he was awarded the Medal of Honor for his heroics.

(Source: 77)

Robins Air Force Base

Robins Air Force Base is located in Houston County, Georgia and is the home of the Air Force Material Command. It was named for Brigadier General Augustine Warner Robins. He received his wings in 1918 and he served as Chief of the Air Corps Material Division between 1935 and 1939. His system for cataloguing supplies is still in force. He died in 1940 while serving as Commandant of the Air Corps Training Center.

Augustine Warner Robins was born in Gloucester County, Virginia on September 29, 1882. His father was William Todd Robins, a Confederate colonel. Both his father and mother were descendents of early settlers of Virginia. The family moved to Richmond when he was six. He graduated from West Point with the Class of 1907. He served in various capacities including teaching at West Point and chasing Pancho Villa. He asked for and was permitted to transfer to the Air Service and he received his wings in 1918.

In 1921 he received serious facial injuries in a plane accident which required six months hospitalization. After his release he was given command of Air Corps Supply Depot at Fairfield, Ohio. In 1935 he was given command of the Material Division. During this four year tour of duty he was responsible for the supply, repair and experimental work as well as the purchase of equipment for the Army Air Forces.

The naming of the base after him is worthy of mention as, at that time most bases were required to be named after the nearest town of their location. The commander of the base wanted it to be named after Robins, so he approached the citizens of the nearby town, Wellston, to have them change the name of the town to Warner. He was successful in this endeavor and the town as well as the base is named after Warner Robins.

(Source: 77, 199, 214)

Schriever Air Force Base

This base located near Falcon, Colorado began in 1983 and was the site of 50th Space Wing, the Joint National Test Facility and the Space Warfare Center.

Brigadier General Schriever was responsible for the ICBM program from June 1954 to April 1959. At that time he was named Commander of ARDC (Air Research and Development). This group along with NASA worked on reliable launching systems for the Atlas and Titan missiles. He is known for his leadership in the development of missiles and satellites.

Bernard Adolph Schriever was born in Bremen, Germany on September 14, 1910. His father was a naval engineering officer and was interned with his ship in New York in 1916. In 1917, his mother and her two sons were able to obtain passage aboard a Dutch ship and joined the father. Later the family moved to Texas and Schriever became a naturalized citizen in 1923. He graduated from Texas A&M in 1931 where he was a part of their ROTC unit. He was commissioned into the Artillery but in 1932 began his flight training and was commissioned into the Army Air Corps in 1933. He was forced out of the service in 1937 because of budget constraints and became a commercial airplane pilot at Northwest Airlines. In 1938 he reentered the service and became a test pilot.

He was sent to the South Pacific for combat where he served in such campaigns as the Bismarck Archipelago, Leyte, Papua, North Solomon, South Philippine and Ryukyu. In 1943 he assumed command of Far East Air Service. He retired in 1964 but continued his interest in the space program. He died on June 20, 2005 at the age of 94.

(Source: 25, 77, 164)

Scott Air Force Base

This base is located in St. Clair County, Illinois which is near St. Louis. It is the headquarters of the Air Mobility Command. It was named for Corporal Frank S. Scott, who was the first enlisted man in the United States Army to lose his life in an aircraft accident.

Frank Scott was born in Braddock, Pennsylvania. He was orphaned in 1889 when his parents were killed in the Johnstown Flood. He joined the Army in 1908 and became a part of the Signal Corps in 1911. He had a medical problem that released him from his duties and upon recovery became the chief mechanic for a Type-B Wright biplane.

On September 27, 1912 he was able to secure a ride in an aircraft that was limited in the weight it could handle. Scott qualified because he had never fully recovered the weight loss he endured from his medical problems. After this flight he was scheduled to fly with another pilot in a solo flight after the plane had first been tested for function ability. When it was declared airworthy Scott and the pilot, Lieutenant Rockwell, took off and when the plane attempted to land, it crashed and killed both persons.

Corporal Scott was twenty eight when he died.

(Source: 77)

Selfridge Air National Guard Base

Selfridge Field is located near Harrison Township, Michigan. It is used by the Michigan Air National Guard as well as various other military reserve entities. It was named for Lieutenant Thomas Selfridge who was the first military officer to die in an airplane crash.

It was active as an Air Corps base during the 1940s but was actually opened in 1916. In 1971 it was transferred to the Michigan Air National Guard.

Thomas Etholen Selfridge was born on February 8, 1882 in San Francisco, California. He graduated from West Point with the Class of 1903 in the same class as Douglas MacArthur. He started off in the Field Artillery and then transferred to the Aeronautical Division of the U.S. Signal Corps. He was one of the first three pilots trained to fly the Army Dirigible Number One. He was Secretary of the Aerial Experiment Association which was chaired by Alexander Graham Bell. He flew in the first recorded flight of a heavier than air craft in Canada.

He designed the "Red Wing" which was the Aerial Association's first powered aircraft. On September 17, 1908, he and Orville Wright flew a plane called the "Wright Flyer." During the flight one of the propellers shattered and in the ensuing crash Selfridge suffered a skull fracture from which he succumbed the following day. Orville Wright had several broken bones and his hospital stay was for seven weeks.

Selfridge was 26 when he was killed.

(Source: 25, 67, 77, 90)

Sewart Air Force Base

Sewart Air Force Base is located near Smyrna, Tennessee and began in 1941. It served the Army Air Corps during World War II and was deactivated at the end of the war. It was reactivated after the Air Corps became the United States Air Force and operated until the 1970's.

It was named for Major Alan J. Sewart, Jr., a native of Nashville, Tennessee. Major Sewart was killed in a bombing run over the Solomon Islands in November of 1942. For his wartime heroics he was awarded the Distinguished Flying Cross, the Silver Star, the Air Medal, and two Purple Hearts.

(Source: 77)

Seymour Johnson Air Force Base

This base is located in Goldsboro, North Carolina and was opened in April 1942. During World War II, it was used as a base to train officers and men for overseas duties. It served as well as Headquarters, Technical School, Army Air Forces Technical Training Command. The base is the only Air Force base to be named after a Naval Officer, Seymour Johnson, who died as a test pilot in a plane crash in 1940.

Seymour A. Johnson was born in Goldsboro, North Carolina on February 4, 1904. He graduated from the local high school and attended the University of North Carolina for three years. He left to enter the United States Naval Academy and graduated with the Class of 1927. He took flight training at Pensacola, Florida, receiving his wings in 1929. He flew as a pilot from battleships and aircraft carriers.

In 1937 he became a test pilot and served in this capacity until his death in 1941. He was flying a Grumman at an altitude of 43,000 when he ran out of oxygen and his plane crashed near Norbeck, Maryland. He was buried at Arlington National Cemetery.

When the Army Air Base at Goldsboro became a reality in 1942, the local leaders petitioned to have the base named in honor of this Goldsboro native. It was officially named in his honor on October 30, 1942.

(Source: 77, 207)

Shaw Field Air Force Base

Shaw Field Air Force Base is located northwest of Sumter, South Carolina. It is the home of the 20th Fighter Wing and the Ninth Air Force. It was named for Second Lieutenant Erwin David Shaw and was established in 1941.

Erwin David Shaw was born in Clarendon County, South Carolina on September 13, 1894 and was the first man from Sumter to go into the Air Service. He went to local schools, then on to Davidson College and Georgia Tech. He joined the Air Service in early 1918 and went to France to serve with the British. On July 9, 1918 he was on a solo reconnaissance mission when he was attacked by three German aircraft. Enemy fire must have severed vital support wiring as the plane flew into pieces and Lieutenant Shaw was killed.

(Source: 77)

Shepherd Air Force Base

Shepherd Air Force Base is located near Wichita Falls, Texas. It is the home of the Euro-NATO Joint Jet Pilot Training Program and has a United States Air Force wing commander and a German Air Force operations group commander in the top two leadership roles. The base was established in October, 1941 and operated as an Army Air Corps training center. It was named for Senator John Morris Shepherd of Texas who had been the Chairman of the Senate Military Affairs Committee. It was deactivated in 1946 but continued to be used by the National Guard. It was reopened for the Korean War to train students in aircraft maintenance and sundry other duties.

Morris Shepherd was born on May 25, 1875 in Morris County, Texas. He studied at the University of Texas, earning a law degree in 1897. He studied further at Yale University. In 1902 he was elected to the House of Representatives to fill his deceased father's seat. In 1913 he was elected to the United States Senate. He was active in the writing of the temperance laws and authored the Shepherd Bill in 1916 to impose prohibition in the United States. He remained in the Senate until his death in 1941.

(Source: 20, 77, 229)

Tinker Air Force Base

This base is located in Oklahoma City, Oklahoma. Worldwide

management of aviation parts is done through Tinker Air Force Base. The base was named in honor of Major General Clarence Leonard Tinker who was part Osage Indian. He was a graduate of Wentworth Academy and went on to become the first general of American Indian descent in U.S. Army history.

He was killed on June 7, 1942 when his airplane was lost as he was leading a squadron of bombers against Wake Island.

Clarence Leonard Tinker was born on November 21, 1887 in Osage County, Oklahoma. He received his early education from Catholic schools at Hominy and Pawhuska, Oklahoma. He graduated in 1908 from Wentworth Academy in Lexington, Missouri and was commissioned a Third Lieutenant in the Philippine Constabulary. In 1912 he received his commission as Second Lieutenant in the U.S. Army. During World War I he served in the Southwestern United States. He transferred to the Air Corps after taking flying lessons. He served in Southeastern United States and rose to the rank of brigadier general. After the Japanese attacked Pearl Harbor he was given command of the Seventh Air Force at Hickam Field, Hawaii. He was killed leading a flight of Liberator bombers flying out of Midway Island. He was the first American general killed in World War II. Among his awards were the Soldier's Medal and the Distinguished Service Medal.

(Source: 69, 77)

Travis Air Force Base

Travis Air Force Base is located in Fairfield, California and handles more military cargo than any other military air base in the United States. The base began operation in 1942 and during the war its primary mission was ferrying planes to the Pacific War zone.

In 1951 it was renamed Travis Air Force Base in honor of Brigadier General Robert F. Travis. Travis was killed along with eighteen others in the crash of a B-29 Super Fortress on August 5, 1950.

Robert F. Travis was born in Savannah, Georgia in 1904. He began his higher education at the University of Georgia, but then received an appointment to the United States Military Academy where he graduated with the Class of 1928. He received his primary air training at Brooks Field and then went to Kelly Field for advanced training. He rose through the ranks as he was assigned various duties. By 1935 he was named Flight Commander of the 49th Bombardment Group. In 1939 he served as Flight Commander of the 72nd Bombardment Group at Hickam Field, Hawaii. During World War II he was in the European Theater and flew thirty five combat missions. After the war he commanded several divisions or wings before becoming the Commanding General of the Fairfield-Suisun Air Force Base.

On August 5, 1950 his B-29 crashed shortly after takeoff from Fairfield-Suisun and the General was killed along with a passenger in the forward compartment. The other crew members and passengers received only minor injuries. He was buried at Arlington National Cemetery. The Fairfield-Suisun base was renamed in his honor.

(Source: 11, 25, 77)

Tyndall Air Force Base

This base is located in Bay County, Florida near Panama City. Its construction began in May of 1941 and was named in honor of Lieutenant Frank B. Tyndall who was a World War I "Ace." He was killed in 1930.

Frank B. Tyndall was born on September 28, 1894 in Sewell's Point, Florida. He enlisted in the military at Atlanta, Georgia on August 1, 1917. On April 10, 1918 he received his commission and became a fighter pilot in World War I. He is credited with shooting down four German airplanes. On July 15, 1930 he was killed when his plane crashed near Mooresville, North Carolina while on an inspection tour. He was the second military airman to parachute from an aircraft. This happened at Seattle, Washington during the test of a MB3A pursuit airplane.

(Source: 74, 77, 97, 105)

114

Vance Air Force Base

Vance Air Force Base is located near Enid, Oklahoma and was renamed in honor of Lieutenant Colonel Leon Robert Vance, Jr. on July 9, 1951. It first was known as the Enid Army Flying Field. It was used to train aviation cadets during World War II and was closed in 1947 when the demand for pilots dropped. It was reactivated in 1948 and was used to train advanced students in multi-engine aircraft.

Leon Robert Vance, Jr. was born on August 11, 1916 in Enid, Oklahoma. As he grew up he wanted to join the Army Air Corps because of his father who was a local flight instructor and also because of his uncle who as a World War I pilot lost his life in France. He began his higher education at Oklahoma University but went on to the U.S. Military Academy at West Point, where he graduated with the Class of 1939.

On the day before D-Day, on a mission over Wimereux, France, his bomber was hit by anti-aircraft fire. Despite the condition of the plane and his own injuries he completed the mission and headed back toward the Channel. Finally feathering the last engine he descended in a glide toward a landing in the Channel. Though his right foot was nearly severed, he was able to complete the glide and land the bomber even with a 500 pound bomb lodged in the bomb bay.

Lieutenant Colonel Vance received the last Medal of Honor given in the European Theater before D-Day. He was killed in an aircraft accident as he was returning to the United States on July 26, 1944. His body was never found.

(Source: 15, 77, 88, 123)

Vandenberg Air Force Base

Vandenberg Air Force Base is located in Santa Barbara County, California. It is responsible for satellite launches for both civilian and military spacecraft. It began in 1941 as Camp Cooke and served as a training site for armored and infantry troops. In 1958 it was renamed in honor of General Hoyt S. Vandenberg who was the second Chief of Staff of the Air Force.

Hoyt Vandenberg was born on January 24, 1899 in Milwaukee, Wisconsin. He graduated from the United States Military Academy with the Class of 1923 and was commissioned a second lieutenant in the Air Service. He graduated from flying school in 1924. In 1929 he went to Schofield Barracks and joined the Sixth Pursuit Squadron. During World War II he received a number of service awards including two Distinguished Service Medals, the Silver Star, the Legion of Merit, the Distinguished Flying Cross, the Bronze Star and five Air Medals.

During World War II he served in a number of assignments including being the operations and training officer of the Air Staff. In 1943 he was assigned to North Africa to assist in the organization of the Air Service there. He flew numerous missions over southern Europe and was awarded the Silver Star and the Distinguished Flying Cross. In August of 1944 he was named the Deputy Air Commander of the Allied Expeditionary Forces. In July of 1945 he was named the Assistant Chief of the Air Staff. He became director of the Intelligence of the Army Air Force and in June of 1946, the Director of the Central Intelligence Agency. He returned to the Air Force in 1947 to become the Deputy Commander in chief of the Air Staff. Later that year he was designated the Vice Chief of Staff of the Air Force.

In 1948 he became the Chief of Staff of the Air Force and served two terms.

He suffered from prostate cancer and retired from the Military on June 30, 1953. He died at Walter Reed Hospital on April 2, 1954 and was buried at Arlington National Cemetery.

(Source: 25, 77)

Volk Field Air National Guard Base

The Volk Field Air National Guard Base is a National Guard Air Base located in Wisconsin. It is named for Lieutenant Jerome A

Volk, USAF.

Volk was born on March 17, 1925 in Harvey, North Dakota. He moved with his family to Milwaukee, Wisconsin and graduated from high school there in 1943. Just out of high school he enlisted in the Reserve Corps and was accepted into the Air Cadet Training program. In late 1943 he was commissioned into the Army Air Corps. He flew P-51 fighters during the war. After the war he went on inactive duty and studied at Marquette University.

In February of 1951 he was recalled to active duty and was sent to Korea. He was killed on November 7, 1951 while flying an F-80 jet. His remains have never been recovered despite many pleas to the North Koreans.

(Source: 105, 248)

F.E. Warren Air Force Base

The F.E. Warren Air Force Base is located near the city of Cheyenne, Wyoming. It was established as a fort in 1867 and was originally named after Brigadier General David A. Russell who served in the Civil War. It is the oldest continuously active station within the Air Force. In 1930 the base was renamed for Francis E. Warren who had been Territorial Governor of Wyoming as well as its first state governor. It became an Air Force Base in 1947 even though it only had a single dirt air strip. Many of the early flyers and celebrities trained here including General Billy Mitchell, General Mark Clark, General Benjamin O. Davis, Sr., Dr. Walter Reed and General Carl Spaatz.

In 1958 a strategic missile wing was established with twenty four Atlas Missile Sites.

Francis Emroy Warren was born in Hinsdale, Massachusetts on June 20, 1844. He joined the Union Army and served with the 49th Regiment, Massachusetts Volunteer Infantry as a noncommissioned officer. He received the Congressional Medal of Honor when he was nineteen at the Siege of Port Hudson. He, despite a serious wound, was able to disable Confederate artillery which had decimated

117

his platoon. After the war he returned to Massachusetts and was engaged in farming and raising stock. In 1868 he moved to the Dakota Territory and settled in Cheyenne. There he became wealthy as he engaged in various businesses including establishing the first lighting system in Cheyenne.

He became involved in politics, becoming the Territorial Governor of the Territory of Wyoming. When Wyoming became a state in 1890 he was elected its first governor. Shortly thereafter he was elected senator and moved to Washington. His daughter Frances Warren married General John J. Pershing. She and three of her daughters perished in a fire at the Presidio in San Francisco. Warren died in 1929 while serving in the Senate. He held the title of the longest serving senator at that time.

(Source: 37, 77, 261)

Westover Air Reserve Base

This base is now a joint use military and general aviation airport located near the City of Springfield, Massachusetts. It was named for General Oscar Westover, Commanding Officer of the Army Air Corps in the 1930s.

Oscar Westover was born on July 23, 1883 in Bay City, Michigan. He enlisted in the Army when he was eighteen as a private and received an appointment to West Point. He graduated with the Class of 1906 and was commissioned a second lieutenant. He rose through the ranks to major and was detailed to the Aviation Section of the Signal Corps in 1919. By 1932 he had received ratings as a balloon observer, airship pilot, airplane pilot, and airplane observer. In 1921 he was the director of aircraft production. In 1924 he became Commander of Langley Field.

He was appointed as assistant director and executive in the Office, Chief of the Air Service. He was Commandant of Langley Air Field and by 1931 was promoted to Brigadier General; then on to Major General in 1935. He was appointed head of the Air Corps.

He died in a plane crash on September 21, 1938 as he was landing at the Lockheed Air Field at Burbank, California. He was awarded the Distinguished Service Medal and the World War I Victory Medal.

(Source: 11, 77)

Wheeler Field, Schofield Barracks

Wheeler Field, Schofield Barracks is located on Oahu, Hawaii. It was a part of the targets of the Japanese when they bombed Pearl Harbor. Most of its planes were lost in the attack. Wheeler Field began as a landing field in 1922. It was named for Major Sheldon H. Wheeler, United States Air Service on November 11, 1922.

Shelton Wheeler was born on April 6, 1889 in New York City. He attended the University of Vermont before procuring an appointment to the United States Military Academy, graduating with the Class of 1914. He spent one year in the Infantry and applied for aviation duty. He progressed rapidly in the Air Service. In 1919 he assumed command of Luke Field, and Ford Island, Pearl Harbor. On July 13, 1921 Major Wheeler was killed in the crash of an observation plane along with Sergeant Thomas A. Kelly.

(Source: 77, 111, 130)

Whiteman Air Force Base

This base is located in Johnson County, Missouri and is the home of the 509th Bomb Wing which operates the B-2 stealth bombers. It began in 1942 as the Sedalia Glider Base. In 1951 it was modified to handle the heavy bombers. It was named in honor of Second Lieutenant George A. Whiteman. He was a native of Sedalia and one of the first American airmen killed in World War II during the attack on Pearl Harbor.

George A. Whiteman was born on October 12, 1919 in Pettis

County, Missouri. He graduated from the Smith-Cotton High School in Sedalia. He enlisted in the Air Corps in 1939 and was sent to Randolph Field. He was commissioned a second lieutenant on November 15, 1940.

On December 7, 1941 he was stationed at Bellows Field, Hawaii and as he attempted to take off in his P-40 to fight the Japanese, he and his plane were hit. The plane went out of control and crashed at the end of the runway. He died from his injuries.

(Source: 12, 77)

Williams Air Force Base

Williams Air Force base is located near Chandler, Arizona. It was built in 1941 as an advanced training base and graduated more pilots and instructors than any other base in the country. The base was closed in 1992. In 1942 the base was named to honor Charles Linton Williams, an Arizona born pilot.

Lieutenant Charles Linton Williams, who was born in 1898, was killed on July 6, 1927 when his Boeing PW-9A pursuit plane crashed into the sea near Fort DeRussy, Hawaii.

(Source: 71, 77, 105, 226)

Wright-Patterson Air Force Base

This base is located near Dayton, Ohio and is the headquarters of the Air Force Material Command. It was named after the Wright Brothers and Frank Stuart Patterson, son and nephew of the co-founders of National Cash Register. It began as the Wilber Wright Field in 1917 and was used to train pilots and gunners during World War I. In 1931 it was renamed Patterson Field to honor Lieutenant Frank Stuart Patterson who was killed in 1918 during a test flight. In 1948 the names were merged and it became Wright-Patterson Air Force Base.

Frank Stuart Patterson was born on November 6, 1897 in Dayton, Ohio. His father and uncle founded the National Cash Register and figured heavily in the building and retaining of the air field in the Dayton area. Many of his ancestors were military men who fought in the Revolutionary War, the War of 1812 and the Civil War. Frank Stuart Patterson enrolled at Yale but left to join the Air Service. He finished his training and was assigned to Fort Sill, Oklahoma for training in aerial observation. On September 14, 1917 he was discharged from the service to be designated a pilot. He was given the assignment to test the fighter planes ability to fire synchronized machine gun bullets through the propeller. During the last of the test dives, the wings separated from the aircraft and the plane crashed, killing all aboard. There was a report that the machine gun bullets had shattered the propeller and the damaged parts hit the wings, shearing them. This report proved to be false. He was buried near his father in Woodland Cemetery in Dayton, Ohio.

Orville and Wilber Wright were brothers who were born on August 19, 1871 and April 16, 1867 respectively. They are given credit for inventing the first successful airplane which made its maiden flight on December 17, 1903. They were not the first to fly experimental aircraft but they made the first controls that made mechanical fixed wing flight possible. Orville was born in Dayton, Ohio and Wilber in Millville, Indiana. They both died in Dayton, Ohio; Orville at age 76 on January 30, 1948 and Wilber on May 30, 1912 at age 45. Neither was married.

Their father was the editor of a church newspaper. They moved often but always returned to their house in Dayton. Wilber suffered two accidents while playing hockey and baseball which kept him homebound for a number of years. At the same time he was taking care of his mother who was dying from tuberculosis. In 1892 the two brothers opened a bicycle shop. Their interest in flying had begun at an early age and they were sure that manned flight was possible. They built the first wind tunnel that was designed for the purpose of testing aircraft. They made the first sustained manned flight at Kitty Hawk, North Carolina in 1903. There were many lawsuits fought over the invention of flying but the Wright Brothers are given credit for being the first to successfully fly an airplane in powered flight.

(Source: 30, 77, 187, 260)

Wurtsmith Air Force Base

This base is a deactivated Air Force Base located in Iosco County, Michigan. It had its beginning in 1923 as Loud-Reames Aviation Field. It was renamed in 1924 as Camp Skeel to honor Captain Burt F. Skeel a World War I pilot. It was renamed again in 1942 as Oscoda Army Air Field and again in 1953 to honor Major General Paul Bernard Wurtsmith. He was a Michigan native who was killed in the crash of his B-25 Mitchell bomber on September 1946 near Cold Mountain, North Carolina. The base was closed on June 30, 1993.

Paul Bernard Wurtsmith was born in 1906 in Detroit, Michigan. He earned a degree in Engineering and in 1927 he enlisted in the Army Air Corps as a cadet. He served in the 94th Pursuit Squadron which was known as the "Hat in the Ring" squadron during World War I. In December of 1941 he took command of the 49th Pursuit Squadron stationed in Australia. His squadron was credited with shooting down seventy eight aircraft. In 1943 he was given command of the 5th Fighter Group. In this Group were two well known fighter pilots, Lt. Col. Thomas J. Lynch and Captain Richard I. Bong. Bong was the leading air "Ace" with 40 planes shot down.

He returned to the United States and on September 13, 1946 he was killed in a B-25 crash while in route to MacDill Field, Florida.

(Source: 11, 77, 101, 167, 226)

Yeager Airport

Yeager Airport is located near Charleston, West Virginia. While it is not a military base it is included so that the name "Yeager" which is synonymous with modern flying could be included in these listings.

Charles Elwood "Chuck" Yeager was born on February 13, 1923 in Myra, West Virginia. He began his military career by enlisting as a private in the U.S. Air Force on September 12, 1941. In 1942 he took pilot training to be an enlisted pilot and graduated as a Flight Officer. He flew P-51 fighters. He became a test pilot after the war and in 1953 flew at Mach 2.4. (Mach One is the speed of sound.) He commanded fighter squadrons and wings in Europe and Southeast Asia. He rose to the rank of Brigadier General and retired on March 1, 1975.

During his combat days in Europe, he was shot down on his eighth mission but escaped to Spain through the help of the French Resistance. While it was not permissible for pilots who had been shot down to return to combat for fear of compromising the French Resistance fighters, he argued successfully with General Eisenhower that the war was far enough along that the Resistance Fighters were now fighting openly alongside the uniformed soldiers and that no compromise would be made. He returned to combat and later credited this decision to helping him become a test pilot. He was the first pilot in his group to become "Ace in a Day", shooting down five enemy aircraft in one day on January 15, 1945. He flew sixty-one missions during the war.

As a test pilot he flew the Bell X-1 breaking the sound barrier on October 14, 1947 after another pilot wanted a great sum of $150,000 to make the attempt. He did this while nursing two broken ribs sustained in a fall off of a horse two days before.

(Source: 77)

United States
Navy
and
Marine Corps
Bases

Camp Smedley D. Butler Marine Corps Base

Camp Butler is located on Okinawa and is named for General Smedley D. Butler, United States Marine Corps. Butler was born on July 30, 1881 in West Chester, Pennsylvania, one of three sons born in a prominent Quaker family. At the age of sixteen, he lied about his age and joined the Marine Corps, and became an officer before he was seventeen. His father was in the United States Congress for thirty one years and was chairman of the House Naval Affairs Committee.

Butler fought in the Boxer Rebellion. He sported a tattoo of the Marine Corps emblem that covered his entire chest.

During the Boxer Rebellion he led a Marine force that opened the gates to a city that allowed larger forces to enter and stop the siege that had trapped the foreign Legations. He was wounded twice and for his bravery he was awarded the rare Marine Corps Brevet Metal. Only twenty two of these medals were ever issued. By the age of nineteen he had been promoted to Captain.

In 1903 he was suffering from malaria but had enough stamina to lead a small bunch of Marines to rescue the U.S. Consular agent in the Honduras. From 1909 to 1912 he served in Central America. He was twice awarded the Congressional Medal of Honor, the first in Veracruz. The second Medal of Honor came for his gallantry in Haiti. In a battle where his small force of Marines were greatly outnumbered and for his attacking and securing a rebel stronghold he was awarded a second Medal of Honor.

During World War I he was not assigned to a combat unit but was asked to organize the debarkation port that funneled all the troops into battle. For his superior handling of this billet he was awarded the Distinguished Service Medal of both the Army and Navy.

After the war he was granted a leave of absence to become the Director of Public Safety in Philadelphia, a city that was known for its corruption. In a short period he cleaned up the city, earning the hatred of those profiting from its corruption. He went back into the Marines and was Commander of the Marine Expeditionary Force in China. He was promoted at the age of 48 to the rank of General, making him the youngest Major General in the Corps. He was nationally known for his methods that caught the public attention. He was outspoken and for this he was passed over as Commandant of the Marine Corps. He retired from active duty in 1931. This did not stop him from speaking his mind. He wrote a book called "War is a Racket" where he condemned "Wall Street" for profiteering during the wars.

General Butler died on June 21, 1940 at the Naval Hospital in Philadelphia. He is buried at Oaklands Cemetery in West Chester, Pennsylvania.

There are camps within the base that are named for Marines who lost their lives during the Battle of Okinawa.

(Sources: 77, 150)

Cecil Field Naval Air Station

Cecil Field began in 1941. It was located in Duval County, Florida and was the largest military base in the Jacksonville area. It was named for Commander Henry Barton Cecil and operated from 1941 until 1999.

Henry Barton Cecil was a graduate of the United States Naval Academy, Class of 1910. He was killed when the U.S. Navy Blimp Akron crashed in New Jersey in 1933.

(Source: 45, 77, 227, 244)

Chase Field Naval Air Station

Chase Field was located at Beeville, Texas and was commissioned in 1943 to train Navy aviators. After the war it was closed until the Korean conflict and again was opened to relieve over-crowding at Nair Station, Corpus Christi. It operated until its closure in 1993. It was named for Lt. Commander Nathan Brown Chase who was killed on a training flight in 1925 at Pearl Harbor, Hawaii.

(Source: 229)

Corry Station Naval Technical Training Center

This training center is located north of Pensacola, Florida and is named for Medal of Honor recipient Lieutenant Commander William M. Corry, Jr.

Corry was born at Quincy, Florida. He graduated from The United States Naval Academy with the Class of 1910. He spent the first five years of his career on the Battleship Kansas. Transferring to the Aviation Section, he earned his wings as Naval Aviator Number 23. He commanded the Naval Air Stations at Brest and Le Croisic. In 1920 he and another pilot crashed near Hartford, Connecticut. He was thrown clear but he returned to pull the other aviator from the plane. He died from the burns received. He was awarded the Congressional Medal of Honor for his heroics.

(Source: 77)

Earle Naval Weapons Station

This base is located in New Jersey and serves as an ammunition loading facility. It was built in 1943 and was named after Rear Admiral Ralph Earle who was the Chief of the Bureau of Ordnance during World War I.

Ralph Earle was born on May 3, 1874 in Worchester, Massachusetts. He graduated from the U.S. Naval Academy with the Class of 1896. He served on battleships and won commendations for his heroism during a turret explosion. He became an expert on guns and explosives and was made Chief of the Bureau of Ordnance just before World War I. He retired and was President of Worchester Polytechnic Institute until his death in 1939.

(Source: 77)

Camp Elmore

Camp Elmore is located near Norfolk, Virginia and is a part of the Sewalls Point Naval Complex. It is the headquarters for Marine Corps Forces, Atlantic/Fleet Marine Force, Atlantic.

It was named in honor of PFC George W. Elmore, United States Marine Corps, a Browning Automatic Rifleman. During the Korean War on February 26, 1951, he left his secure position to move into the open where he could inflict heavier fire on the enemy. This allowed the remaining members of his squad to move forward. He suffered wounds that cost him his life. He was awarded the Navy Cross, the country's second highest award for bravery.

(Source: 105)

Henderson Hall Marine Corps HQ

Henderson Hall is located in Arlington, Virginia near the Pentagon. It hosts the Marine Corps Barracks and a number of education facilities. It was named for Commandant of the Marine Corps Archibald Henderson. Henderson was born on January 21, 1783 in Colchester, Virginia. He was made a Second Lieutenant in the Marine Corps on June 4, 1806 and served aboard the USS Constitution in its fight against the British ship, Java, during the War of 1812. In 1818 he was appointed acting Commandant of the Marine Corps. In 1819 he was given the permanent position. He held it for thirty eight years, the longest Commandant in the history of the Marine Corps. At one time there was an attempt to integrate the Corps into the Army. Henderson fought this and insured that the Marine Corps remain a part of the Navy.

He fought in the Indian campaigns in 1836 and 1837. It is said he left a note on his office door, "Gone to Florida to fight the Indians. Will be back when the war is over."

Henderson was given credit for the well coordinated Marine Corps activities during the Mexican War, turning the Corps into a true fighting force. After the war he directed the Marines in many expeditions to the Far East. He died on January 6, 1859 and was interred at the Congressional Cemetery in Southeast Washington, DC. Among the large throng present at his funeral was James Buchanan, President of the United States.

(Source: 1, 62, 77, 83, 146, 147)

Camp Lejeune Marine Corps Base

Located near Jacksonville, North Carolina, Camp Lejeune is a major Marine Corps installation. It is located in an area with some fourteen miles of beaches making it ideal for amphibious assault training. Two nearby deep water ports makes fast deployment easy. The base construction began in May of 1941. It was named for John A. Lejeune, the 13th Commandant of the Marine Corps.

John A. Lejeune was born on January 10, 1867 in Batchelor, Louisiana. He graduated from Louisiana State University, Baton Rouge. He then received an appointment to the U.S. Naval Academy, graduating with the Class 0f 1888. He went to sea as a Cadet Midshipman and two years later was commissioned into the Marine Corps. He served in the Marine Guard on U.S. Naval vessels until 1900. He served at the Pensacola Marine Barracks as well as the Norfolk Barracks. After a number of tours at various barracks and Navy ships he was ordered to the Philippines to command the Marine Barracks and Naval Prison at Cavite. He was given command of the First Brigade and promoted to Lieutenant Colonel shortly thereafter.

He had a number of tours in Cuba, Mexico and Panama. He returned to Washington to become Assistant to the Major General Commandant of the Marine Corps and was promoted to Brigadier General. During the First World War he commanded the 4th Brigade of the 2nd Division. Shortly thereafter he was given command of the 2nd Division. His leadership abilities were recognized by the medals he received during the war that included the French Legion of Honor and the Croix de Guerre. General John J. Pershing presented him with the Army Distinguished Service Medal. He received also the Navy Distinguished Service Medal.

He was appointed and served two terms as Commandant of the Marine Corps from 1920 until 1929. His nicknames of "The Greatest of all Leathernecks" and "The Marine's Marine" attest to his love for the Marines. After retirement he served as Superintendent of the Virginia Military Institute.

(Source: 77)

Moffett Federal Airfield

Moffett Air Field is located in Santa Clara County, California. It is presently owned by the NASA Ames Research Center. The base was opened in 1931 as a base for the Airship USS Macon. It became an airfield when it was discovered that it was open for flying many times when the surrounding areas was closed because of fog. It was originally called Airbase Sunnyvale CAL but renamed to honor Rear Admiral William A. Moffett. Many anti-submarine flights were flown out of Moffett Field. It was closed in 1994 and became the NASA Ames Research Center.

William Adger Moffett was born in Charleston, South Carolina on October 31, 1869. He graduated from the U.S. Naval Academy with the Class of 1890. He served on the USS Charleston in the Battle of Manila Bay. He received the Medal of Honor for his heroic action as Captain of the USS Chester at Veracruz, Mexico. During World War I he was commander of the Great Lakes Naval Training Center and while there established an aviator training program. While he was not an aviator, he was known for his love of flying. He was a leader in the Navy's Bureau of Aeronautics and helped develop tactics for naval aircraft. He introduced the aircraft carrier and fought successfully to have a separate naval air arm.

(Source: 77)

Camp Pendleton Marine Corps Base

Camp Pendleton is the major Marine Corps base on the West Coast and is located at Oceanside, California. It was established in 1942 to train Marines for World War II service.

The base is named for Joseph Henry Pendleton who was born on June 2, 1860 in Rochester, Pennsylvania. He was appointed to the U.S. Naval Academy and graduated with the Class of 1884. He was commissioned as a Second Lieutenant in the Marine Corps. He served at various barracks and aboard U.S. Navy ships in the early part of his career. In 1899 he was promoted to Captain and to Major in 1903. In 1904 he joined the First Brigade of Marines in the Philippines. He was given command of the Marines on Guam in 1906 and then commanded the Marine Barracks at Puget Sound, Bremerton, Washington. He was promoted to Lt. Colonel and returned to the Philippines. In 1911 he was promoted to Colonel. He saw service in Cuba and Nicaragua in 1912 and 1913.

He was in command of all Naval Forces ashore in Santo Domingo in 1916. He was promoted to Brigadier General in that same year. In 1921 he served as Commander of the Department of the Pacific as well as the Commanding Officer of the Fifth Brigade of Marines. In June of 1924 he retired at the age of 64 as a Major General. He served as Mayor of the City of Coronado from 1928 to 1930. He died at age 81 on February 4, 1942. For his gallantry in battle he was awarded the Navy Cross and the Distinguished Service Medal.

(Source: 77)

Saufley Field,

NAS Pensacola

Saufley Field is located about ten miles north of NAS Pensacola and is used for practice landings of aircraft from other fields. It opened in 1940 and became a Naval Auxiliary Field in 1943. In 1968 it was re-designated as a Naval Air Station. It was decommissioned in 1976, but was reactivated in 1979 as Naval Education and Training

Program Training Center, Naval Air Station Whiting Field.

Saufley Field was named for Lt. (jg.) Richard C. Saufley, who was born on September 1, 1884. He was a pioneer in naval aviation and set many endurance and altitude records. He graduated from the United States Naval Academy with the Class of 1908. He saw duty on the USS Kansas, USS Biddle and USS Terry before returning to the Academy for aviation training. He became a pilot and was designated Naval Aviator No. 14. He served on the USS Mississippi and USS North Carolina where he specialized in the advancement of aviation technology. On June 16, 1916, he died in a plane crash attempting to set a new endurance record at Pensacola, Florida. He was married to the former Helen O'Rear who, in 1915, was the first female to pilot an airplane over New York City. This was with Lawrence Sperry, inventor of the Sperry Gyroscope. Lt. Saufley had been assisting Sperry in the testing of his gyroscope and invited his wife to take his place during a portion of the test.

(Source: 77, 112, 220)

The David Taylor Model Basin

The David Taylor Model basin is located near Washington, DC and was designed to test ship models of the United States Navy. It is used to test models before the actual ship is built and can predict its performance within a few percent. This allows the ship's designer to make changes beneficial to its final performance before it is constructed.

The model basin is named for David Taylor who was born in Louisa County, Virginia on March 4, 1864. In 1896 the Washington Navy Yard was appropriated $100,000 to build a "Model Tank for Experiments." The supervisor of the project was a young naval officer by the name of David Watson Taylor. Later as a rear admiral he served as Chief Constructor and Chief of the Bureau of Construction from 1914 to 1922. More than 1000 ship designs were tested between those dates.

By the 1930s it was obvious that the existing water tanks near the

Anacostia River were inadequate for the testing of modern ships. A new facility was built as Carterock, Maryland just west of Bethesda. This became known as the David Taylor Model Basin.

(Source: 284)

Whiting Field Naval Air Station

This Naval Air Station is located in Milton, Florida and is one of the Navy's primary training centers. It was named for Captain Kenneth Whiting.

Kenneth Whiting was born on July 22, 1881 in Stockbridge, Massachusetts. He graduated from the United States Naval Academy and was commissioned an Ensign in 1908. He first served on submarines and commanded the Porpoise, Shark, Tarpon and Seal. While serving on submarines he proved the feasibility of escape from a submarine through one of its torpedo tubes. He swam out of a torpedo tube of the Porpoise while it was submerged at twenty feet in Manila Bay.

In 1914 he turned to aviation and was taught to fly by Orville Wright. He was designated Naval Aviator No. 16 He commanded naval stations during World War I in England and the 1st Naval Air Unit in France. He was awarded the Navy Cross for his meritorious service.

After the war he was one of those responsible for the conversion of the Collier Jupiter into the Navy's first aircraft carrier, the Langley. He made the first catapult launch from the Langley while it was at anchor in the York River. He later commanded the Langley as well as the Saratoga. He retired from active duty in 1940, but stayed on as General Inspector of Naval Aircraft, Eastern Division.

He was assigned to command the Naval Air Station, New York and was at that post at the time of his death on April 24, 1943.

(Source: 77, 105, 117)

SERVICE
ACADEMIES

United States
Air Force
Academy
Colorado Springs,
Colorado

Arnold Hall

(Cadet Social Center)

This hall is named after General Henry H. "Hap" Arnold, commanding general of the US Army Air Forces during WWII. (This is a repeat of the biography of General Arnold first listed under Air Force Bases.)

Henry Harley "Hap" Arnold was born on June 25, 1886 in Gladwyne, Pennsylvania. He went to Lower Merion High School in Ardmore, Pennsylvania. He took a competitive exam to enter West Point and received the appointment after the person ahead of him was not allowed to enter because of being married. He graduated with the Class of 1907. He ended up being commissioned into the Infantry, rather than his choice of Cavalry, as he stood in the lower half of his class. While on assignment in the Philippines he volunteered to help Captain Arthur Cowan of the Signal Corps, map the Island of Leyte. Afterwards Cowan returned to the United States and chose Arnold as one of two persons to receive pilot training.

It took two years before the transfer to the Signal Corps became a reality and he was sent to Dayton, Ohio where he was instructed to fly by the Wright Brothers. He became the second rated pilot in the Army Air Corps. In September, 1911 he became the first pilot to carry mail. He had many near fatal crashes and ended up with a phobia of flying. He returned to the Philippines and there became a close friend of George Catlett Marshall.

On his return to the United States he was offered the rank of Captain by Major William T. Mitchell, if he would return to the Signal Corps. He was asked to go to the Panama Canal to find a suitable place for an air field. While on his way there the United States declared war on Germany. He asked for overseas duty but the need for qualified officers at headquarters overrode his request. In June of 1917 he was promoted to Major and two months later to Colonel, becoming the youngest full colonel in the Army.

He fought to get a large appropriations bill for the Air Service through Congress. This was a failure but the experience learned would stand him in good stead in later years. After the war he was ordered to demobilize the air unit. He fought for its preservation. At Rockwell Field he met many of the officers who would later become his aides. During this time the battle raged between the Army and the advocates of Air Service. Arnold was banished to a western post and there he met Major General James Fechet who intervened to have Arnold's exile ended. By 1929 he became executive officer of the Air Material Division and on November 27, 1931, the Commander of March Field, California. One of his assignments was to heal the rifts that occurred between the base and the citizens of nearby Riverside. He accomplished this though relief efforts and having his personnel join in the local service clubs.

In 1935 he took command of the First Wing of the newly created Air Corps. By 1935 he had become Assistant Chief of the Air Corps. His boss, General Westover, was killed in a plane crash and Arnold became Chief of the Air Corps. Arnold fought for an expansion of the Air Corps into a unit equal to the Army ground units.

In June of 1941 the United States Army Air Forces was created and Arnold was chosen to be commander. He became a member of the Joint Chiefs of Staff. It was through his leadership that the growth of the Army Air Corps during World War II made it an air fighting force unequalled in the world.

During the war he suffered numerous heart attacks, some of which were not reported as he might be taken from his duties as "the Chief." He worked long hours, particularly trying to solve the problems associated with the B-29 Super Fortress.

In 1945 he founded Project RAND which became a think tank called the RAND Corporation. He retired in 1946 onto a small ranch in California. On May 7, 1949 he was honored to be named also the General of the Air Force, making him the only five star general in two military services. He died on January 15, 1950 and is buried at Arlington National Cemetery.

(Source: 77)

Doolittle Hall

Doolittle Hall, the Headquarters of the Academy's Association of Graduates, is named after General "Jimmy" Doolittle.

James Harold "Jimmy" Doolittle was born on December 14, 1896 in Alameda, California. He moved to Nome, Alaska and was known for his boxing skills. He came back to California and attended Los Angeles City College. He went from there to the University of California. In 1917 he left college to join the Signal Corps Reserve and was commissioned a second lieutenant on March 11, 1918.

During World War I he was a flight instructor at various fields in the United States. After the war he remained in the service and completed schools at Kelly Field and McCook Field, Ohio. He completed his college degree at the University of California. During the 1920's he became known for his flight achievements and was the first to take off, fly and land using instruments only. He won a number of racing cups. He was the first to perform an outside loop.

In the 1930's he retired from active duty and worked with Shell Oil Company to develop high octane fuels which were needed for the modern aircraft engines.

When World War II started he was recalled to active duty and promoted to Lieutenant Colonel. He was given the assignment to plan retaliatory raids against the Japanese mainland. He led the top-secret attack of 16 B-25 bombers that took off from the USS Hornet and bombed Tokyo, Yokohama, Kobe and Nagoya. After the bombing runs the planes were to land in China. Many of the airplanes' crew had to bail out as fuel ran out. Doolittle bailed out also and landed in a rice paddy. Most of the crew reached safety through the help of friendly Chinese, though many were captured and killed.

Doolittle received the Medal of Honor which was bestowed on him by President Roosevelt at the White House. Doolittle went on to fly many other combat missions, receiving four Air Medals.

In July of 1942, Jimmy Doolittle was promoted to General, bypassing the rank of Full Colonel. He went on to command the Twelfth Air Force in North Africa and then on to become the Commanding General of the Northwest African Strategic Air Forces.

In January 1944 he took command of Eighth Air Force operation out of England.

Doolittle was known for his innovative decisions including having pursuit planes run strafing missions on German ground facilities as they returned from escorting bombers on their missions. After the war he returned to civilian life having been the highest ranking reserve officer to serve in the Armed Forces.

His awards include the Medal of Honor, the Silver Star, three Distinguished Flying Crosses, the Bronze Star, four Air Medals, and decorations from various allied nations. He is the only person to win the Medal of Honor and the Medal of Freedom. Jimmy Doolittle had two sons, both of whom served in the Air Force.

General Jimmy Doolittle died in Pebble Beach, California on September 27, 1993 and is buried at Arlington National Cemetery.

(Source: 25, 77)

Fairchild Hall

Fairchild Hall, the main Academic building at West Point, was named in honor of Air Force Vice Chief of Staff, General Muir S. Fairchild, a native of Bellingham, Washington. (This is a repeat of the biography of General Fairchild first listed under Air Force Bases.)

Muir Stephen Fairchild began his Army service in 1916 when he joined the Washington National Guard as a sergeant. He shortly became a flying cadet and earned his wings in time to fly bombing missions in World War I.

After the war he served at various Army Air Fields including Langley Field, Virginia, McCook Field, Ohio, and Mitchel Field, New York. He was a part of the Good Will Tour to South America and for this was awarded the Distinguished Flying Cross.

By 1939 he had risen to be Director of Air Tactics and Strategy. In March of 1942 he was assigned the duty of Director of Military Requirements. Later he was a member of Joint Strategic Survey Committee of the Joint Chiefs of Staff.

After the war he was named commandant of the Air University at

Maxwell Field. In 1948 he became Vice Chief of Staff at Fort Myer, Virginia. He died while on active duty on March 17, 1950.

(Source: 11, 77, 105, 167)

Goldwater Visitor Center

The Goldwater Visitor Center was named for a longtime proponent of the Academy, Senator Barry Goldwater.

Barry Morris Goldwater was born on January 1, 1909 in Phoenix, Arizona Territory. He attended local schools as well as Staunton Military Academy, Staunton, Virginia. He attended the University of Arizona in 1928, and then went into the family business. He joined the United States Army Air Corps at the onset of the Second World War, serving in the Asiatic Theater in India. At the end of the war his rank was Lieutenant Colonel with a pilot rating. He organized the Arizona National Guard and stayed in the Air Force Reserve, rising to the rank of Brigadier General. He was promoted to the rank of Major General and retired in 1967.

After service in local political duties he was elected to the United States Senate in 1952. He was the Republican nominee for President in 1964, losing to Lyndon Johnson. He was reelected to the Senate in 1968 and served until 1987. He was known as "Mr. Conservative" during his tenure as Senator.

He was a strong advocate of a separate Air Force Academy. He died on May 29, 1998 at Paradise Valley, Arizona.

(Source: 37, 77)

Harman Hall

Harman Hall, the Primary Administration Center, is named after Lieutenant General Hubert R. Harman, first superintendent of the Air Force Academy.

Hubert Reilly Harmon was born on April 3, 1892 in Chester,

Pennsylvania, a member of a prominent military family. His father was a graduate of the United States Military Academy and was Commandant of Cadets at the Pennsylvania Military Academy. Two brothers preceded him at West Point, one of whom was lost over the Pacific in World War II.

Hubert Reilly Harman graduated from West Point with the Class of 1915, the same class as that of Dwight D. Eisenhower. He first was a part of the Coast Artillery Corps but transferred to the Air Service the year following his graduation. He earned his wings in 1917 and was a pursuit pilot in France during World War I. He was one of the advocates of a strong air service. In 1920 he was an assistant executive in the Office of the Chief of the Air Service. In 1924 he attended and graduated from the Command and General Staff School at Fort Leavenworth, Kansas. By 1936 he was appointed commander of the 19th Bombardment Wing. In 1940 he was Commander of the Advanced Flying School and promoted to Brigadier General.

In 1942 he was the Commanding General of the 6th Air Force. He later was Deputy Commander of the Air Forces in the South Pacific. In January of 1944 he became Commander of the 13th Air Force. In 1947 he was appointed as senior member of the Military and Naval Staff Committee of the United Nations. He retired in 1953 but was called back in the following day for the same duty. He retired again but was called back into service later that year to be the special to the Chief of Staff for Air Academy Matters. On August 14, 1954 he became the first Superintendent of the newly established Air Force Academy. He returned to retired status on July 31, 1956 and died on February 22, 1957 at Lackland Air Force Base, Texas.

(Source: 89)

Mitchell Hall

Mitchell Hall, the Cadet Dining Hall, was named after General Billy Mitchell who was born on December 29, 1879. His father was the only child of a millionaire banker and this may have played a part of the independent streak that Billy Mitchell showed during his military career. As a graduate of George Washington University, he entered the service and rapidly rose through the ranks to become the youngest person ever appointed to the General Staff. (This is a repeat of the biography of General Mitchell first listed under Air Force Bases.)

Billy Mitchell was born in Nice, France. His father was a Wisconsin senator. He enlisted in the Army as a Private at the age of eighteen. Using his father's influence he gained a commission in the Army Signal Corps. As early as 1906, he predicted that future wars would be fought with air power. In 1908 he observed Orville Wright at a flying demonstration at Fort Myer, Virginia. By 1917 he was a lieutenant colonel and while in France he studied the leadership of Lord Hugh Trenchard.

By the end of the war he commanded all American Air Forces in Europe. He had earned his pilot's license at his own expense at age 36 in 1916. His outspoken ways got him into trouble with superiors as he fought for the United States to concentrate on becoming an air power, arguing that superior air power would mean a lesser role for the land troops as well as the Navy. He argued that World War I was not the war to end all wars but that the country that amassed air power could control not only a continent but the entire world.

In 1921 he proposed the testing of air power by bombing surplus ships from World War I. One of the ships attempted to be sunk was the unsinkable German battleship Ostfriesland. The result was in favor of the air power with all ships targeted being sunk. The battle was joined between the advocates of air power and the Navy. Before it was through, Billy Mitchell said such incendiary things that in 1925 he was court marshaled and he resigned from the service. He continued his fight for air power but died at an early age on February 19, 1936. While he did not live to see the vindication of his efforts, the need for superior air power came to fruition in World War II. In 1942, President Roosevelt elevated him posthumously to major general and the B-25 bomber was called the "Mitchell" bomber, the only aircraft to be named after a person. He is buried at Forest Home Cemetery in Milwaukee, Wisconsin.

(Source: 77, 90, 91, 155)

Sijan Hall

Sijan Hall was named after Captain Lance Sijan, United States Air Force Academy Class of 1965 and the first U.S. Air Force Academy graduate to win the Medal of Honor.

Lance Peter Sijan was born in Milwaukee, Wisconsin on April 13, 1942. His father was Serbian, his mother Irish. He graduated from Bay View High School and opted for the Air Force Academy after first considering Annapolis. He played football in high school as well as at the Air Force Academy. He graduated from the Air Force Academy with the Class of 1965 and entered pilot training.

Flying out of Da Nang Air Base in Vietnam with the 366th Wing, he finished fifty one missions before being downed on his 52nd. It was at this point his spirit and character were evidenced as he attempted to elude the North Vietnamese Army. He was almost picked up by search and rescue helicopters but he couldn't hold on to the rescue line long enough to be rescued before the rescuers were driven off by enemy fire. He refused to allow them to return, not wanting to put anyone else in danger.

He avoided capture for 45 days as he slid on his back from spot to spot, living without food the entire time. A mangled hand, a broken leg and a skull fracture contributed to his difficulties. Once captured, he managed to escape by assaulting the guard with his one good hand. He was recaptured a few hours later.

He was taken to a POW camp at Hanoi where he continued his resistance even in his weakened condition. He, to the end, adhered to the Code of Conduct taught to him at the Air Force Academy, giving only the information allowed by the Geneva Convention. He survived the beatings that came because of his resistance but finally his health broke. He, according to his captors, died on January 22, 1968. His remains were repatriated on April 22, 1974 and he is buried at the Arlington National Cemetery.

The Air Force has created the Lance P. Sijan Award given to individuals who have shown the highest qualities of leadership in their jobs and in their lives. As a part of their training, all Fourth Class Cadets at the Air Force Academy are required to learn the story of Captain Lance Peter Sijan.

(Source: 12, 77)

Vandenberg Hall

Vandenberg Hall was named in honor of General Hoyt S. Vandenberg who was the second Chief of Staff of the Air Force. (This is a repeat of the biography of General Vandenberg first listed under Air Force Bases.)

Hoyt Vandenberg was born on January 24, 1899 in Milwaukee, Wisconsin. He graduated from the United States Military Academy with the Class of 1923 and was commissioned a second lieutenant in the Air Service. He graduated from flying school in 1924. In 1929 he went to Schofield Barracks and joined the Sixth Pursuit Squadron. During World War II he received a number of service awards including two Distinguished Service Medals, the Silver Star, the Legion of Merit, the Distinguished Flying Cross, the Bronze Star and five Air Medals.

During World War II he served in a number of assignments including being the operations and training officer of the Air Staff. In 1943 he was assigned to North Africa to assist in the organization of the Air Service there. He flew numerous missions over southern Europe and was awarded the Silver Star and the Distinguished Flying Cross. In August of 1944 he was named the Deputy Air Commander of the Allied Expeditionary Forces. In July of 1945 he was named the Assistant Chief of the Air Staff. He became Director of the Intelligence of the Army Air Force and in June of 1946, the Director of the Central Intelligence Agency. He returned to the Air Force in 1947 to become the Deputy Commander in Chief of the Air Staff. Later that year he was designated the Vice Chief of Staff of the Air Force.

In 1948 he became the Chief of Staff of the Air Force and served two terms.

He suffered from prostate cancer and retired from the Military on June 30, 1953.

He died at Walter Reed Hospital on April 2, 1954 and was buried at Arlington National Cemetery.

(Source: 25, 77)

UNITED STATES COAST GUARD ACADEMY NEW LONDON, CONNECTICUT

Chase Hall

Chase Hall is named after Salmon P. Chase, Secretary of the Treasury during the Civil War. It is the barracks for the entire Corps of Cadets at the Coast Guard Academy.

Salmon Portland Chase was born on January 13, 1808 in Cornish, New Hampshire. His father died when he was nine and Chase spent his youth in Ohio with his uncle. He graduated from Dartmouth College in 1826 and studied law under William Witt, the Attorney General of the United States. He was a lawyer in Cincinnati and was known for his knowledge of Ohio law. In 1836 he began an association with the anti-slave movement and gave of his services free to those who were fugitive slaves on Ohio. He became known for his defense of slave laws that limited the ability of a slave owner to cross state lines to recover slaves. He helped start a new party in an effort to keep the Democratic Party from further extending slavery. He was elected to the United States Senate in 1849.

He was the first Republican Governor of Ohio from 1855 to 1859 and was an early advocate of public education, prison reform and women's rights. He fought unsuccessfully to become the presidential nominee of the Republican Party in 1860. Abraham Lincoln was the winner and appointed him Secretary of the Treasury. It was during this time that two fundamental changes in the money system occurred; the establishment of a national banking system and the issue of legal tender paper money.

In 1864 he retired as Treasury Secretary and was appointed Chief Justice of the United States Supreme Court. It was his decision that the United States was made of "an indestructible union composed of individual states." He also presided over the impeachment trial of Andrew Johnson, insisting that it be done in a most dignified manner. He died in New York City on May 7, 1873. The "Chase Manhattan Bank" was named for him by Banker John Thompson for his passing the National Bank Acts of 1863. His portrait was on the now obsolete $10,000 bill.

(Source: 47, 128, 178, 230)

Dimick Hall

Dimick Hall is named for Professor Chester E. Dimick who was the head of the Mathematics Department from 1906 to 1945. Professor Dimick was affectionately known by Cadets as "The Dean." He was responsible for much of the Core Curriculum at the Academy.

(Source: 47)

Hamilton Hall

Hamilton Hall is named for Alexander Hamilton, the first Secretary of the Treasury and considered the father of the Coast Guard. (This is a repeat of the biography of Alexander Hamilton first listed under Army Bases.)

Alexander Hamilton was born in the British West Indies, out of wedlock to Rachel Lavien and James A. Hamilton in 1755 (or 1757). Because of his lack of legal parentage he was not allowed to attend the church school. As a result he received private tutoring and became a student of the family library of books. Abandoned by his father and shortly thereafter the death of his mother, Hamilton worked as a clerk at an import-export company.

In 1772 he was able to make his way to New Jersey where he attended a grammar school and later King's College (now Columbia University). His first political writings were against the writings of a Church of England clergyman who defended the Tory cause. While he was on the side of the revolutionaries, he defended those on the other side from mob vengeance.

As the Revolutionary War began he joined a New York volunteer militia. He studied tactics and military history and made successful attacks on British batteries. He asked for and became an aide to General Washington and rose to the position where he was allowed to issue orders over his own signature.

He wanted a command post and was finally given command of a New York Light Infantry division. He was heavily responsible for the surrender of Cornwallis at the Battle of Yorktown. At the

149

end of the war he was frustrated with the weakness of the Articles of Confederation and proposed a stronger central government, especially one with the ability to tax. Many soldiers and service providers were not paid for their efforts and he supported their efforts to receive payment. He surrendered his commission and became a representative from New York to the Congress of the Confederation.

As a way to a more centralized government, Hamilton proposed that the articles of Confederation be revised. This led to the call for a constitutional convention. He drafted a constitution based on the convention debates. While it was never presented, most of its features found their way into the Constitution. He, along with John Jay and James Madison, wrote some 85 essays defending the proposed constitution. These came to be known as the Federalist Papers.

In 1789 he became the first Secretary of the Treasury and served until 1795. Active and very vocal in politics, he made many enemies. He considered himself more than just a Secretary. He lobbied for a strong central banking system and helped establish the U.S. Mint.

One of the first sources of tax funds was that an excise tax on whiskey. This led to the Whiskey Rebellion led by whiskey manufacturers in Western Pennsylvania. A strong showing by military forces squelched the rebellion and showed the power of a strong central government.

Known for his temper, over the years Hamilton had challenged others to duels. In the end he had a duel with Aaron Burr, the Vice President of the United States. The duel was fought along the west bank of the Hudson River near the same spot where Hamilton's oldest son had lost his life in a duel.

It has been argued that Hamilton deliberately missed the first shot of the duel. Burr's shot did not miss and Hamilton died from its effect the following day.

(Source: 47)

Henriques Room

Henriques Room was named for Captain John A. Henriques, the first Superintendent of the Coast Guard Academy. John Henriques was born in1826 and joined the Merchant Marine in 1841. In 1854 he enlisted in the Revenue Marine and was selected to run the Cadet training ships. He served as Superintendent of the Revenue Cutter School until 1883. He served on the Connecticut during the Spanish American War. He died in 1906 and is buried in Cedar Grove Cemetery in New London, Connecticut.

(Source: 47, 200)

Johnson Hall

Johnson Hall is named after Rear Admiral Harvey F. Johnson from the Coast Guard Academy Class of 1908. He was Engineer-in-Chief of the Coast Guard from 1935 to 1946.

Harvey F. Johnson was born in Wheatley, Arkansas on August 27, 1882. In 1906 he graduated from Cornell University and then began his Coast Guard career as an Engineering Cadet in the U.S. Coast Guard. He was commissioned in 1908.

He served during World War I on the Aphrodite. Afterwards he saw shore duty at the Coast Guard Headquarters. He returned to sea duty on the Cutter Pequot. He was assigned to the Philadelphia Navy Yard working on the reconditioning of the destroyer Jouett and later was its engineering officer. He returned to the Philadelphia Navy Yard where he saw duty in the reconditioning of destroyers destined to become a part of the Coast Guard.

After another tour of duty at Coast Guard Headquarters in 1928-31 he became Inspector of Machinery at Trenton, New Jersey. He then became Chief Inspector at the Defoe Shipbuilding Company in Bay City, Michigan who was constructing the cutter Escanaba.

He retired from active service on August 1, 1946 at the age of sixty two. He was awarded the Legion of Merit on February 28, 1946.

(Source: 47, 210, 235)

Leamy Hall

Leamy Hall was named for Rear Admiral Frank Leamy who graduated with the Class of 1925. He was Superintendent of the Academy from 1957 to 1961.

Frank A. Leamy was born on May 13, 1900 in Philadelphia, Pennsylvania. He attended public schools in Ardmore, Pennsylvania, graduating from high school in 1918. He enlisted in the Tank Corps and was discharged in early 1919. He began his secondary education at the University of Delaware, transferring to Temple University, then on to the Coast Guard Academy in 1922. He was active in many extracurricular activities including football, baseball, and crew and as manager of the track team. He was Class Vice President and Associate Editor of the year book "Tide Rips."

He graduated with the Class of 1924 and received regular promotions until he reached the rank of Rear Admiral in 1954.

He saw duty aboard the destroyer Beale. In 1926 he was assigned to the U.S. Navy and saw duty as a Gunnery and Small Arms Observer aboard the USS Worden in Cuba and Haiti. After this duty he returned to the Coast Guard where he was responsible for establishing the first small arms training school for destroyer personnel.

In 1927 he became Executive Officer of the Coast Guard Base in Biloxi, Mississippi where he was credited with training his detachment in the skills needed to traverse treacherous flood waters. In 1934 he was in charge of the rescue operations to save the passengers of a burning cruise ship Morro Castle. In 1936 he became a Coast Guard Aviator.

He earned the Distinguished Flying Cross for his heroics in rescuing a critically injured person from a fishing trawler. This award is seldom given in peace time and represents the heroic actions of those who protect persons and ships in peril on our waters. In 1939 he became Commander of the U.S. Coast Guard Station in San Diego, California. He went from there to command the Coast Guard Air Station in Miami, Florida.

From 1939 to 1943 he served as Chief, Aviation Section at Coast Guard Headquarters. In 1943 he requested overseas duties with the Amphibious Forces. He participated in the assault landings of Southern France as Commander of the APA Joseph T. Dickman and for his service against the enemy was awarded the Navy Commendation Medal with Combat Star. He then took the Dickman to the South Pacific and was a part of the Okinawa landings. At the end of the war he helped bring home the troops in what was called Operation Magic Carpet.

In 1957 he became Superintendent of the Coast Guard Academy and was responsible for a number of curriculum changes. He was responsible for the meetings and interchange of ideas with the other Service Academies. He retired from active service in February, 1960.

Admiral Leamy died on June 24, 1966 in Bethesda, Maryland. He is buried at Arlington National Cemetery.

(Source: 47, 236)

McAllister Hall

McAllister Hall is named for Admiral Charles Albert McAllister, who was the Chief of Engineering for the Coast Guard from 1902 to 1919.

Charles Albert McAllister was born on May 29, 1867 in Dorchester, New Jersey. He received a degree in Mechanical Engineering from Cornell University in 1887. He was appointed Second Assistant Engineer in the United States Revenue Service in 1892 and was commissioned as First Lieutenant Assistant Engineer in 1895. He became a Chief Engineer in 1897. He participated in the Spanish-American War as well as World War I. In 1905 Commander McAllister became Engineer-in-Chief of the Revenue Cutter Service which was merged with the Lifesaving Service and became the U.S. Coast Guard in 1915. He retired on July 12, 1919.

(Source: 47, 236)

Michel Hall

Michel Hall was named for Rear Admiral Carl Michel who was the Chief Medical Officer of the Academy as well as Chief Medical Officer for the Coast Guard.

(Source: 47)

Munro Hall

Munro Hall was named for Signalman First Class Douglas Albert Munro, the only Coast Guard person to be awarded the Medal of Honor. He received the medal for his heroics in saving a group of Marines on Guadalcanal during World War II. He was a part of a Coast Guard Force that was given the assignment of transporting Marines and equipment to those embedded on the island.

Douglas A. Munro was born on October 11, 1919 in Vancouver, British Columbia. He grew up in Cle Elum, Washington and joined the Coast Guard in September 1939. He served on the Cutter Spencer until 1941, where he earned his signalman rating. He became a part of an integrated Navy and Coast Guard group and served aboard the APA Hunter Liggett. The ship was an attack transport weighing 13,712 Tons and carrying 700 officers and men.

In August of 1942 the United States decided to counter the Japanese successes in the South Pacific by making an assault on Guadalcanal. Munro was assigned to the staff of Rear Admiral Richmond Kelly as the Hunter Liggett served as the command post. After the initial landing, Munro went ashore along with the staff and set up base on a small house on a coconut plantation.

As a part of the drive to seize control of an area, Munro was given the duty of transporting a number of U.S. Marines inland. Overwhelming Japanese forces forced an attempted withdrawal. The same landing craft that had landed the Marines was assigned the duty of extracting them. During this action Munro was hit by enemy fire. He lived long enough to ask, "Did they get off?" For his heroic action he was posthumously awarded the Medal of Honor. The date of his death was September 27, 1942.

(Source: 47, 77, 169, 236)

Satterlee Hall

Satterlee Hall was named for Captain Charles Satterlee who graduated with Class of 1898. He was Commanding Officer of the USCGC Tampa which was one of the vessels protecting the transports across the Atlantic during World War I. The Tampa was sunk off the coast of Great Britain by a German submarine and all hands were lost.

Charles Satterlee was born on September 14, 1875 in Essex, Connecticut, the son of Charles Avery Satterlee. He became a Cadet at the Revenue Cutter Service School of Instruction in 1895 and was commissioned Third Lieutenant on January 17, 1898. For a period he served aboard the Cutter Levi Woodbury and was a part of the North Atlantic Squadron commanded by Admiral Samson. He received the Bronze Medal for his meritorious action.

In 1899-1900 he served aboard the Steamer Corwin and participated in patrols in the Bering Seas and the Arctic Ocean. In 1909 he became the Executive Officer of the Cutter Tahoma which operated out of Seattle, Washington. While on duty there he received a commendation for assisting the American Schooner Robert R. Hind which was disabled with a full cargo. From 1910 to 1913 he served in the New England area where he was promoted to Captain of the Cutter Acushnet.

By the time the Revenue Cutter Service had become the Coast Guard in 1915, he had been promoted to Captain. He was given command of the Coast Guard Cutter Miami which later had a name change to Coast Guard Cutter Tampa. He commanded the ship until it was sunk while on its eighteenth convoy duty on September 26, 1918. The loss of 115 crew members was the greatest single loss of men by the Navy or Coast Guard during World War I. Also lost were sixteen other persons, civilians or from the British military.

Besides Satterlee Hall, there have been two United States Navy ships named after him.

(Source: 47, 77, 117, 211, 235. 236)

Smith Hall

Smith Hall was named for Coast Guard Academy graduate Rear Admiral Edward H. "Iceberg" Smith. He was known for his knowledge of Oceanography and iceberg behavior. He studied ice in the Arctic through a number of expeditions. He won the Distinguished Service Medal during World War II.

Edward Hanson Smith was born on Vineyard Haven, Massachusetts on October 29, 1889. Before entering the Revenue Cutter service School, he attended the Massachusetts Institute of Technology for one year. He graduated in 1913 and in a few years joined the International Ice Patrol. He served in the European and Mediterranean Theaters during World War I. After the War he became the Navigator of the Cutter "Seneca" which was beginning an ice patrol. He began experiments on ocean currents as well as weather details. It is here that he picked up the nickname of "Iceberg." His work was recognized by Norway shipping groups and he went there to study. In 1931 he was the only American member of the scientific staff on the Graf Zeppelin Polar Flight.

His charts of iceberg travel routes were used to establish the movements of icebergs south of Newfoundland. In 1934 he received from Harvard the first doctorate given in the United States in Oceanography.

During World War II he became commander of Task Force 24 which was known as the Greenland Patrol. The Distinguished Service Medal was given to him in recognition for his work in keeping Greenland out of German hands. Admiral Smith retired from the Coast Guard in 1950 but continued his interest in ocean research. He died on his birthday in 1961 but the cooperation between the Coast Guard and those institutions studying the ocean continued.

(Source: 47, 77, 236, 256, 259)

Waesche Hall

Waesche Hall was named after Admiral Russell R. Waesche who graduated from the Coast Guard Academy with the Class of 1906. He was Commandant of the Coast Guard in World War II and met with General MacArthur and instructed Marine and Navy personnel on landing procedures for troops. He received the Distinguished Service Medal as well as Knighthood from the King of England.

Russell Waesche was born on January 6, 1886 in Thurmont, Maryland. He attended Purdue University to study Electrical Engineering before going to the United States Revenue Cutter Service School. After he graduated in 1906 he served in the North Atlantic, Great Lakes and the Pacific. In 1915 he was assigned to the Coast Guard headquarters and kept this assignment throughout World War I. He commanded various cutters and destroyers after the war until 1924.

In 1928 he became the Chief Ordnance Officer for the Coast Guard. In 1936 he worked to assure the integration of the U.S. Lighthouse Service into the Coast Guard. During World War II he was responsible for the unprecedented growth of the Coast Guard. He strove to insure the prompt return of the Coast Guard to the Treasury Department after the war.

He was awarded the Distinguished Service Medal as he served to create the unprecedented growth of the Service during the War. He was Commandant of the Coast Guard during World War II.

He retired from the Coast Guard in1946 and died on October 17, in that year. He is buried at Arlington National Cemetery.

(Source: 47, 133, 235, 236)

Yeaton Hall

Yeaton Hall is named after Captain Hopley Yeaton, the first officer commissioned into the United States Navy. Much of the details of his life are sketchy. His commission was signed by both George Washington and Thomas Jefferson on March 21, 1791. After the

Revolutionary War the Continental Navy was disbanded and the only seagoing naval defense was the Revenue Cutter Service. This became the United States Coast Guard when it merged with the United States Life Saving Service in 1915 and Yeaton is considered the "Father of The Coast Guard." Yeaton was born in 1739 in New Hampshire and grew up in Maine. After being commissioned he was given command of the revenue Frigate "Scammel," whose activity centered on smuggling suppression and tax collecting. He also was responsible for the establishment of a lighthouse known as the West Quoddy Light, which is still in operation.

Yeaton died on May 12, 1812 and was buried in North Lubec, Maine along side of the remains of his wife, Comfort Marshall Yeaton. His remains were dug up and reinterred at the Coast Guard Academy in 1976, though his wife's remains are at the original burial site near other members of her family. The Cadets at the Coast Guard Academy, whose grades are in need of improvement, will take up vigil over his grave, as legend has it he will bestow on them an improvement of their knowledge sufficient for them to pass their exams.

(Source: 39, 47, 77, 108, 124, 142, 196, 236)

United States Military Academy West Point, New York

Arvin Gym

Arvin Gym is named after Captain Carl Robert Arvin who was First Captain of the Corps of Cadets and Captain of the Wrestling Team when he was at the Military Academy. Arvin graduated with the Class of 1965 and during the Vietnam War was an advisor with the 7th Airborne Battalion. He received the Silver Star for his actions during a battle on September 5. 1967. Though wounded himself he dragged a fellow soldier to safety and then returned to direct helicopter gunship strikes.

He recovered from his wounds and insisted upon returning to action. During a second battle on October 8, 1967 he was mortally wounded during the attack where he again directed gunship fire onto enemy positions while disregarding his own personal safety. This led to the awarding of a second Silver Star and a posthumous promotion to Captain. He was born in Ypsilanti, Michigan on January 19, 1943 and died on October 8, 1967. There is a memorial in his name at the Boy Scout Headquarters in Ann Arbor, Michigan.

(Source: 22, 246, 253)

Blaik Field

Blaik Field is named for "Colonel" Earl "Red" Blaik, Army football coach from 1941 to 1958. Blaik was born on February 15, 1897 in Detroit, Michigan. He attended Miami University of Ohio for two years before going to West Point, where he was selected as a third-team All American. He graduated from the Academy with the Class of 1920. After graduation he served in the United States Cavalry for a period before returning to Ohio where his father was a contractor. In 1924 he began his coaching career as a part-time assistant at Miami University. In 1927 he joined the coaching staff at West Point. In 1934 he became head coach at Dartmouth College where he coached for seven seasons.

In 1941 he became the head coach at West Point and was instrumental in having some height-to-weight restrictions removed

Mark W. Royston

that that were a requirement for all Cadets at West Point. This restriction limited the size of the linemen and made it difficult to be competitive against those teams without these restrictions.

During his coaching career at West Point, the football teams went 121-32-10, including a 32 unbeaten win streak from 1944-1947. The team won the National Championship in 1944 and 1945. He coached three Heisman Trophy winners and twenty of his assistant coaches went on to become head coaches at other colleges, universities or professional teams.

In 1959, Blaik resigned from coaching and became a vice-president of Avco Corporation. He was inducted into the Football Hall of Fame in 1964 and in 2004 a statue was dedicated in his honor at its home in South Bend, Indiana. He died on September 25, 1999 and is buried at the U.S. Military Cemetery at West Point.

(Source: 77, 96, 106, 183)

Cristl Arena

Cristl Arena is a multi-purpose arena that seats over 5000 and was named after First Lieutenant Edward C. Cristl, Jr.

Edward Cristl was the Captain of his basketball team at West Point, leading his team to a perfect 15-0 record his senior year. He graduated with the Class of 1944 and was killed in action in Austria during World War II, while a member of the 65th Division. He received the Distinguished Service Cross for his heroic action during combat.

(Source: 6, 77)

Cullum Hall

Cullum Hall was built in 1898 and was named for Major General George Washington Cullum who graduated from West Point with the Class of 1833.

George Cullum was born in New York City on February 25, 1809. Upon graduation from the Military Academy he entered the Engineering Corps and superintended the building of the fortifications in New London, Connecticut and Boston Harbor. He was engaged in the War with Mexico as an engineer. In 1848 he returned to the Academy and taught Military Engineering.

During the Civil War he was Chief Engineer of the Department of Missouri as well as Chief Engineer of the Siege of Corinth. He served on many inspection boards.

After the war he served on boards whose duties were to improve the defenses of many cities. He became known for his work on summarizing the careers of the graduates of West Point. He died on February 28, 1889 in New York City.

(Source: 86, 141, 239)

Doubleday Field

Doubleday Field was dedicated to honor West Point Graduate Abner Doubleday when it opened in 1939.

Abner Doubleday was born at Ballston Spa, New York on June 26, 1819 and went to schools in Auburn and Cooperstown, New York. He graduated from the United States Military Academy with the Class of 1842. After graduation he served in the War with Mexico and the campaign against the Seminoles in Florida. He was stationed at Fort Sumter at the outset of the Civil War, aiming the first Union gun that was fired. Later in the war he served with Union troops in the Shenandoah Valley and led Union troops in the Second Battle of Bull Run. He was in the Battles of South Mountain, Antietam, and Fredericksburg. At Gettysburg he led the Union troops until reinforcements arrived. He retired from the military in 1873 and moved to San Francisco where he started the first cable car in that city. He then moved to New Jersey where he died on January 26, 1893. He is buried at Arlington National Cemetery.

He is given credit for the invention of baseball in 1835. It was said that he laid out a field when he was a Cadet at West Point in 1839.

(Source: 25, 237, 230, 239)

Eisenhower Hall & Eisenhower Monument

The Eisenhower Hall and Monument were named for General Dwight David Eisenhower, Supreme Commander of the Allied Forces in Europe and the thirty fourth President of the United States.

Dwight Eisenhower was born on October 14, 1890 in Denison, Texas. The German translation of his surname is "Iron worker." Eisenhower graduated from Abilene, Kansas in 1909 and entered West Point in 1911, graduating with the Class of 1915. He had wanted to go to the Naval Academy but he was past the age limit. Fifty nine of the graduates of that class became generals.

At the "Point" he wanted to fulfill a childhood dream of playing baseball. He didn't make the baseball team but did play running back and linebacker on the football team.

After graduation he served with the Infantry. During the First World War he joined the Tank Corps. He spent the war training crews without seeing combat. He was assigned to the Panama Canal Zone and was stationed there until 1924. He attended Command and General Staff Schools and was assigned duty in the Philippines under Douglas MacArthur. In 1941he was promoted to Brigadier General for his administrative abilities. One of those recognizing his great administrative abilities was General George Catlett Marshall. Marshall was one of those responsible for Eisenhower getting senior command posts.

In 1944 he was promoted to be General of the Army partly because of his ability to work with other senior officers, as well as the senior officers of other allied nations.

He was responsible for Operation Overlord which was the name given to the invasion of Europe and the defeat of Germany. He was ready to take the blame if the Normandy Invasion did not succeed.

After the surrender of Germany he was appointed Military Governor of the U.S. Occupied Zone. He gave the orders to document the atrocities of the Nazis that were discovered in the concentration camps. He was an early supporter of the Morgenthau Plan to limit the growth of industrialization in Germany so as to reduce their potential to wage future wars.

In 1952 he was persuaded to run for the presidency against Adlai Stevenson. It was a landslide victory for this popular general. While President he was responsible for the continuation of many of the New Deal programs. In 1956 he signed the bill authorizing the Interstate Highway System. Perhaps his zeal for this program came from his early military days when he was a part of the War Department's First Transcontinental Motor Convoy. He was a promoter of integration, proposing to Congress the Civil Rights Acts of 1957 and 1960. He sent Federal troops to Arkansas schools to enforce the non-segregation of public schools.

During his presidency two states were admitted to the Union, Alaska and Hawaii.

In his final address to the nation he warned against the "military-industrial complex" gaining unwarranted influence in the country.

He retired to his farm adjacent to the Battlefield at Gettysburg, Pennsylvania. He died on March 28, 1969 and was buried alongside of his wife Mamie and an infant son, Dowd, who died at the age of three.

(Source: 72, 77, 255)

Gillis Field House

The Gillis Field House was named for William G. Gillis, Jr. who graduated with the Class of 1941 at the Military Academy. He was born in Cameron, Texas and was a graduate of the Schreiner Institute where he excelled at athletics, being awarded the name of Best-All-Around Cadet. While at West Point he was captain of the 1940 football team and a three year letterman in track.

He was killed in action on October 1, 1944 in Gremercy Forest in France. He was the holder of the Distinguished Service Cross, two Purple Hearts, Distinguished Service Order, as well as France's Croix De Guerre, Silver Gilt and Vermillion Stars.

(Source: 32, 214)

Grant Hall

Grant Hall was named for General Ulysses S. Grant, the leading general of the Civil War as well as the eighteenth President of the United States.

Grant was born on April 27, 1822 in Clermont County, Ohio. His original name was Hiram Ulysses Grant but the Congressman making out the application papers for Grant to enter West Point put down "Ulysses S." and that was the name he was given at the Point. He graduated from the United States Military Academy with the Class of 1843, standing 21st out of 39 graduates. After graduation he served under Zachary Taylor in the War with Mexico where he received applause for his bravery. When the War was over he was transferred to Western posts but could not afford to have his wife join him. He resigned from the Army and tried his hand at other businesses.

When the Civil War started he offered his services and recruited a company of volunteers and marched to Springfield, Illinois. After accepting the position to train the recruits, he was appointed a colonel in the Illinois Militia. He went to Missouri to protect the railroads and shortly thereafter he was appointed Brigadier General to command the District of Southeast Missouri.

He seized the town of Paducah, Kentucky. The state had declared for neutrality but another town in the state had been occupied by the South. He fought a number of battles for control of river ports and his decisiveness in battle was quickly noticed. In one battle, 12,000 Southern troops surrendered to his demand for an unconditional surrender. When this became public news he was acclaimed and called "Unconditional Surrender" Grant. Grant had problems with a superior officer who believed the stories of Grant's consumption of whiskey. He was relieved of command but it was restored by Lincoln.

At the Battle of Shiloh he was initially overwhelmed by the superior numbers of the attackers. He regrouped and counterattacked and the battle was won. Once again the superior officer used the battle as an excuse to demote Grant from command and Grant pressed for duties elsewhere. In time this superior officer was promoted and moved to Washington. Grant was given command of the Army of the Tennessee. He was successful in a number of battles and he was able to split the confederacy in two. Grant was promoted to major general effective July 4, 1863.

Lincoln was looking for a leader who wanted to fight, as many of his first appointees in the east did more planning than fighting. In March, 1864 Grant became general-in-chief of the entire Union Army. Grant moved to the East and devised strategies to defeat the Southern Forces. It pitted Grant against Robert E. Lee and the battles through Virginia and as far south as Georgia raged relentlessly. Finally the war was over when Lee surrendered to Grant at Appomattox Courthouse on April 9, 1865.

Very soon thereafter Grant had the sad honor of being pallbearer at Lincoln's funeral. Grant continued as Commanding General of the Army when Vice President Johnson was sworn in to take Lincoln's place as President. In 1868 Grant ran for President and at the time of his inauguration he was the youngest man that had been elected to that office. His term of office was a mixture of successes and failures as he faced the continuing battle of Reconstruction. The Ku Klux Klan was a force with which to be reckoned in the South and he signed a number of orders in an attempt to restrict their activities. There were many splits in both the North and the South that made it difficult to achieve success in restoring the unity of the country.

During his terms in office he signed into law orders making Christmas a Federal holiday and the establishing of Yellowstone as the first National Park. The Panic of 1873 hit and Grant appeared indecisive in his efforts to control it. He was fighting division at every turn and it appeared that he could not make decisions. Grant worked to reduce the national debt created by the funding of the

War. There were scandals such as those created by Wall Street manipulators and the Whiskey Ring of 1875. The reader is left to pursue the details of these online or at the library.

He left the Presidency in 1877 and died on July 23, 1885.

(Source: 57, 77, 208)

James K. Herbert Alumni Center

The James K. Herbert Alumni Center is named for James K. Herbert, a West Point graduate from the Class of 1930. Herbert was born on February 25, 1909 and entered West Point in 1926. At the Academy he distinguished himself in athletics and academics. He was Cadet Captain during his first class year and was a "star" man (One who maintains a certain high academic average.). He graduated sixth in his class and became a member of the Corps of Engineers.

He rose to the rank of Brigadier General and received the Distinguished Service Medal as Commander of the Port of Los Angeles Embarkation. He retired from active service in 1946 and became an executive with the Schenley's Roma Wine Division. He retired from this in 1957 but was still active in the business world of the San Joaquin Valley in California.

He was a philanthropist and gave to many charities. He died on January 22, 1990 and as a part of his will gave for the establishing of an Alumni Center at West Point.

(Source: 254, 239)

Holleder Center

The Holleder Center houses the basketball court and the ice skating rink. It is named for Major Donald W. Holleder who was killed in action during the Viet Nam Conflict.

Donald Walter Holleder was born August 30, 1934 in Irondequoit, New York. He went to high school at Aquinas Institute and was recruited by many colleges and universities for his athletic abilities. He chose West Point and graduated with the Class of 1956. While at West Point he was named to the All America team as an end. His last year Coach Blaik asked him to switch to quarterback as they had no one to replace the graduated quarterback of the past year. After a bit of "thinking-it-over" he agreed to the switch knowing he would give up his chance of repeating as an All-American. Coach Blaik's choice brought lots of criticism but he was vindicated when Holleder led the Army team to a final game win over a favored Navy team that was led by All American George Welsh and Ron Beagle.

After graduation he served as a combat infantryman and rose to the rank of Major. On October 17, 1967 he was headed into the Vietnamese jungle in a helicopter as he observed an ambush of American soldiers. He landed and went straight toward the wounded, encouraging a medic to follow him. He was killed by automatic weapon fire as he tried to get to the wounded. He is buried at Arlington National Cemetery. The West Point Athletic Center is named in his honor. Also in his honor, the "Black Lions" Award is given annually to a member of the Army football team. Thanks to a high school football coach the same award is available to any youth, middle school or high school team.

(Source: 25, 52, 106, 167, 243, 246)

Kosciuszko Monument

The Kosciuszko Monument base was erected in 1828 by the West Point Corps of Cadets to honor Thaddeus Kosciuszko, Polish born American Revolutionary War hero. His statue was added by the Polish clergy and laity of the United States in 1913. Kosciuszko was born in Poland on February 4, 1746. He attended the Cadet Academy in Warsaw and then an engineering school in France. In 1776 he offered his services to the Continental Congress and was given the task of fortifying the various battle sites.

He was so moved by reading the Declaration of Independence that he sought out Thomas Jefferson on a trip to Virginia. They were to become close friends. It was through his fortification of Saratoga that the Colonies were able to defeat the British, a battle which was to become the linchpin of the American war efforts. In 1778 Kosciuszko was made engineer at West Point and saw to its fortification. It was so well protected that the British were never able to penetrate it.

In 1783 George Washington presented Kosciuszko with the Cincinnati Order Medal. In 1784 he returned to Poland to help his own country in their battle for independence. There he was wounded and taken prisoner by the Russians. When he was released he returned to America in 1797. He was a great believer in equality and in his will, asked that the proceeds be used to buy freedom for slaves. He died in Switzerland on October 15, 1817. He is buried in Wawel Castle in Krakow, Poland.

(Source: 192, 239)

Lichtenberg Tennis Center

The Lichtenberg Tennis Center was named after brothers Alan Lichtenberg and Herbert Lichtenberg. Alan graduated from the U.S. Military Academy with the Class of 1951, and Herbert with the Class of 1955. Both joined their father's business after their military careers and became well known philanthropists. They were responsible for spearheading the new tennis center which bears their name. Alan went into the Army after graduation and served in Korea. Herbert went into the U.S. Air Force and served four years. Herbert was declared a Distinguished Graduate in 2006 along with seven other graduates. In 1965 Herbert became a member of those supporting a Jewish Cadet Chapel that became a reality in 1984. Alan died of Alzheimer's disease in 2001.

(Source: 8, 89, 106, 125, 183, 254)

MacArthur Monument

The MacArthur Monument is a sculpture of General Douglas MacArthur and was dedicated in 1969 by his wife, Jean.

Douglas MacArthur was born in Little Rock, Arkansas on January 26, 1880, the son of General Arthur MacArthur, Jr. and Mary Pinkney Hardy MacArthur. His father was later stationed at San Antonio, Texas and Douglas attended West Texas Military Academy. He went to West Point and was commissioned a Second Lieutenant in the Army Corps of Engineers. He stood first in the Class of 1903.

His first tour of duty was the Philippines. He later joined his father who was serving in the Far East. In 1906 he became aide-de-camp to President Roosevelt. By the time of the First World War MacArthur commanded the 42nd Division and was decorated thirteen times. In 1918 he became the youngest Division Commander in France.

MacArthur returned to the United States and served as Superintendent of the Military Academy where he modernized its curriculum. As he moved up the ranks he was always the youngest to hold that position. He was the Army's youngest general when he returned to the Philippines to take over the Military District of Manila. In 1928 he was appointed President of the American Olympic Committee.

He was appointed Chief of Staff in 1932 and attempted to modernize the Army. He saw Communism as an enemy and was known for his right wing views. He had a running battle with journalist Drew Pearson and entered into a law suit against him. His political views brought him against President Roosevelt and he retired from service in 1937 to become the military advisor to the Philippines. He was recalled to active service in 1941 and was given freedom to modernize the Philippine Army. When the Japanese attacked Pearl Harbor, they also attacked the Philippines the following day, destroying half of MacArthur's troops.

After the Japanese invaded the Philippines, MacArthur was forced to leave Bataan and retreat to Australia. After the forces were reorganized, MacArthur became supreme Commander of the Southwest Pacific Area and Admiral Chester Nimitz became Commander-in-Chief of the United States Pacific Fleet.

Douglas MacArthur was awarded the Medal of Honor and he and his father were the first father-son duo to be awarded the Medal of Honor. (Later in 2001 Theodore Roosevelt was awarded one for his gallantry in the Spanish American War as he joined his son Theodore Roosevelt, Jr. as holders of the Medal of Honor.)

In 1944 MacArthur returned to defeat the Japanese in the Philippines and he followed with the bloody conquest of Okinawa. At the end of the war he was appointed Supreme Commander of the Allied Powers and he received the formal surrender of the Japanese on the Battleship Missouri. He was given the duties of being head of the Allied occupation of Japan.

At the outbreak of the Korean War he was given command of the United Nations forces. As the Korean War progressed he and President Truman disagreed on the United Nations decision to limit the war to Korea itself.

By April 1951, MacArthur was removed from his command and he returned to the United States, a foe of Truman. His last public appearance was before Congress where he uttered the most memorable words, "Old soldiers never die, they just fade away..." After his retirement he was President of the Rand Corporation. As his life waned he made trips to Washington and the Philippines, but it was at West Point he gave his last speech where he gave his last advice to the assembled Corps of cadets. He dwelt on the theme, "Duty, Honor, Country." He died on April 5, 1964 and he and his wife Jean are both buried in Norfolk, Virginia.

(Source: 77, 213, 239)

Michie Stadium

Michie Stadium was completed in 1924 and named for Dennis Mahan Michie, a Cadet who started football at West Point. Michie was the son of Peter Michie who was a professor at the Academy and who had graduated with the Class 1863.

West Point played only one game in 1890, that first year of football, and lost to Navy 24-0. Navy had been competing in football for a number of seasons and their experience told as they were organized as a team. Army had only three players who had previously played football and the Corps of Cadets was canvassed to find players. To show the ethics that existed in those times, Navy used a fake punt to score one touchdown. Army protested to no avail that the punter was honor bound to punt because that was the formation that was called. Michie was also a member of the team that first beat Navy in 1891.

Michie graduated and went into the Army. He was killed at the age of twenty eight in Cuba (as was the captain of the 1890 Naval Academy team) during the War with Spain.

(Source: 20, 27, 76, 106, 241)

Patton Monument

The Patton Monument was dedicated in the honor of General George S. Patton, Jr. in 1950. George Smith Patton, Jr. was born on November 11, 1885 in San Gabriel, California. He attended the Virginia Military Academy for one year before going to West Point where he graduated with the Class of 1909.

In 1912 he was a part of the United States Olympics Team competing in the Pentathlon. At this time the event was open only to military officers and consisted of pistol shooting, sword fencing, swimming, horseback riding and a cross country run. He placed fifth even with a poor showing in the pistol shooting. (He was charged with missing the target and he argued that his bullet went through an existing hole that had been enlarged by previous fire.)

One of his early assignments, under the command of General John J. "Blackjack" Pershing, was the pursuit of Pancho Villa. In 1917, Pershing took Patton with him to France as commander of his headquarter troops. He was given the task of organizing the United States Tank Corps and leading a tank corps in the battle at St. Mihiel. He was wounded at the beginning of the Meuse-

Argonne and was awarded the Distinguished Service Medal and the Distinguished Service Cross. He was a strong advocate of the use of tanks thereafter.

The period between the wars was filled with schools and base assignments. His advocacy of a strong mobile armored corps fell on deaf ears until the beginning of the hostilities leading to World War II. The Armored Force was formed in 1940 and Patton given its command in 1941. In 1942 he led the Tank Corps in the invasion of North Africa. He later commanded the invasion of Sicily and along with the British Eighth Army, defeated the Germans there.

In 1944 he was given Command of the Third Army and it raced across Western Europe. He was known for having German civilians come and witness what horrors he found in the Concentration Camps as they were liberated.

In October, 1945 he was given command of the 15th Army in Germany. On December 9, 1945 he was in a Jeep accident which cost him his life twelve days later. He was buried alongside soldiers who lost their lives in the Battle of the Bulge, in Hamm, Luxembourg.

(Source: 77, 100, 109, 239)

Fort Putnam

Fort Putnam is one of the fortifications built to defend West Point during the Revolutionary War. The commander of the team that built the Fort was Rufus Putnam and the fort was named for him.

Rufus Putnam was born on April 9, 1738 in Sutton, Massachusetts. During the French and Indian War he served with a Connecticut regiment and saw action in the Great Lakes Region. After that war he returned to the New England area and worked as a millwright, while educating himself. Becoming a surveyor he travelled to the Pensacola, Florida area and surveyed land that was to be given to the veterans of the French and Indian War.

At the beginning of the Revolutionary War he was commissioned a Lieutenant Colonel. During the Battle of Saratoga, he commanded two regiments and in 1778 he was given the task of laying out fortifications that included those at West Point, which came to be known as Fort Putnam.

After the war he returned to Rutland, Massachusetts where he helped found an organization for the development of the Western Lands, including Ohio. He was responsible for the development of much of Ohio as well as the Northwest Territory and his rectangular assignment of surveyed lines would become the standard in the laying out of the territory. He has been called the "Father of Ohio." He died in Marietta, Ohio on May 4, 1824 and is buried in Mound Cemetery in that city.

(Source: 77, 178, 217, 231)

Sedgwick Monument

Sedgwick Monument is named for Major General John Sedgwick who was killed at the Battle of the Spotsylvania during the Civil War. It is said that a Cadet deficient in studies only has to go to the monument at midnight and spin the rowels of the General's spurs and his grades will improve. (To compare the magic of monuments to improve grades, the reader is referred to the Naval Academy's Tecumseh Figurehead Monument and the Coast Guard Academy's Yeaton Hall.)

John Sedgwick was born in Cornwell Hollow, Connecticut on September 13, 1813, and taught for two years before attending the United States Military Academy, graduating with the Class of 1837. He became a part of the Artillery Corps and participated in the Seminoles Wars and the War with Mexico. In 1860 he was directed to build a fort on the Platte River in what is now Colorado. He was successful in this endeavor even though there were little supplies available.

At the onset of the Civil War he served as Assistant Inspector General of the Military Department of Washington. Illness precluded him from some of the early battles but he fought in the Battle of Antietam. There he was wounded three times and again was out of action until the Battle of Fredericksburg. In the Battle of

Fredericksburg he fought against Major General Jubal Early's forces and a portion of Lee's Second Corps, commanded by General J.E.B. Stuart.

He was in the latter part of the Battle of Gettysburg and was in the final counter attacks against the Confederate Troops.

On May 9, 1864 he was killed by a sharp shooter as he was directing artillery emplacements. The bullet hit him just after he was joking to those who were dodging as the bullets sung by, about the inability of any bullet finding a target. His death was mourned by both sides as his abilities were known to all. He is buried at his home place of Cornwell Hollow, Connecticut. Sedgwick County, Kansas is named for him.

(Source: 53, 56, 57, 77, 162, 206, 239)

Shea Stadium

Shea Stadium is a multi-use stadium at West Point situated near the Hudson River. It was named for Richard Thomas Shea who graduated from the United States Military Academy with the Class of 1952.

He was born in Portsmouth, Virginia on January 3, 1927 and graduated from Churchland High School. He studied at Virginia Tech and then went into the enlisted ranks of the United States Army. He rose to the rate of Sergeant and then entered the United States Military Academy and graduated with the Class of 1952. While at the Academy he excelled at athletics and was an All American in track. He was a distance runner and won Heptagonal and IC4A titles. He declined the opportunity to compete in the 1952 Olympics at Helsinki, Finland to join his comrades fighting in the Korean War.

He was a part of the action at Pork Chop Hill and was killed on July 8, 1953 while leading a counterattack against the enemy. During this time he killed three enemy soldiers singlehandedly and though wounded, refused to be evacuated. He was last seen fighting hand to hand combat against the enemy.

175

For his heroics he was posthumously awarded the Medal of Honor.

(Source: 5, 29, 77, 106, 167, 245)

Tate Rink

The Tate Rink is a part of the Holleder Center at West Point and is named after Brothers Joseph S. Tate, Class of 1941 and Frederick H.S. Tate, Class of 1942. Both brothers were shot down in action during World War II. Construction on the Rink began April 22, 1983 and the first game was skated on October 25, 1985.

(Source: 28)

Thayer Monument

The Thayer Monument was erected in 1883 to honor Sylvanus Thayer, who is given the title, "Father of the Military Academy."

Sylvanus Thayer was born June 9, 1785 in Braintree, Massachusetts. At the age of eight he went to live with his uncle. There he met General Benjamin Pierce, a veteran of the Revolutionary War. Thayer went on to Dartmouth College where he graduated first in his class. Just at that time he was given an appointment to the United States Military Academy at the behest of General Pierce. He was able to complete the course at West Point in one year and graduated with the Class of 1808.

During the War of 1812 he directed the building of fortifications at Norfolk, Virginia. After the War he went on an inspection tour of Europe. Upon his return he was made Superintendent of West Point where he served from 1817 to 1833, the longest tour of any superintendent at the Academy. While there he was responsible for the transformation of the Academy to a preeminent school of engineering. He reorganized the academic as well as the military aspect of the Academy. He recruited professors who served with distinction, including Dennis Hart Mahan, whose son, Alfred Thayer Mahan, became the noted historian at the Naval Academy.

Thayer resisted outside attempts to change his modifications at West Point leading to his resignation in 1833.

He returned to fortification duties and then went on to establish an engineering school at Dartmouth. Thayer died on September 7, 1872 and is buried at the West Point Cemetery. In 1958 the Sylvanus Thayer Award was established to honor his achievements and is awarded to deserving Cadets at the Academy.

(Source: 18, 20, 58, 77, 78, 92, 167, 239)

Washington Monument

The Washington Monument at West Point was unveiled in 1916. It was moved from its original location to a point near the Cadet Dining Hall. It is named for George Washington, the first President of the United States and the "Father of our Country."

George Washington was born in Westmoreland County, Virginia on February 22, 1732, the oldest son of Augustine Washington and Mary Ball Washington. He spent his early years near the Potomac River on his father's plantation. He received little formal education but studied the classics, mathematics and surveying. His father died in 1743 and young George went to live with his half brother, Lawrence, at Mount Vernon which was adjacent to Belvoir, the home of Lord Fairfax.

In 1748 George turned to surveying and made several survey trips into the Shenandoah Valley at the request of Lord Fairfax as the Lord attempted to extend his holdings by finding more western sources for the headwaters of the Potomac.

George's brother, Lawrence, died in 1752 and George inherited the Mount Vernon estate. The French and Indian War was on the horizon and George became a part of it by volunteering to be an adjutant of one of Virginia's military districts. He was sent on an unsuccessful mission to warn the French against further encroachment on territory claimed by the British.

His first taste of battle came against the French as he attempted to set up a post at the forks of the Ohio. Finding the French already there he hastily built a fort elsewhere, naming it Fort Necessity. The French overwhelmed his troops there and he was allowed to return to Williamsburg by the terms of the surrender.

He resigned his commission but the next year he volunteered to join General Braddock in an expedition against the French. Braddock was killed during this campaign and his body buried in the wagon road itself so that it would be difficult for the enemy to find its location. During the French and Indian War he honed his skills as a military leader. He left the Army in 1758, returning to Mount Vernon. He married Martha Dandridge Custis, a wealthy widow with two small children. They were to have no children of their own.

The rift between the colonies and Great Britain became more serious and Washington was a leader in opposing their actions against the colonies. When the Continental Congress convened he was one of the delegates. In June, 1775 he was named Commander in Chief of the Continental forces. His actions during the Revolutionary War have been well chronicled and it was his strength and perseverance that won in the end. On October 19, 1781 the American victory was assured with the surrender of Cornwallis at Yorktown, Virginia.

In 1789 the country was ready for its first President and he was unanimously elected to that position. He took office in New York City and set about a methodical building of the structure of the country. He was reelected in 1792. During the second administration, serious differences between America and the British were settled with the signing of the Jay Treaty. His reaction to those who opposed the excise tax placed on the sale and manufacture of alcohol came to a swift conclusion when the United States Army acted to put down the Whiskey Rebellion in Western Pennsylvania.

By the time of his departure from politics (He refused to serve a third term.) the power of the central government was well established both domestically and abroad. He retired to Mount Vernon in 1797 and lived in retirement until his death on December 14, 1799. It was Henry Lee who said at the funeral oration that Washington was "first in war, first in peace, and first in the heart of his countrymen."

(Source: 77, 79, 203, 253, 255)

UNITED STATES
NAVAL
ACADEMY
ANNAPOLIS, MARYLAND

Armel-Leftwich Visitor Center

This visitor center at the U.S. Naval Academy is named for two of the author's classmates who graduated from the U.S. Naval Academy, Class of 1953. (The author was honored to stand in the same company rank and file with one as he responded to the commands of the other who served as Brigade Commander.) It is also an honor to receive first hand details from those close to Captain Lyle Armel, USN, and Lt. Col. William Groom Leftwich, USMC, both deceased. It was decided to leave the details received from the Lyle's widow intact as it tells not only the story of a Naval hero, but that of the spouse, as it was seen through the eyes of a service wife who was an integral part of her husband's life and through his untimely death just six years after his retirement.

Biographical Sketch of Lyle Armel, Capt. USN
By his Widow, Barbara Lee Rhodes Armel Rieley.
Lyle was born in Topeka, Kansas and grew up in Lawrence, Kansas where his father was a professor. His father was in the U.S. Navy Reserve and when World War II came, he served in the Pacific Theater. After the war, the family moved to Washington, DC as a part of his father's transfer. Lyle went to Woodrow Wilson High School for his 10, 11, and 12th grades. Among the many friends he made there was myself and we fell in love. But I was always to know, the Navy came first. His main goal was to be a Naval Officer. He attended classes at a prep school for a few months his senior year and then with an appointment to the U.S. Naval Academy as a son of a deceased war vet, he was accepted into Annapolis. There he made many friends but had a few real close ones including his roommate, Ross (H. Ross Perot)

His first duty after graduation was on the destroyer, USS Hickox (DD 673) out of Newport, Rhode Island; so, on our honeymoon we stopped and secured an apartment. His entire career was a "tin can" sailor. He was fortunate to be chosen Flag Lt. to Des-Lant Arleigh Burke. A funny story, when he was driving Bobbie and Admiral Burke to Washington from Newport, Rhode Island, the Admiral dictated a letter in which he accepted the post as Chief of Naval Operations. Well, Lyle swerved the car and slammed the brakes on hearing this and Admiral Burke laughed as he apologized for the shock.

Various duties included Intelligence School, which made Intelligence his second choice after Destroyer duty. He then went to CNO Briefer-under Burke. Next to California, to be exec of the Turner Joy (C. Turner Joy DD 951). While on duty in the Pacific, they caught and surfaced the first Russian submarine, held them in sight until others came and escorted the ship to Vladivostok, USSR. This operation was known only as "Operation X" because the Cuban missile crisis was in progress, therefore no "press." But very quietly to the ship came:

"Virginia Gentlemen
Carry the
Congratulations of
Commander in Chief, Pacific
Admiral Harry D. Felt, USN"

in recognition of their feat.

Lyle then received his first command the USS Evans, a DE (Destroyer Escort)(DE 1023) which was named for a full-blooded Indian. He liked that. He came back to Washington, Plans and Policies, as Aide to Admiral Andrew Jackson and on to command of the USS Waddell (DDG 24), happy as a lark, as we moved back to California. Soon the Division was home ported to Japan and we lived in Yokosuka a year. Lyle was home maybe six weeks.

Plane guard was a part of the duties and a Navy pilot called me one evening in Yokosuka to say how grateful he was to Capt. Armel and wished to thank him. It seems his plane was downed in Tonkin Bay and he was circled by sharks when a ship came straight for him, a boat hook appeared and scooped him to safety. This was the Waddell. The pilot wanted me to know how the usual ship handling was-other pilots had waited for a dinghy to be put into the water and several, due to timing, were lost to the sharks. He felt so indebted-Bless his heart.

All the men that Lyle served with seem to appreciate his guidance and integrity-Warrants, Chiefs, Petty Officers and Sailors all told me how they admired and respected him. But as one Chief said "When the Captain had had it-watch out, his temper flared.

Lyle loved the Navy and volunteered for "in-country" service in Vietnam in the Ruing Sat District where he flew "helos" to village chiefs. Well, he got an Air Medal-which he cherished, being a "tin can" sailor.

He retired in 1983 after thirty years of service. We had three children, Thomas C. Armel, Capt. USN, Lyle O Armel, III Col. USMC and daughter Martha Lee Kennedy. There were eight grandchildren and one great grandchild, Lyle O. Armel IV.

It was sad that he died at fifty-eight and never got to see his boys reach flag rank or to walk his daughter down the aisle at her wedding.

(Missing out of Barbara's biography was service on the USS Wren, DD 568. He commanded the USS Piedmont, AD 47 from 1975–78.) Awards received by Captain Lyle O. Armel II were Legion of Merit, Bronze Star with Combat "V" – two Awards, Navy Unit Commendation with two Awards, Occupation Ribbon, National Defense Ribbon with 2 Awards, Armed Forces Expeditionary Medal, Vietnam Service Medal with 6 Stars, and Navy Distinguished Service Medal.

BIOGRAPHICAL SKETCH OF MY FATHER WILLIAM G. LEFTWICH JR.

(By his son Bill Leftwich)

William G. Leftwich Jr. was born on April 28, 1931 in Memphis, Tennessee to William G. Leftwich, Sr. and Mattie Howard Scrape Leftwich. His father was a graduate of Sewanee, a stock broker and a World War One veteran. Both mother and father hailed from Aberdeen, Mississippi.

Dad grew up an only child in Memphis, Tennessee. He attended Central High School, achieving the distinction of serving simultaneously as Class President, Governor of Boys State, Co-Captain of the Football Team, and Commander of the JROTC unit. One of his classmates described him as "the all-American boy" .... Everybody liked him. He earned their respect." Dad's impact on his classmates was such that at his high school class' Fifty Year Reunion in 1999, a classmate compiled and distributed a collection of articles, pictures, distinctions and letters about Dad, entitled "Memphis Central High's 'American Hero': William Groom Leftwich, Jr. 1931-1970."

From an early age, Dad wanted to enter the military service. However, no one was quite sure why he wanted either to join the Marines or go to the Naval Academy. There was no family tradition involved with either. In any case, he entered the Naval Academy and distinguished himself, earning the rank of Brigade Commander and receiving a commendation for displaying "exemplary officer-like qualities" upon graduation in 1953.

Commissioned a Marine Corps Second Lieutenant in 1953, Dad had an eventful career over the next ten years, serving as an infantry officer with tours as a platoon and company commander, Company Officer at the Naval Academy, and Aide de Camp to the Commanding General, Second Marine Division and the Commandant, Marine Corps Schools, Quantico.

He reported for duty in Vietnam in January 1965, as assistant senior advisor to a Vietnamese Marine Brigade. During this tour, he was awarded the Navy Cross, Legion of Merit with Combat "V," Air Medal with Gold Star, Purple Heart, Vietnamese Distinguished Service Order, Honor Medal First Class and three Vietnamese Cross of Gallantry. General Westmoreland called him the "best Advisor" in Vietnam and a later military historian, even called him "legendary."

After his return from Vietnam, Dad served as an instructor at The Basic School in Quantico, Virginia, graduated with honors from Marine Corps Command and Staff College and served as Marine Aide to the Under Secretary of the Navy. In 1970, he returned to Vietnam and served first as Commanding Officer, 2nd Battalion, 1st Marines and then as Commanding Officer, 1st Reconnaissance Battalion.

He was killed on November 18, 1970 when his helicopter crashed as he was extracting a reconnaissance team. During his second tour, Dad received the Silver Star (posthumously), Legion of Merit with Combat V and two Purple Hearts.

Dad is buried in Forest Hill Cemetery in Memphis, Tennessee. He received many honors after his death: Memphis named its tennis courts the Leftwich Tennis Center, the U.S. Navy commissioned the *USS Leftwich* (DD984) in 1979, the Marine Corps established the Leftwich Trophy for Outstanding Leadership and erected a statue – sculpted by Felix DeWeldon – at The Basic School, and the Naval

Academy established the Armel-Leftwich Visitor Center. Dad's photograph with a brief bio and a copy of the Leftwich trophy is also found in the National Marine Museum in Quantico.

I am sometimes asked what my father did to receive so much recognition after his death in 1970. All I can answer is that he was not recognized for one specific achievement but for his overall personal and professional character and ability. Simply, my father was a leader who led by example. He was an outstanding leader because he worked hard at being one. A Marine recalled that "all of us would follow him anywhere;" another remembered him as a "father figure." Still another friend stated he was "genuine . . . he never took airs and was always the same person." A former Midshipman remembered that "He taught us what it means to be an officer and gentlemen"; finally, another Marine called him the "epitome of integrity." Childhood friends recall his friendliness but also his competitiveness; Dad played to win. He loved sports, particularly tennis and squash. He was a fine writer and an excellent speaker, regularly publishing articles in service journals. A talented artist, he used to paint pictures of soldiers and send them to friends as gifts.

(Source: Personal)

Bancroft Hall

Ask any Midshipman about George Bancroft and the reply will center on the fact that it was George Bancroft who was the founder of the Naval Academy in 1845. Bancroft Hall was named for him and is the building that houses all of the Midshipmen.

George Bancroft was selected by President James K. Polk as his Secretary of the Navy. He desired to establish an academy for the purpose of instructing future naval officers. He met the resistance from the Congress by acting under the rule that is characteristic of naval officers, "You can do anything except what the rule book tells that you cannot do." Out of these actions came the Naval Academy. He did by finding he had at his disposal sufficient funds to find a place where Midshipmen could await orders. And while they were there, instructors could give them instructions.

Many of those future naval officers are not aware of the impact that Bancroft had on the country as it went through the trying days of reunification of the country after the Civil War. He was one of the best known historians of the nineteenth century and was called upon to deliver the eulogy before Congress after the assassination of President Lincoln. His treatise enumerated the nation's struggle as it rid itself of the one stain which kept it from truly assuming the role as a leader in the world powers.

Bancroft was born on October 3, 1800 in Worchester, Massachusetts, the son of Reverend Aaron Bancroft. He graduated from Harvard at the age of seventeen and went abroad for further studies in Germany and Greece. His specialty was history and he received his PhD from the University of Gottingen. He returned to the United States in 1822 and taught Greek one year at Harvard. He was elected to State Congress without his knowledge and refused to serve. He also declined the nomination to the State Senate.

In 1834 he published his first volume of "The History of the United States." By 1838 he had completed the second volume. He ran for Governor of Massachusetts but lost while winning a large amount of votes. He was appointed Secretary of the Navy and though he only served in that capacity for less than two years he fully impacted the nation with his actions. Besides founding the Naval Academy, while acting as Secretary of the War Pro-tem, he ordered the Army to march into Texas. He gave the only order ever given to take possession of California upon the start of hostilities with Mexico.

In 1846-49 he served as Minister to Great Britain. Later he was Minister to Prussia. He was important in the settlement of the northwestern boundary of the United States with England. He was responsible in obtaining the treaty signed first by Prussia and then by Great Britain that allowed for individual emigration from those countries to the United States. Until that time these countries refused to allow any of their citizens to throw off their native allegiance and immigrate to the United States. Even though the War of 1812 was fought over this premise (that Great Britain could board any American vessel and if one of their previous citizens was found, he could be removed by force if necessary), Great Britain insisted that the emigrant could not throw off his British citizenship. He thus remained subject to British laws and rules.

In 1849 he removed himself from public service and concentrated his efforts on history. He was asked by both houses of Congress to give the eulogy before Congress after the assassination of Abraham Lincoln. The eulogy was a plea for unity as it explored the causes of the Civil War.

George Bancroft died in Washington, DC on January 17, 1891.
(Source: 5, 77, 86, 105)

Wesley Brown Field House

The Wesley Brown Field House was named for Wesley Brown, the first African American to graduate from the United States Naval Academy. Wesley Brown was born in Baltimore, Maryland on April 3, 1927. He attended Dunbar High School where he was Cadet Corps Battalion Commander. He graduated from the Naval Academy with the Class of 1949. He was the sixth African American to attend the Academy and the first one to graduate.

After graduation he entered the Navy's Civil Engineering Corps. In that duty he was responsible for housing projects in Hawaii, roads in Liberia, a nuclear power plant in Antarctica and desalination plant at the United States Naval base in Guantanamo Bay, Cuba. He retired after twenty years service as a Lieutenant Commander. He presently resides in the District of Columbia.

(Source: 77, 117, 185, 252)

Chauvenet Walk

Honors all Academy Graduates who died in service during the first century of the Academy. Named for William Chauvenet who took charge of the "Philadelphia Asylum" School in 1842. (See Chauvenet Hall)

Chauvenet Hall

This is one of the newer halls that is named for William Chauvenet. While the establishment of the Naval Academy in 1845 is generally credited to George Bancroft, a case can be made for that title being given to William Chauvenet.

Chauvenet graduated from Yale University in 1840 and became a Professor of Mathematics in the U.S. Navy in 1841. He served on the USS Mississippi before being appointed to the Chair of Mathematics at the Naval Asylum in Philadelphia, Pennsylvania. While there he was instrumental in the founding of the United States Naval Academy. He remained there even though being offered professorships at his alma mater, Yale.

In 1859 he did accept the Chair of Mathematics at Washington University in St. Louis, Missouri.

Chauvenet's parents were Mary Kerr and William Marc Chauvenet. The son would most likely have followed his father's footsteps in business except the operator of the private school which he attended convinced the parents that Chauvenet should pursue studies at Yale.

While a professor at the Naval Asylum in Philadelphia he was convinced that the students should follow a four year course, rather than the eight month course in existence at the time. He began to promote a separate naval school devoted exclusively to academics. An abandoned Army base at Fort Severn, Annapolis, was chosen as it was sufficiently remote from diversions to allow the students to concentrate on their studies.

When the school was established in 1845, he became its Head of Mathematics.

He was a writer of precise textbooks and an original member of the American Association for the Advancement of Science. The Chauvenet Prize was created in 1925 in the Mathematical Association of America.

(Source: 77, 222, 288)

Robert Crown Sailing Center

The Robert Crown Sailing Center was named after the late Captain Robert Crown, USNR. After his retirement from the Navy he was National President of the Navy League in 1961 and 1963. He earned two Navy Distinguished Service Awards for his humanitarian efforts.

(Source: 241)

Dahlgren Hall

Dahlgren Hall was named for named for John Dahlgren, the father of modern naval ordnance.

John Adolphus Bernard Dahlgren was born on November 13, 1809 in Philadelphia, Pennsylvania, the son of the Swedish Council. He joined the Navy in 1827 and by 1834 was promoted to the Coastal Survey. In 1847 he was assigned to the Ordnance Department in Washington, D.C. and became the head of the Washington Navy Yard at the onset of the Civil War. He was instrumental in the redesign of naval weaponry and is known as the father of modern naval ordnance. He was a favorite of President Lincoln and it was not unusual for the President to drop in on Dahlgren at the Navy Yards just for a visit, to the consternation of Gideon Welles, the Secretary of the Navy. There was much controversy as to why the President spent so much time with Dahlgren, but it was found that the President was intrigued by gadgets and munitions and these abounded at the Naval Yard.

Dahlgren had a son, Colonel Ulric Dahlgren who lost his life in a raid on the Southern Capitol of the Confederacy, Richmond, Virginia with the argued purpose of capturing Jefferson Davis. After the Civil War, Admiral Dahlgren commanded a naval squadron off the west coast of South America. He returned to Washington where he again served as head of the Bureau of Ordnance. He died on July 12, 1870.

(Source: 55, 77, 159)

Dewey Basin & Dewey Field

Dewey Basin and Field were named for Admiral George Dewey.

George Dewey was born in Montpelier, Vermont on December 26, 1837. After a very active youth where "chance taking" seemed to be an obsession, he entered the United States Naval Academy and graduated with the Class of 1858. He went through the ranks of Midshipman, Passed Midshipman, Lieutenant, Lieutenant Commander, Commander, Captain, Commordore, Rear Admiral and Admiral. On March 2, 1899 he was made Admiral of the Navy, the only officer to ever hold that rank. During the Civil War he saw service on the USS Mississippi, USS Agawan, USS Colorado, USS Kearsarge, and USS Canadiagua.

After the war he saw duty at the United States Naval Academy and in 1870 took command of the USS Narragansett. Later he was to command the USS Juniata, the USS Dolphin and the USS Pensacola. In 1889 he became chief of the Bureau of Equipment. In November of 1897 he took command of the Asiatic Station with his flag aboard the USS Olympia. It was on that vessel that he gave the command at the onset of hostilities at Manila against the Spanish Fleet to its captain, Charles V. Gridley, "You may fire when ready, Gridley." This quotation, as a plaque, along with many others, hung in Luce Hall at the Naval Academy.

Dewey became a celebrated hero and by Act of Congress was given the rank of Admiral of the Navy with the provision that such rank would cease to exist upon Dewey's death. He died on January 16, 1917 and is buried at Arlington National Cemetery.

(Source: 117)

Farragut Field

Farragut Field is the parade field at the Academy and is named for Admiral David Glasgow Farragut.

David Glasgow Farragut was born James Glasgow Farragut near Knoxville, Tennessee, the son of Jorge Farragut, who fought in the

Revolutionary War and the War of 1812. James Glasgow Farragut would change his name to David Glasgow to honor his mentor Captain David Porter. David Porter befriended the Farragut family when they helped to rescue Porter's father from a drifting boat. David Glasgow Farragut came under the guardianship of David Porter and went to sea when he was only eight. He was named a Midshipman at the age of nine and at twelve actually commanded a prize ship during the War of 1812. Later in his life he was known as a very aggressive commander and earned the wrath of Captain David Porter for his overzealous actions.

At the beginning of the Civil War, he agonized over the choice of sides as he had a definite Southern background. He finally decided to stay with Union and was given command of the West Gulf Blockading Squadron. On July 16, 1862 he was given the rank of Admiral, the first to have that rank in the United States Navy. He was instrumental in the Union having control of the Mississippi. It was during the Battle of Mobile Bay that one of his many sayings became a household phrase. When warned that the area was heavily mined (Mines at that period were called torpedoes.), he ignored the danger, giving the command, "Damn the torpedoes, full speed ahead."

In 1868, he was such a hero that he was asked to run for President of the United States. He declined, stating that he had no desire for political office. He died at the age of 69 on April 14. 1870. More than twenty five cities, buildings, ships and monuments have been named in his honor as is the athletic field at the Naval Academy.

(Source: 77, 182)

Halligan Hall

Halligan Hall was named for Commander John Halligan, Jr., Class of 1898, United States Naval Academy.

John Halligan, Jr. was born on May 4, 1876 in South Boston, Massachusetts. He graduated first in his class at the Academy and was commissioned an ensign in 1900. He served during the Spanish

American War on the flagship of Commodore Winfield S. Schley. He received the Distinguished Service Medal for his performance during the First World War where he served as Chief of Staff to the Commander of the U.S. Naval Forces in France.

Between the wars he commanded the Battleship Ohio, the USS Saratoga and was Chief of the Bureau of Engineering. He was made Commander of the 13th Naval District. He died on December 11, 1934 while in this command.

(Source: 77, 117, 168, 241)

Halsey Field House

The Halsey Field House is named after Admiral William Frederick Halsey, Jr. He was known by the nickname of "Bull" Halsey as well as "Bill." William Halsey was born on October 30, 1882 in Elizabeth, New Jersey. He attended the United States Naval Academy and graduated with the Class of 1904. He was not known for his academic skills but excelled as an athlete, winning the Thompson Trophy as the most outstanding athlete that year. While some of his first years of service were spent on battleships and patrol craft, he spent most of his next twenty five years on destroyers. During World War I he commanded the Destroyers, USS Shaw and USS Benham. He was the commander of the USS Reina Mercedes, the station ship at Annapolis.

Between the two world wars he commanded another destroyer and then two destroyer squadrons. He became a Naval Aviation Observer and was designated a Naval Aviator in 1935 and then commanded the USS Saratoga. In 1938 he was promoted to Rear Admiral and commanded carrier divisions.

Halsey was at sea on the USS Enterprise when Pearl Harbor was attacked. He was ordered to command Task Force Sixteen which escorted the Carrier USS Hornet to within 800 miles of Japan so that that the initial bombing of Japan, led by Jimmy Doolittle, could be effected. His World War II service was entirely in the Pacific where he commanded a number of carrier squadrons, including command of the Third Fleet. His flag was flying at the masthead of the USS Missouri when the formal Japanese surrender was signed on its decks. On December 11, 1945 he was made Fleet Admiral, the fourth and last officer to hold that rank.

Admiral Bull Halsey retired on March 1, 1947 but remained active in military and civic affairs until his death on August 16, 1959. He is buried at Arlington National Cemetery. Among his decorations were The Navy Cross, Distinguished Service Medal with three gold stars, Army Distinguished Service Medal, Presidential Unit Citation, Mexican Service Medal, Victory Medal, Asiatic-Pacific Campaign Medal, World War II Victory Medal, National Defense Service Medal, and Philippine Liberation Medal.

(Source: 25, 117)

Herndon Monument

The Herndon Monument was erected in 1859. It was named for Commander William Louis Herndon who went down as Captain of his ship, the Mail Steamer "Central America" in a storm off Cape Hatteras in September, 1857.

Herndon was born in 1813 in Fredericksburg, Virginia and joined the Navy as a Midshipman in 1828. His brother-in-law was Matthew F. Maury, head of the Naval Observatory. He and Lardner Gibbon were instructed in 1851 by the Secretary of the Navy to explore the entire watershed of the Amazon.

Shortly after his death, in 1857 a small town was formed to serve the Alexandria, Loudoun and Hampshire Railroad. One of the residents was a survivor of the sinking of the Mail Steamer "Central America" and he suggested that the town be named after William Herndon. The name Herndon, Virginia was accepted by the Post Office Department in July of 1858.

(Source: 113, 194)

Hubbard Hall

Hubbard Hall is named for the Navy Oar Stroke on Admiral Porter's crew, Admiral John Hubbard, who led an Academy rowing team to victory in 1870. John Hubbard was the commander of the USS Minnesota during the travels of the "Great White Fleet" which left Hampton Roads, Virginia on December 16, 1903. He was also a part of the United States force that was present when Panama became independent. The presence of German forces, who sought a power position in Central and South America made it necessary for a strong personality to represent the United States. Such a man was John Hubbard. He graduated with the Class of 1870 and attained the rank of Rear Admiral. He died in May of 1932.

(Source: 77)

Ingram Field

Ingram Field was named after Admiral Jonas Howard Ingram.

Jonas Ingram was born in Jeffersonville, Indiana on October 15, 1886. He attended Jeffersonville High School and the Culver Military Academy, in Culver, Indiana. He was appointed to the United States Naval Academy and graduated with the Class of 1907. At the Academy he was a member of the football team as well as rowing and track. He scored the lone touchdown to beat Army in 1906 to give Navy their first victory against Army in six years. He was inducted into the College Football Hall of Fame in 1968.

After his graduation he served on a number of battleships, destroyers and cruisers. He was on the Battleship Arkansas when it landed a battalion of men at Veracruz, Mexico. For his action there, he was awarded the Medal of Honor.

He came back to the Academy and was its football coach from 1915 to 1917. During World War I, he was on the staff of the Commander, Division Three, Battle Force of the Atlantic Fleet. For his heroics there he was awarded the Navy Cross. He went on to command the USS Pennsylvania. He was promoted to Captain in

1935, becoming an aide to the Secretary of the Navy. He went back to sea as Commander of the USS Tennessee.

He was promoted to Rear Admiral in 1941 and became Commander Task Force Three. Promoted to Vice Admiral, he was given command of the South Atlantic Force. He was known for his ability to coordinate his fleet and the activities of the Brazilian air and surface units. For this he received the Distinguished Service Medal.

He retired from active duty on April 1, 1947 and died on September 9, 1952 at San Diego, California.

(Source: 77, 167, 172)

Isherwood Hall

Isherwood Hall, which was razed in 1982, was named for Admiral Benjamin Franklin Isherwood. Isherwood was born on October 6, 1822 in New York City and was responsible for much of the designs to convert ships to steam propulsion. He first worked for the Utica and Schenectady Railroad. He also designed and constructed railroads for the Treasury Department. In 1844 he joined the Navy and served on the USS Princeton as First Assistant Engineer during the Mexican American War. After the war he was assigned to the Washington Navy Yard where he assisted in studying the use of steam for propelling Navy ships. He compiled data, using the empirical results to analyze the existing engines.

During the Civil War he was involved in the attempt to bring the "Merrimac" out of the Norfolk Navy Yard as the war threatened. While he finished the necessary engine repairs the ship was sunk by the retreating Union forces at the onset of the War. By War's end, the Navy had some 600 steam powered vessels. For eight years he served as head of the Bureau of Steam Engineering. He retired as a Commodore on June 6, 1884. He died on June 19, 1915. Isherwood Hall was built in 1905 and was the main engineering building at the Academy.

(Source: 77, 88)

King Hall

King Hall is the Midshipmen dining hall, capable of seating the entire Brigade at one time. It was built in 1937 and was recently renovated.

King Hall was named for Fleet Admiral Ernest J. King who was born in Lorain, Ohio on November 23, 1878. He was appointed to the United States Naval Academy and graduated with the Class of 1901. He served on many surface vessels before becoming Commander of the USS Terry. In 1928 he received flight training and was appointed Assistant Chief of the Bureau of Aeronautics. In 1930 he took command of the aircraft carrier, USS Lexington.

In 1933 he became chief of the Bureau of Aeronautics and commanded the Battle Fleet's aircraft carriers. While he was known for his aeronautical experience he also was involved with the submarine service, and was commander of a submarine division. While he never earned his "Dolphins" he is given credit for design of the insignia. He was known for his incisiveness and the ability to get to the essence of any problem. This earned him opposition in his desire for a strong Navy during peacetime. He was appointed to the General Board, though he had hopes of becoming the Commander-in-Chief of the U.S. Fleet. The General Board was a place where senior officers waited retirement.

When Pearl Harbor came, Admiral Stark, remembering the command abilities of Admiral King recalled him to be the Commander-in-Chief of the Atlantic Fleet. It was said that when he received this call he retorted that "When the going gets rough, you yell for the sons-a-bitches." He shortly thereafter was given command of the U.S. Fleet, becoming Chief of Naval Operations. There were many criticisms thrown at him during his career but being indecisive was not one of them. It was said that he was one of the most disliked leaders of World War II, topped only by British Field Marshal Montgomery. There was no question he was an organizational genius and World War II needed men of his talents.

He retired on December 15, 1945 but was recalled as an advisor to the Secretary of the Navy in 1950. He died of a heart attack in

Kittery, Maine on June 26, 1956 and is buried at the United States Naval Academy Cemetery at Annapolis.

(Source: 77, 240)

Lawrence Field

Lawrence Field where Navy baseball is played was named after Captain James Lawrence, famous for his order, "Don't give up the ship."

James Lawrence was born in Burlington, Vermont on October 1, 1781. He joined the fledgling United States Navy in 1798 as a Midshipman. He was commissioned as a lieutenant in 1802 and served on the schooner Enterprise during the War with Tripoli. Later he commanded the Warships Argus, Vixen and Wasp. He commanded the Sloop Hornet in the War of 1812 where he captured a privateer and participated in blockades. He was given command of the Frigate Chesapeake and while doing battle with the Royal Navy Frigate Shannon, he was mortally wounded. As he was taken below his last orders were "Don't give up the ship." He died of his wounds three days later.

(Source: 17, 168)

Leahy Hall

Leahy Hall is named after Admiral William Daniel Leahy. William Daniel Leahy was born in Hampton, Iowa on May 6, 1875 and though wanting to go to West Point, he missed getting an appointment to the U. S. Military Academy. He was able to secure an appointment to the Naval Academy and graduated with the Class of 1897, placing 15th in a class of 47. After completing the required two years sea duty he was commissioned an ensign during which he saw duty on the USS Oregon. He spent time in the Pacific and was involved in fighting for our country during the Philippine Insurrection and the

Boxer Rebellion. In 1902 he was on the USS Tacoma and the USS Boston which were stationed in Panama during the construction of the Canal.

In 1915 he took command of the USS Dolphin and at that time established a relationship with Franklin D. Roosevelt, who was Assistant Secretary of the Navy. In 1918 he commanded a troop ferrying ship that transported troops to France. After shore duty he returned to sea in command of the USS St. Louis. By 1927 he had achieved flag rank and became Chief of the Bureau of Ordnance. By 1937 he was appointed Chief of Naval Operations and in August, 1939 he was put on the retired list.

Immediately thereafter he was appointed Governor of Puerto Rico and in 1940 was appointed Ambassador to France. In July of 1942 he was recalled to active duty as Chief of Staff to the Commander in Chief, President Roosevelt. He was present at the meetings of the heads of the Allied Powers. In December of 1944 he was given the rank of Fleet Admiral. He retired again in 1949 but served in an advisory position to the Secretary of the Navy. He died on July 20, 1959.

(Source: 78, 117)

Lejeune Hall

This hall was named for John A. Lejeune, the 13th Commandant of the Marine Corps. (This biography is a repeat of that written for General Lejeune under the United States Navy and Marine Corps Bases.)

John A. Lejeune was born on January 10, 1867 in Batchelor, Louisiana. He graduated from Louisiana State University, Baton Rouge. He then received an appointment to the U.S. Naval Academy, graduating with the Class 0f 1888. He went to sea as a Cadet Midshipman and two years later was commissioned into the Marine Corps. He served in the Marine Guard on U.S. Naval vessels until 1900. He served at the Pensacola Marine Barracks as well as the Norfolk Barracks. After a number of tours at various barracks and Navy ships he was ordered to the Philippines to command the Marine Barracks and Naval Prison at Cavite. He was given command of the First Brigade and promoted to Lieutenant Colonel shortly thereafter. He had a number of tours in Cuba, Mexico and Panama. He returned to Washington to become Assistant to the Major General Commandant of the Marine Corps and was promoted to Brigadier General. During the First World War he commanded the 4th Brigade of the 2nd Division. Shortly thereafter he was given command of the 2nd Division.

His leadership abilities were recognized by the medals he received during the war including the French Legion of Honor and the Croix de Guerre. General John J. Pershing presented him with the Army Distinguished Service Medal. He received also the Navy Distinguished Service Medal.

He was appointed and served two terms as Commandant of the Marine Corps from 1920 until 1929. His nicknames of "The Greatest of all Leathernecks" and "The Marine's Marine" attest to his love for the Marines. After retirement he served as Superintendent of the Virginia Military Institute.

(Source: 77)

Commodore Uriah P. Levy Center

The Commodore Uriah P. Levy Center and Jewish Chapel were named for Uriah Phillips Levy. Uriah Levy was born in Philadelphia, Pennsylvania on April 22, 1792 and was the first Jewish Commodore in the United States Navy. Levy ran away from home and served as a cabin boy on various Navy ships. He became a sailing master and fought in the War of 1812. He, along with a crew of a commandeered ship, was captured by the British and he was held captive for sixteen months. When he was returned to America he was named Captain of the ship Franklin and elevated to the rank of Lieutenant.

Anti-Semitism was a strong force in the Navy at that time and he was court-martialed six times. Each time he was able to defend his conduct and had his rank of Captain restored. Later he was promoted to Commodore. One of his achievements was the abolition of flogging in the Navy.

By 1826 he had achieved some wealth in investments and he used some of this wealth to acquire the estate of Thomas Jefferson, Monticello. The place was in a state of almost ruins and it had been put up for sale by Jefferson's daughter. Levy was a great admirer of Jefferson and he restored the buildings over time and repurchased much of Jefferson's original furniture. Levy was only able to visit Monticello on vacations but his mother lived there and is buried in its cemetery.

The statue of Jefferson which stands in the Capitol Rotunda in Washington was also donated by Commodore Uriah Levy and is the only privately commissioned artwork in the Capitol.

Upon Levy's death 1862, his will was confusing and it took time for its disposition. One of its confusing details was the dictate that there be an agricultural school for the purpose of educating "farmers children of the warrant office of the United States Navy whose fathers are dead." Failing that, the estate would go to the State of Virginia. Failing that, the mansion would go to the Portuguese Hebrew congregations of New York, Philadelphia and Richmond to be used as an agricultural school for orphans. It wasn't until the 1980's that Levy's role in the preservation of Monticello was recognized. Levy is buried in the Cypress Hills Cemetery in New York.

(Source: 77, 158, 167)

Luce Hall

Luce Hall was named for Admiral Stephen B. Luce who founded the Naval War College. Luce was born on March 25, 1827 in Albany, New York. He went into the naval service in 1841 as a Midshipman. He served with the Atlantic Coast Blockaders during the Civil War.

In 1862 he was an instructor at the Naval Academy and at that time prepared one of the first seamanship textbooks on the subject. He was instrumental in establishing the training manuals and methods to ready the seamen and petty officers for sea duty.

In 1884 the Naval War College was established at his urging and he became its first president. He also helped start the U.S. Naval Institute. He retired from active duty in 1889 but returned to teach at the War College in 1901. Luce died on July 28, 1917 at Newport, Rhode Island.

(Source: 77, 148, 171, 242)

MacDonough Hall

MacDonough Hall was built in 1903 and was named for Thomas MacDonough, Jr., hero of the Battle of Lake Champlain. Thomas MacDonough, Jr. was born on December 21, 1783 near New Castle, Delaware. He was the son of a physician, Major Thomas MacDonough, who had fought in the Revolutionary War. Thomas Senior died when Thomas Junior was eleven and Thomas Jr. obtained a commission as a Midshipman in the United States Navy.

He served a number of years on the USS Constellation which was fighting against Tripoli in the Barbary Coast Wars and which was captained by Alexander Murray. During this time he became knowledgeable in seamanship, navigation and gunnery. He also served under Stephen Decatur on the Enterprise.

When the War of 1812 came, he was given command of a division of gunboats. By September of 1812 he was given command of all United States vessels on Lake Champlain, which amounted to two gunboats and three transport sloops. He formed an association with a New York ship builder and rapidly built a stronger squadron though the conversion of existing steamers into men-of-war. One brig was built in a record of seventeen days.

When the British fleet entered the lake, MacDonough, though outgunned, maneuvered his ships so as to outdo the British. After the victory he was honored for his prowess. This was the high point of his career as he began to suffer from tuberculosis. After the war he served in mostly shore stations. He died on November 10, 1825.

(Source: 77, 98)

Mahan Hall

Mahan Hall was named for Alfred Thayer Mahan, a noted naval historian and promoter of naval sea power. Mahan was born on September 27, 1840 at West Point, New York where his father served as a professor at the United States Military Academy. He studied at Saint James School, an Episcopalian college preparatory school. He attended Princeton for two years, and then entered the United States Naval Academy, graduating second in the Class of 1859.

His record as a seagoing officer did nothing to signify that he would later be known as the Naval Sea Power strategist. He was involved in a number of ship mishaps including collisions. He disliked the move to steam ships, preferring the old square-rigged vessels. He served aboard the Pocahontas during the Civil War which managed to drift into an anchored Union Sloop. Another of his misadventures was the collision of his ship, the Wasp, with a barge in Montevideo, Uruguay.

In 1885 he became a lecturer at the Naval War College. During this time he made meticulous notes and the lectures were published as a book titled, "The Influence of Sea Power upon History, 1660-1783," published in 1890. In 1892, the book, by Mahan, "The Influence of Sea Power upon the French Revolution and Empire" was published. Mahan was an advocate that the control of seaborne commerce would control the outcome of wars. He proposed that the destruction of an enemy's major combatant vessels would allow the rest to be hunted down and destroyed. Today there are those who argue the points of his theories but his books influenced the major powers during the early and mid twentieth century.

Alfred Thayer Mahan died on December 1, 1914 as a Captain. He was given the rank of Rear Admiral after his retirement.

(Source: 20, 42, 77, 78, 118)

Maury Hall

Maury Hall was named for Matthew Fontaine Maury, who was known as "the Pathfinder of the Seas."

Maury was born near Fredericksburg, Virginia in Spotsylvania County on January 24, 1806. When he was four the family moved to Tennessee where he was educated. His older brother was a naval officer and Maury dreamed of following in his footsteps. At the age of nineteen he joined the Navy as a Midshipman. He made three "around the world" type trips, sailing to Europe, South America and into the Pacific. On these trips he became interested in navigation and oceanography, keeping voluminous records of sea currents and winds. He was able to find ways of avoiding the doldrums that were so pervasive around the tip of South America. Soon many sea captains were using his findings to cut days, even weeks, off the sailing time.

At that time the accepted navigation aids were those published by Bowdich, which were mostly empirical. Maury's methods were more analytical and became accepted by many ship's captains.

He returned to America in 1830 and married Ann Hull Herndon in Virginia. As he returned from this trip to Virginia, he was involved in a stage coach accident which permanently injured a leg. This prevented him from further sea duty. He was given the assignment as Superintendent of Charts and Instruments which in time became the Washington Observatory. He asked ships' navigators and captains to report their logs in such a way that he could accumulate statistical information. From this information he was able to prepare "Pilot's Charts" which came to be used by all ships.

He was an early proponent of forming a Naval Academy and is given credit as one of its founders.

As a native Virginian he was swayed to become a part of the Confederacy when the Civil War broke out. He resigned his commission and entered into service in the Confederate Navy. He served in the Harbor Defense. He designed an improvement in underwater mines, then known as "torpedoes," and was the first person to detonate a torpedo by electricity. After the war he fled to Mexico and encouraged others to follow. This idea was not successful and after President Johnson's Amnesty Proclamation he returned to Virginia where he taught at the Virginia Military Institute. He died in Lexington, Virginia on February 1, 1873. He was first buried in

Lexington but was reinterred at Hollywood Cemetery in Richmond, Virginia.

(Source: 4, 20, 80, 117, 119, 178, 262)

Melville Hall

Melville Hall is one of the halls demolished during the modernization of the Academy. At one time it was a part of the Engineering Buildings where Midshipmen went to classes. It was named after Rear Admiral George W. Melville who gained fame as the Engineer of the ill-fated Polar expedition ship the Steamer "Jeanette." The Jeanette Monument in the Academy Yard is also dedicated to those who died during that expedition. Melville was born in New York City on January 10, 1841. He graduated from the Brooklyn Collegiate and Polytechnic Institute. He joined the Navy in 1861 and served in the Engineering Departments of various ships.

During the Civil War he served on two sloops of war and finished the war working on torpedo boats. In 1873 he served on the Steamer "Tigress" as it searched for survivors of a Polar expedition. He returned to the Arctic in 1879 to search for survivors of the steamer Jeanette. While the Jeanette was privately owned it was crewed by United States Naval personnel under the command of George Washington DeLong. The vessel sank when it was crushed by ice as it searched for an open sea passage route to the North Pole. The crew attempted to drag three small boats across the ice searching for open water. One of the boats sank with loss of all aboard. The other two, commanded by DeLong and Melville survived that episode but DeLong and Melville split up in an attempt to reach land. DeLong's crew perished and Melville's survived. Melville returned in an attempt to find the others but only found their remains. They erected a cross on the spot where they found them. Later a monument would be erected out of granite and marble at the Academy and be called the Jeanette Monument.

Melville was assigned other engineering duties as he rose to the rank of Rear Admiral, including Chief of Bureau of Steam

Engineering. He was responsible for the transfer from sail to steam and the modern propulsion that was necessary to build a modern Navy.

He retired from the Navy in 1903 and moved to Philadelphia where he died on March 18, 1912.

(Source: 77, 117, 249, 256)

Michelson Hall

Michelson Hall was built in 1968 as a part of the modernization program at the Naval Academy. It is named for Albert Abraham Michelson, a Naval Academy graduate and the first to discover the speed of light.

Albert A. Michelson was born in Strzelno in the Kingdom of Poland to Polish-Jewish parents on December 19, 1852. The family moved to the United States in 1855 and he grew up in the western mining towns of Murphy's Camp, California and Virginia City, Nevada. He went to high school in San Francisco where he stayed with his Aunt Henriette Michelson Levy, who was the mother of author Harriet Lane Levy.

He was given an appointment to the U. S. Naval Academy by President Ulysses S. Grant where he graduated with the Class of 1873. At the Academy he became interested in measuring the speed of light, and conducted his first experiments as a class project in 1877. After graduation and two years at sea, he returned to the Academy and became an instructor in physics and chemistry. He resigned from the Navy in 1881 and became a professor of physics at the Case School of Applied Science in Cleveland, Ohio. He went on to become a professor at Clark University in Worchester, Massachusetts. He worked with others to conduct many scientific experiments and many of his associates became famous for their work. He received the Nobel Prize in Physics, becoming the first American to receive a Nobel Prize.

He continued experiments to refine his calculations of the speed of light including using Mount Wilson and Mount San Antonio

(Baldy) in California. There were some discrepancies in this test cause by a shift in the baseline.

Michelson died on May 9, 1931 and the results of some of his last experiments were published after his death. While he is best known for his measurement of the speed of light, he was also very active in other projects including inventing a range finder that became a standard in the Navy. He was instrumental in setting the standard for the length of a meter, and became the first to be able to determine the diameter of a star.

(Source: 73, 77, 179, 241)

Rip Miller Field

Rip Miller Field was named for Edgar E. "Rip" Miller who was associated with Naval Academy athletics for 48 years. He was one of the "Seven Mules" who along with the "Four Horsemen" were a legend at Notre Dame. He came to the Naval Academy as an assistant to Bill Ingram and together they gave Navy its only National Championship in 1926. He was the football coach at Navy for two years in 1931-32 and later its assistant athletic director until his retirement in 1974.

He was born in Canton, Ohio on June 1, 1901 and died on October 1, 1990. He was inducted into the Football Hall of Fame in 1966.

(Source: 61, 77, 80, 172, 193, 240)

Mitscher Hall

Mitscher Hall was named for Vice Admiral Marc "Pete" Andrew Mitscher. He was born on January 26, 1887 in Hillsboro, Wisconsin but was reared in the Washington, DC area. He received an appointment to the U.S. Naval Academy, graduating with the Class of 1910. After his two year compulsory sea duty he was commissioned an Ensign. He served on the Battleships Colorado and California and later on two destroyers. In 1915 he took pilot training and was designated Naval Aviator Number 33. By 1919 he was a part of the Aviation Section of the Office of the Chief of Naval Operations. In 1919 he was a pilot of one of four sea planes that crossed the Atlantic from Newfoundland to the Azores. For this operation he received the Navy Cross.

When World War II began he was commander of the USS Hornet and he was commander of that ship when Jimmy Doolittle took off from its deck to bomb Tokyo.

In January 1944 he was commander of Carrier Division Three which later became Task Force 58. He was offered the post of Chief of Naval Operations but turned it down to continue sea duty as Commander of the 8th Fleet and later Commander-in-Chief, Atlantic Fleet.

Admiral Mitscher died on February 3, 1947 and is buried at Arlington National Cemetery.

(Source: 25, 77)

Nimitz Library

The Nimitz Library was named for Fleet Admiral Chester William Nimitz. Nimitz was born in Fredericksburg, Texas on February 24, 1885. As a youth he had wanted to go to the U.S. Military Academy but failed to get an appointment. While still in high school, he received an appointment to the U.S. Naval Academy and graduated seventh in the Class of 1905. While there he excelled at athletics especially in rowing. After his compulsory two year sea duty which he served on the USS Ohio, he was commissioned Ensign and began his naval career. He commanded the Gunboat USS Panay and later the USS Decatur.

In 1909 he entered the submarine service and by 1912 commanded the Atlantic Submarine Flotilla. He was one who recommended that the submarines be switched to diesel engine propulsion. In 1918 he received shore duty which put him in the office of the Chief of Naval

Operations. He became Chief of Staff to both the Commander Battle Forces and Commander-in-Chief U.S. fleet.

After three years teaching in the newly founded Reserve Officers Training Corps, he again went to sea in the submarine program. He later became Commander of the Cruiser USS Augusta. By 1935 he was Assistant Chief of the Bureau of Navigation.

In December of 1941 he was given command of the Pacific Fleet where he served through most of the War. On September 2, 1945 he was the United States signatory on the USS Missouri when Japan surrendered. In December, 1945 he became Chief of Naval Operations. After his term he moved to the San Francisco area and continued to serve the country at local and national levels.

Fleet Admiral Nimitz died on February 20, 1966.

(Source: 117, 186, 213)

Norman Scott Natatorium

The Norman Scott Natatorium was named for Rear Admiral Norman Scott who received the Medal of Honor for his heroic action during the Naval Battle of Guadalcanal. Scott was born in Indianapolis, Indiana. He graduated from the United States Naval Academy with the Class of 1911. While at the Academy he was given credit for introducing intercollegiate swimming. His early service was aboard the USS Idaho, then on to destroyer billets. During World War I he was aboard the USS Jacob Jones which was sunk by a German submarine. After the war he was commander of a division of Eagle Boats.

Between the World Wars he saw sea duty on the Battleship USS New York and on destroyers. He commanded the USS MacLeish and the USS Paul Jones. Prior to World War II he commanded the USS Pensacola. By 1942 he was promoted to Rear Admiral and held a series of commands in the South Pacific. He was commander of a cruiser-destroyer that fought the successful Battle of Cape Esperance. On November 13, 1942 he was second in command of the Navy's force that fought the Battle of Savo islands during the Battle for Guadalcanal. His flagship, the USS Atlanta, suffered terminal damages from gunfire and torpedoes.

Admiral Scott was killed during this engagement and was awarded the Medal of Honor for exceptional heroism and conspicuous intrepidity. He is listed as Missing in Action and his name is listed on the "Tablets of the Missing."

(Source: 88, 117, 121, 123, 167)

Preble Hall

Preble Hall was named for Commodore Edward Preble. Preble was born in what is now Portland, Maine on August 15, 1761. He was the son of General Jedidiah Preble. In 1779 he entered the Massachusetts Navy as a Midshipman and served on the "Protector." He became a British prisoner when that ship was captured by the British. He was released and served on the "Winthrop" where he led a raiding party to capture a British brig. After the war he saw sea duty in the commerce trade and by 1799 he was promoted to captain and given command of the Essex.

During the Tripolian War he served as Squadron Commander with distinction and many of those under him went on to naval fame. He was known as a strict disciplinarian and insisted that his ship be kept in a state of readiness. Those who served under him called themselves "Preble's Boys." Many of his discipline procedures became standard for the fledgling Unite States Navy. It was said that he saved Captain Steven Decatur's life by shielding him from a sword attack.

In poor health he resigned from active duty in 1804 and returned to America where he did shipbuilding activities in Portland, Maine. He died in Portland on August 25, 1807. Six ships have been named after him as well as counties, townships and towns.

(Source: 77. 129, 170)

Ricketts Hall

Ricketts Hall is named after Admiral Claude Vernon Ricketts who played end on the Naval Academy's football team. He came into the Academy from the "Fleet," and graduated with the Class of 1929. During the attack on Pearl Harbor, he, as gunnery officer, was credited with saving the USS West Virginia from sinking by stabilizing the ship with counter-flooding. This quick action saved the ship from capsizing. In 1955 he commanded the USS Saint Paul and later became Commander Second Fleet. He also served as Vice Chief of Naval Operations. He died on July 6, 1964.

(Source: 77, 95)

Rickover Hall

Rickover Hall is named for Admiral Hyman G. Rickover. Hyman Rickover was born in Makow, Russia (now Poland) on January 27, 1900. At the age of six he immigrated with his parents to the United States, settling in Chicago. He received a Congressional appointment to the Naval Academy and graduated with the Class of 1922. He served aboard two ships before returning to the Academy for postgraduate studies in Electrical Engineering. He received his submarine training in 1930 and in 1937 assumed command of the USS Finch.

During World War II he served as head of the Electrical Section of the Bureau of Ships. This gave him the experience necessary to promote the development of the world's first nuclear submarine.

He received his nuclear training at Oak Ridge, Tennessee in 1947 and was asked to explore the possibility of nuclear ship propulsion. In 1949 he was appointed director of Naval Reactors Branch of the Bureau of Ships. Out of this, in 1955 came the world's first nuclear submarine, the USS Nautilus. He was promoted to the rank of Vice Admiral in 1958 and as such exerted great influence over the design of the vessels as well as the choice of those who served on them.

He retired in 1982 after sixty-four years of service in the Navy.

He died in 1986 and is buried at Arlington National Cemetery. The attack submarine the USS Hyman G. Rickover is named for him.

(Source: 132, 289)

Samson Hall

Samson Hall houses the English and History Department and is named for Captain William Samson.

William Samson was born in Palmyra, New York on February 9, 1840, the eldest of seven children. As a youth he worked with his hands helping his father lay bricks, build roads and farming. He was known at an early age for his staying with a project to its completion and while unable to afford to go to college, he caught the attention of a local resident who managed an appointment for him to the Naval Academy. He graduated with the Class of 1861 and for his last three years stood number one in his class. He caught the attention of Alfred Thayer Mahan who was two years his senior and who saw the potential of this young Midshipman. During his last year at the Academy and while acting in his position of commanding officer of the cadet battalion he fought back a Southern mob wanting to take control of the Academy.

His first service was at the Washington Naval Yard where he served under Commander John Dahlgren. He was sent to the Brooklyn Naval Yard where he served as one of the Masters of the USS Potomac. He went to sea serving along side of Winfield Scott Schley, who ranked one number above him. He and Schley would have much divisiveness in their lives later in their careers. In the summer of 1863 he served on the Frigate Macedonian which was commanded by Stephen B. Luce. During this Trans-Atlantic cruise the ship, disguised as a Spanish ship, attempted to sink the Confederate ship Alabama. They were not successful and the Alabama was later sunk by the USS Kearsarge.

In 1864 he joined the South Atlantic Blockading Squadron as executive officer of the ironclad monitor Patapsco. This ship had suffered damages in earlier battles in the South and was in need of serious repair. Sampson studied the condition of the vessel and made numerous recommendations as to the improvements of ironclads. The ship was sunk in January 1865 by a submerged mine. During this sinking Samson distinguished himself for his bravery.

After the Civil War he continued to make outstanding progress in the Navy even as it suffered from post-war reduction. He served aboard the Colorado, a steam frigate and later taught at the Naval Academy. He became head of the newly formed Department of Physics and Chemistry. It was at Samson's urging that Michelson began in serious his quest to discover the speed of light.

In the early 1880's Samson served as Assistant Superintendent of the United States Naval Observatory. It was during this time that the Western Union installed a wire to obtain exact time signals and using this divided the United States into five time zones. Before this the railroads used as many as fifty-three zones. On November 18, 1883 all of the railroads reset their clocks, with the government and businesses following shortly thereafter. Later he represented the United States in the settling on Greenwich, England as the Prime Meridian for longitude calculating.

The U. S. Navy began its building of modern ships in the 1880's and Sampson was a part of the team. He was also responsible for the institution of the post-graduate Naval War College. He proposed the strengthening of Coastal and Great Lakes defenses. In 1886-90 he was Superintendent of the Naval Academy and was responsible for the modernization of its facilities. He was promoted to Captain in 1890 and served on the USS San Francisco off the Chilean waters. His ship was responsible for the saving of Chilean lives and also provided a haven for political refugees.

It was during these times that major breakthroughs in the manufacture of armor plate were made, resulting in ships that could be built with thinner armor plate. As usual, Sampson was in the middle of this progress as he pressed for better ships.

The United States declared war on Spain on April 21, 1898 and Sampson, by this time an Admiral, went to sea in the Flagship New York in search of the Spanish fleet. When the Spanish fleet was found and challenged, Admiral Sampson happened to be ashore. The American fleet under the acting command of Admiral Winfield Scott Schley destroyed the Spanish fleet. Admiral Sampson in his report took full credit for the win and didn't mention Schley. A personal battle ensued between Samson and Schley that finally ended in court. While Sampson was exonerated, Schley was elevated to being a national hero.

Samson retired from Service in 1902 and died on May 6 that year. He is buried at Arlington National Cemetery. Four destroyers have been named after him.

(Source: 25, 77, 211)

Tecumseh Court

Guarding the entrance to the assembly area in front of Bancroft Hall is a bronze replica of the figurehead of the USS Delaware. Known to all as Tecumseh, the figure head was actually that of the Delaware Chief, Tamanend. The bronze version of the statue was presented to the Academy in 1930 by the Class of 1891and it quickly became the god of 2.5 which for so many years was a passing grade at the Academy. Formations of Midshipmen would toss coins at the figurehead as they left the area to attend classes and take exams.

Tamanend was the Delaware Chief that welcomed William Penn when he arrived in 1682.

Born in 1768 near what is now Springfield, Ohio, Tecumseh was a Pawnee Chief who helped to defend Canada during the War of 1812. He attempted to form an alliance with other Indian Nations to keep the white settler out of the Northwest Territories. He was well known for his oration abilities which brought many of the Indian Nations to his side. One of his great claims was that the United States was paying off the Revolutionary War debts by selling off Indian land.

At one time he had over 5,000 warriors under his command and he sought to become a buffer nation between Canada and the United States. His central location was Tippecanoe, Indiana. It was there that William Henry Harrison attacked his stronghold and successfully ended Tecumseh's attempts. He was killed in 1813 while he was fighting for the British against the United States in the War of 1812.

(Source: 77, 137, 152, 249, 294)

Thompson Stadium

Thompson Stadium served as the football Stadium at Annapolis from 1912 to 1959 when it was replaced by the Navy-Marine Corps Memorial Stadium.

This stadium was named for Colonel Robert M. Thompson, U.S.M.C., Class of 1868, U.S. Naval Academy.

Robert Means Thompson was born on March 2, 1849 in Corsica, Pennsylvania and graduated tenth in the Class of 1868. He was commissioned Ensign in 1869 and promoted to Master in 1870. He resigned from the Navy in 1871 to be a lawyer. He was admitted to the Pennsylvania Bar in 1872 and continued his study of law at Harvard, graduating in 1874.

Thompson became very active in naval affairs including athletics at the Naval Academy. He was the donor of the Thompson Cup which recognizes the Midshipman who contributes most to the advancement of athletics at the Naval Academy. He helped found the New York Naval Academy Alumni Association and served as trustee of the Alumni Association at Annapolis. He was president of the Society of Naval Architects and Marine Engineers and President of the Navy League. He was considered the first great U.S. Naval Academy philanthropist. He was the founder of the Naval Academy Athletic Association.

He died in Fort Ticonderoga, New York on September 5, 1930.

(Source: 77, 198)

Ward Hall

Ward Hall is named for Commander James H. Ward, first Executive Officer of the U. S. Naval Academy.

James Harmon Ward was born at Hartford, Connecticut on September 25, 1806. He became a Midshipman in 1823 and sailed on ships in the Mediterranean, off Africa and the West Indies. He was a student of science and taught at the Naval School in Philadelphia. In 1845 Lieutenant Ward became the first executive officer at the new Naval Academy at Annapolis. He was also a professor, teaching gunnery and steam engineering.

In 1848 he took command of the USS Cumberland and then the steam gunboat Vixen. During the 1850's he was on shore duty at the Washington and Philadelphia Naval Yards. On the outset of the Civil War he commanded a small squadron which operated on the Potomac River. In late June, 1861 he fought with the Confederates and was mortally wounded. He became the first U. S. Naval Officer killed in the Civil War.

The USS Ward was named in his honor as well.

(Source: 117, 77)

Glenn Warner Soccer Center

The Glenn Warner Soccer Facility was named for Glenn Warner, soccer coach at the Naval Academy for thirty years. Glenn Warner coached the Midshipmen to nine NCAA tournaments, winning the National Championship one time. He had a stretch of 48 consecutive season victories. The team had twenty eight winning seasons during his coaching career. He is in the Soccer Hall of Fame and the winner of the Honor Award, soccer's top award.

(Source: 77, 172)

Wilson Park (Smoke Park)

Wilson Park was better known as "Smoke Park" where Midshipmen of all classes could smoke in days of yore. It was named for Admiral Henry B. Wilson, former Superintendent of the U.S. Naval Academy, who extended smoking privileges to all classes. Henry Brad Wilson was born in Camden, New Jersey on February 23, 1861 and graduated from the Naval Academy with the Class of 1881.

He served on various ships and in 1916 he was given command of the USS Pennsylvania. When the United States entered World

War I he was given command of American naval forces in France. He ferried troops to France during the war without the loss of any lives. In 1919 he became Commander of the Atlantic Fleet.

He died on January 30, 1954 and is buried at Arlington National Cemetery.

(Source: 25, 198)

Worden Field

Worden Field is the Parade Field at the U.S. Naval Academy and is named for Admiral John L Warden. John Lorimer Worden was born on March 12, 1818 in Sparta Township, Westchester County, New York. He became a Midshipman in 1834 and served in various naval squadrons including, Brazil, Mediterranean, and Pacific. In 1846 he was promoted to Lieutenant and served off California during the War with Mexico. He served on the USS Cumberland in the Mediterranean, returning to the Naval Observatory in 1850. He was then assigned to the Home Squadron and at the outbreak of the Civil War he was taken prisoner by the South as he returned from Pensacola. By February 1862 he was released and returned to active duty. He was given command of the Ironclad Monitor and was the commander when it went into battle against the CSS Virginia, another ironclad.

He suffered serious eye injuries and relinquished command. Afterwards he returned to the Monitor and used it to bombard Fort McAllister, Georgia. He spent the rest of the Civil War supervising the construction of ironclads. He became a Commodore in 1868 and for five years he was Superintendent of the U. S. Naval Academy. Promoted to Rear Admiral during his tour at the Academy, he later became commander of the European Squadron. He was then assigned to shore duty and he retired in 1886. He died in Washington, DC on October 18, 1897. Besides Worden Field at the Naval Academy, there have been four ships named in honor of John Worden.

(Source: 77, 117)

SOURCES
Faces Behind the Bases

1. 123exp-biographies.com
2. 173fw.ang.af.mil/history
3. 186arw.ang.af.mil/resources
4. 1911encyclopedia.org
5. 2020site.org
6. 65thdiv.com
7. absoluteastronomy.com/topics
8. accessmylibrary.com
9. acepilots.com
10. aerofiles.com
11. af.mil/bios
12. af.mil/history/person
13. af.mil/news
14. airfields-freeman.com
15. airforcehistory.hq.af.mil
16. ameddregiment.amedd.army.mil
17. americanheritage.com/articles
18. americanhistory.si.edu/westpoint
19. amphilsoc.org
20. answers.com/topic
21. answersingenesis.org
22. aogusma.org
23. aqetcsv.us
24. archives.state.al.us/Markers
25. arlingtoncemetery.net
26. army.mil/pao

27. armyfootballclub.org

28. armyhockeyfan,com

29. armyrotc.vt.edu/Cadets

30. ascho.wpafb.af.mil

31. associatedcontent.com

32. athletics.schreiner.edu/HALLHONOR

33. atterburybakalarairmuseum.org

34. austinchronicle.com

35. bakalar.org

36. barksdale.af.mil/library

37. bioguide.congress.gov/scripts

38. bluegrayfootball.com/history

39. brainyhistory.com/events/1791

40. brandonu.ca/hillman

41. buckley.af.mil/library

42. c250.columbia.edu

43. cadetstory.biogspot.com

44. calgensoc.blogspot.com

45. cecilcap.org

46. cem.va.gov/CEMs

47. cga.edu

48. cga.edu/display

49. changemagazine.net/articles

50. check-six.com/lib

51. chesapeake.va.us

52. chronicle.augusta.com/stories

53. chs.org

54. ci.austin.tx/austinairport

55. civilwarartillery.com/inventors

56. civilwarbattlefields.us/Spotsylvania

57. civilwarhome.com

58. civilwarinteractive,com/Biographies

59. clanmcalister.org

60. cnac.org

61. collegefootball.org

62. congressionalcemetery.org

63. c-spanarchives.orgbille.us/Annapolis

64. dean-boys.com

65. delrionewsherald.com

66. dcmilitary.com/dcmilitary

67. detnews.com

68. detrick.army.mil

69. digital.library.okstate.cdu

70. dmairfield.com/people

71. doney.net/aroundaz

72. dwightdeisenhower.com

73. ead.lib.uchicago.edu

74. earlyaviators.com

75. ehistory.osu.edu/world

76. en.allexperts.com

77. en.wikipedia.org

78. encarta.msn.com/encyclopedia

79. enchantedlearning.com/history

80. encyclopedia.com

81. endyorks.gn.apc.org

82. enmobile.wikipedia

83. everything2.com

84. explorenorth.com/library

85. Fairbanks-alaska.com

86. famousamericans.net

87. files.usgwarchives.net

88. findagrave.com

89. findarticles.com

90. firstflight.org/shrine

91. firstworldwar.com/bio

92. flicker.com/photos/thayerschool

93. floridagenealogyproject.com

94. fly2houston.com

95. football.ballparks.com/NCAA

96. footballfoundation.com/news

97. fpc.dos.state.fl.us

98. galafilm.com/1812

99. genealogytrails.com

100. generalpatton.com/biography

101. generals.dk/general

102. geocities.com

103. georgiaencyclopedia.org

104. georgiainfo.galileo.usg.edu

105. globalsecurity.org

106. goarmysports.com

107. golddusteddreams.tripod.com

108. gravematter.com

109. grolier.com

110. groups.dcs.st-and.ac.uk

111. hawaii.gov/hawaii/aviation

112. helpfulsolutions.com

113. herndonweb.com

114. hickam.af.mil/library
115. hill.af.mil/library
116. history.army.mil
117. history.navy.mil
118. historynet.com
119. historypoint.org
120. historysandiego.edu
121. hmdb.org/marker
122. holloman.af.mil/Library
123. homeofheroes.com
124. homepage.mac.com
125. hometextilestoday,com/article
126. hunts-upgrade,com
127. imdb.com/name
128. impeach-andrewjohnson.com
129. infoplease.com
130. innatschofield.com
131. invention.psychology.msstate.edu
132. inventors.about.com
133. jacksjoint.com
134. johnbrashear.tripod.com
135. jsc.nasa.gov.bios
136. kirkland.af.mil/library
137. knowledgerush.com
138. lasvegassun.com/news/1997
139. legendsofamerica.com
140. leisureguy.wordpress.com
141. lib.utexas.edu
142. lighthousedepot.com

143. lojto.com/Fayetteville

144. lucidcafe.com/library

145. maotis.ang.af.mil

146. marineheritage.org

147. marines.com

148. maritimequest.com

149. mccordairmuseum.org

150. mclm.com

151. members.fortunecity.com

152. members.tripod.com

153. michigan.gov/mdot

154. militarymuseum.org

155. mitchellgallery.org

156. mishalov.com

157. mnbeef.org

158. monticello.org

159. mrlincolnswhitehouse.org

160. mtnlakes.org/Library

161. mybaseguide.com

162. mycivilwar.com

163. mysanantonio.com

164. nationalaviation.blade6.donet.com

165. nationalchamps.net

166. nationalmuseum.af.mil

167. nationmaster.com

168. navsource.org/archives

169. navymars.org/pacific

170. navysna.com/awards

171. navysna.org/awards

172. navysports.cstv.com

173. ncmarkers.com

174. nelis.af.mil/library

175. nga.org/portal

176. ngb.army.mil

177. niulib.niu.edu

178. nndb,com/people

179. nobelprize.org

180. npg.si.edu

181. npr.org/templates

182. nps.gov/archive

183. nytimes.com

184. oknapc.org/usna

185. ova.dc.gov

186. pbs.gcn.in

187. pbs.org/kcet/chasingthesun

188. perrinairforcebase.net

189. perrinfield.org

190. petitiononline.com

191. philippecolin.net

192. polishamericancenter.org

193. pqasb.pqarchiver.com

194. probertencyclopaedia.com

195. query.nytimes.com

196. quoddyvacation.com/history

197. radioreference.com

198. Reef Points 1949-50

199. robins21.org/synopsis

200. rootsweb.ancestry.com

201. s9.com/Biography

202. savethechapelmcclellanafb.org

203. sc94ameslab.gov/TOUR

204. scaahof.org

205. scard.buffnet.net

206. sedgwickcounty.org

207. seymourjohnson.af.mil/library

208. shopthepoint.com

209. shorpy.com

210. sname.org/sections/Chesapeake

211. spanamwar.com

212. sparslysageandtimely.com

213. spartacus.schoolnet.co.uk

214. spock.com

215. statelibrary.der.state.nc.us

216. strategic-air-command.com/bases

217. surveyhistory.org

218. swco.ttu.edu

219. switchboard.com

220. tailhhook.org

221. tampagov.net

222. tamug.edu

223. techbastard.com/afb

224. texashistory.unt.edu

225. themilitaryzone.com/bases

226. time.com/time/magazine

227. tngenweb.org

228. tripatlas.com

229. tshaonline.org

230. tulane.edu

231. unc.edu

232. united-publishers.com

233. us95th.org/ww1history

234. usa-patriotism.com

235. uscg.mil/history/people

236. U,S. Coast Guard-Public Info Div.

237. us-civilwar.com

238. usgwararchives.org

239. usma.edu/Tour

240. usna.com

241. usna.edu

242. ussluce.org

243. veterantributes.org

244. vic.com

245. virginiasportshalloffame.com

246. virtualwall.org

247. visitfayettevillenc.com

248. volkfield.ang.af.mil

249. wapedia.mobi

250. wapiti.com

251. warbirdinformationexchange.org

252. washingtonpost.com

253. waymarking.com

254. westpointaog.net

255. whitehouse.gov/history

256. whoi.edu

257. wingsmuseum.org

258. wingsoverkansas.com/legacy

259. worldatwar.net/nations/Greenland

260. wright-house.com/wright-brothers

261. wyoarchives.state.wy.us

262. xroads.virginia.edu

263. indianamilitary.org

264. politicalgraveyard.com

265. aphill.army.mil

266. google.com

267. benefits.military.com/history

268. tripod.com/history

269. sentinelandenterprise.com

270. facilities.utah.edu

271. course-notes.org

272. saintmarys.com

273. ohiohistorycentral.org

274. jackson.army.mil

275. buffnet.net

276. fortpickett.net

277. keyhole.com

278. thepepper.com

279. davismonthanafb.net

280. fas.org

281. mitchellairport.com

282. msmeri.ang.af.mil

283. klamathfallsairport.com

284. ASME International

285. 2.hickam.af.mil/library

286. 2.military.hill.af.mil/library

287. 2.holloman.mil/library

288. groups,dcs.st-and.ac.uk

289. military.com

290. nh.gov.nhdhr/publications

291. all-biographies.com

292. americanpresidents.org

293. ushistory.org

294. Eminent Americans, Namesakes of the Polaris Submarine Fleet

Appendix A
Names of Bases, Persons, Sorted by Date of Birth of Person

Base, Hall or Monument Name	Base Type	Named For	Year Born
Dover Air Force Base	USAF	Location, Date of Town	1683
Fort Belvoir	Army	Location, Lord Fairfax	1693
Fort Lee, New Jersey	Army	Lee, Charles	1732
Washington Monument	USMAcad	Washington, George	1732
Fort Putnam	USMAcad	Putnam, Rufus	1738
Yeaton Hall	USCGAcad	Yeaton, Hopley	1739
Jefferson Barracks Military Post	Army	Jefferson, Thomas	1743
Kosciuszko Monument	USMAcad	Kosciuszko, Thaddeus	1746
Fort Knox	Army	Knox, Henry	1750
Fort Hamilton, Ohio	Army	Hamilton, Alexander	1755c
Fort Hamilton, New York	Army	Hamilton, Alexander	1755c
Hamilton Hall	USCGAcad	Hamilton, Alexander	1755c
Fort Monroe	Army	Monroe, James	1758
Fort Stewart	Army	Stewart, Daniel	1761
Preble Hall	USNAcad	Preble, Edward	1761
Fort Jackson	Army	Jackson, Andrew	1767
Tecumseh Court	USNAcad	Techumseh	1768
Fort Lewis	Army	Lewis, Meriwether	1774

Lawrence Field	USNAcad	Lawrence, James	1781
Henderson Hall Marine Corps HQ	USMC	Henderson, Archibald	1783
MacDonough Hall	USNAcad	MacDonough, Thomas	1783
Thayer Monument	USMAcad	Thayer, Sylvanus	1785
Fort Eustis	Army	Eustis, Abraham	1786
Fort Riley	Army	Riley, Bennett C.	1790
Commodore Uriah P. Levy Center	USNAcad	Levy, Uriah P.	1792
Fort Sam Houston	Army	Houston, Sam	1793
Fort Dix	Army	Dix, John Adams	1798
Bancroft Hall	USNAcad	Bancroft, George	1800
Farragut Field	USNAcad	Farragut, David Glascow	1800c
Fort Polk	Army	Polk, Leonidas	1806
Maury Hall	USNAcad	Maury, Matthew Fontaine	1806
Ward Hall	USNAcad	Ward, James H.	1806
Fort Campbell	Army	Campbell, William Bowen	1807
Fort Lee, Virginia	Army	Lee, Robert E.	1807
Chase Hall	USCGAcad	Chase, Salmon P.	1808
Fort Carson	Army	Carson, Christopher "Kit"	1809
Cullum Hall	USMAcad	Cullum, George Washington	1809
Dahlgren Hall	USNAcad	Dahlgren, John Adolphus	1809
Fort Douglas	Army	Douglas, Stephan A.	1813
Sedgwick Monument	USMAcad	Sedgwick, John	1813

Herndon Monument	USNAcad	Herndon, William Louis	1813
Fort Benning	Army	Benning, Henry L.	1814
Fort Bliss	Army	Bliss, Wiliam Wallace Smith	1815
Fort George G. Meade	Army	Meade, George C.	1815
Fort Rucker	Army	Rucker, Edmund	1815c
Chauvenet Walk /Hall	USNAcad	Chauvenet, William	1815c
Fort Bragg	Army	Bragg, Braxton	1817
Fort Ord	Army	Ord, Edward Otho Cresap	1818
Worden Field	USNAcad	Worden, John Lorimer	1818
Doubleday Field	USMAcad	Doubleday, Abner	1819
Fort Devens	Army	Devens, Charles A.	1820
Beale Air Force Base	USAF	Beale, Edward Fitzgerald	1822
Grant Hall	USMAcad	Grant, Ulysses S.	1822
Isherwood Hall	USNAcad	Isherwood, Benjamin Franklin	1822
Fort A. P. Hill	Army	Hill, Ambrose Powell	1825c
Fort Pickett	Army	Pickett, George E.	1825
Fort McClellan	Army	McClellan, George Brinton	1826
Henriques Room	USCGAcad	Henriques, John A.	1826
Luce Hall	USNAcad	Luce, Stephen B.	1827
Fort McPherson	Army	McPherson, James Birdseye	1828
Fort Myer	Army	Myer, Albert James	1828
Fort Crook	Army	Crook, George	1829

Camp McCoy	Army	McCoy, Bruce E.	1829
Fort Hood	Army	Hood, John Bell	1831
Schofield Barracks	Army	Schofield, John MacAllister	1831
Fort Sheridan	Army	Sheridan, Phillip Henry	1831
Fort Sill	Army	Sill, Joshua Woodrow	1831
Fort Gordon	Army	Gordon, John B.	1832
Chanute Air Force Base	USAF	Chanute, Octave	1832
Fort Benjamin Harrison	Army	Harrison, Benjamin	1833
Langley Air Force Base	USAF	Langley, Samuel Pierpont	1834
Dewey Basin & Dewey Field	USNAcad	Dewey, George	1837
Mahan Hall	USNAcad	Mahan, Alfred Thayer	1840
Samson Hall	USNAcad	Samson, William	1840
Melville Hall	USNAcad	Melville, George W.	1841
Fort Chaffee	Army	Chaffee, Adna R.	1842
F.E. Warren Air Force Base	USAF	Warren, Francis E.	1844
Hubbard Hall	USNAcad	Hubbard, John	1848c
Thompson Stadium	USNAcad	Thompson, Robert Means	1849
Michelson Hall	USNAcad	Michelson, Albert Abraham	1852
Fort Hunter Liggett	Army	Liggett, Hunter	1857
Fort Leonard Wood	Army	Wood, Leonard	1860
Camp Pendleton Marine	USMC	Pendleton, Joseph Henry	1860

Corps Base

Wilson Park (Smoke Park)	USNAcad	Wilson, Henry Brad	1861
Patrick Air Force Base	USAF	Patrick, Mason Matthews	1863
The David Taylor Model Basin	USN	Taylor, David	1864
Camp Atterbury	Army	Atterbury, William Wallace	1866
Fort Irwin	Army	Irwin, George Leroy	1867c
Wright-Patterson Air Force Base	USAF	Wright, Wilber	1867
Camp Lejeune Marine Corps Base	USMC	Lejeune, John A.	1867
McAllister Hall	USCGAcad	McAllister, Charles Albert	1867
Lejeune Hall	USNAcad	Lejeune, John A.	1867
Moffett Federal Airfield	USNAS	Moffett, William A.	1869
Michie Stadium	USMAcad	Michie, Dennis Mahan	1870c
Wright-Patterson Air Force Base	USAF	Wright, Orville	1871
Kirtland Air Force Base	USAF	Kirtland, Roy C.	1874
Earle Naval Weapons Station	USN	Earle, Ralph	1874
Shepherd Air Force Base	USAF	Shepherd, John Morris	1875
Dimick Hall	USCGAcad	Dimick, Chester E.	1875c
Satterlee Hall	USCGAcad	Satterlee, Charles	1875c
Leahy Hall	USNAcad	Leahy, William Daniel	1875
Camp Blanding / Fort Blanding	Army	Blanding, Albert H.	1876

Fort Ritchie	Army	Ritchie, Albert Cabell	1876
Halligan Hall	USNAcad	Halligan, John, Jr.	1876
Mitscher Hall	USNAcad	Mitscher, Marc Andrew "Pete"	1877
Kelly Air Force Base	USAF	Kelly, George E.M.	1878
King Hall	USNAcad	King, Ernest J.	1878
Fort Drum	Army	Drum, Hugh A.	1879
General William Mitchell Airport	USAF	Mitchell, William	1879
Pope Air Force Base	USAF	Pope, Harley Halbert	1879
Mitchell Hall	USAFAcad	Mitchell, William "Billy"	1879
Gunter Air Force Base	USAF	Gunter, William	1880c
MacArthur Monument	USMAcad	MacArthur, Douglas	1880
McChord Air Force Base	USAF	McChord, William C.	1881
Camp Smedley D. Butler Marine Corps Base	USMC	Butler, Smedley D.	1881
Whiting Field Naval Air Station	USNAS	Whiting, Kenneth	1881
Robins Air Force Base	USAF	Robins, Augustine Warner	1882
Selfridge Air National Guard Base	USAF	Selfridge, Thomas	1882
Johnson Hall	USCGAcad	Johnson, Harvey F.	1882
Halsey Field House	USNAcad	Halsey, William Frederick, Jr. "Bull"	1882
Fort Lesley J. McNair	Army	McNair, Lesley J.	1883

Camp Wallace	Army	Wallace, Elmer J.	1883c
Westover Air Reserve Base	USAF	Westover, Oscar	1883
Andrews Air Force Base	USAF	Andrews, Frank Maxwell	1884
K.I. Sawyer Air Force Base	USAF	Sawyer, Kenneth Ingalls	1884
Scott Air Force Base	USAF	Scott, Frank E.	1884
Saufley Field, NAS Pensacola	USNAS	Saufley, Richard C.	1884
Davis-Monthan Air Force Base	USAF	Davis, Samuel H.	1885c
Davis-Monthan Air Force Base	USAF	Monthan, Oscar	1885
Hickam Air Force Base	USAF	Hickam, Horace Meek	1885
Lackland Air Force Base	USAF	Lackland, Frank	1885
Patton Monument	USMAcad	Patton, George Smith, Jr.	1885
Nimitz Library	USNAcad	Nimitz, Chester William	1885
Arnold Air Force Base	USAF	Arnold, Henry Harlay "Hap"	1886
Arnold Hall	USAFAcad	Arnold, Henry H. "Hap"	1886
Waesche Hall	USCGAcad	Waesche, Russell R.	1886
Ingram Field	USNAcad	Ingram, Jonas Howard	1886
Bolling Air Force Base	USAF	Bolling, Raynal C.	1887
Tinker Air Force Base	USAF	Tinker, Clarence Leonard	1887
Cecil Field Naval Air Station	USNAS	Cecil, Henry Barton	1888c
Corry Station Naval Technical	USNAS	Corry, William M.	1888c

Training Center

Fort Detrick	Army	Detrick, Frederick L.	1889
Fitzsimons Army Hospital	Army	Fitzsimmons, William T.	1889
Ellington Field	USAF	Ellington, Eric Lamar	1889
MacDill Air Force Base	USAF	MacDill, Leslie	1889
Wheeler Field, Schofield Barracks	Army Air	Wheeler, Sheldon H.	1889
Smith Hall	USCGAcad	Smith, Edward H. "Iceberg"	1889
Norman Scott Natatorium	USNAcad	Scott, Norman	1889c
Rickenbacker International Airport	Non-Mil	Rickenbacker, Eddie	1890
Michel Hall	USCGAcad	Michel, Carl	1890
Eisenhower Hall & Eisenhower Monument	USMAcad	Eisenhower, Dwight David	1890
Goodfellow Air Force Base	USAF	Goodfellow, John J., Jr.	1891
Cannon Air Force Base	USAF	Cannon, John Kenneth	1892
Davison Army Air Field	Army Air	Davison, Donald A.	1892
George Air Force Base	USAF	George, Harold H.	1892
Maxwell Air Force Base	USAF	Maxwell, William C.	1892
Harman Hall	USAFAcad	Harman, Hubert R.	1892

Lawson Army Air Field, Fort Benning, Georgia	Army Air	Lawson, Walter Ralls	1893
Fairchild Air Force Base	USAF	Fairchild, Muir S.	1894
Hill Air Force Base	USAF	Hill, Ployer Peter	1894
Lowry Air Force Base	USAF	Lowry, Francis	1894
McClellan Air Force Base	USAF	McClellan, Hezekiah	1894
Offutt Air Force Base	USAF	Offutt, Jarvis	1894
Shaw Field Air Force Base	USAF	Shaw, Erwin David	1894
Tyndall Air Force Base	USAF	Tyndall, Frank B.	1894
Camp Roberts	Army	Roberts, Harold W.	1895
Brooks Air Force Base	USAF	Brooks, Sidney Johnson, Jr.	1895
Elmendorf Air Force Base	USAF	Elmendorf, Hugh Merle	1895
Chase Field Naval Air Station	USNAS	Chase, Nathan Brown	1895c
Bellows Air Force Station (Bellows Field)	USAF	Bellows, Franklin Barney	1896
Brookley Field AFB	USAF	Brookley, Wendell H.	1896
Eaker Air Force Base	USAF	Eaker, Ira Clarence	1896
Keesler Air Force Base	USAF	Keesler, Samuel Reeves, Jr.	1896
March Air Reserve Base	USAF	March, Peyton C., Jr.	1896
Perrin Field	USAF	Perrin, lmer D.	1896

Richards-Gebaur Air Force Base	USAF	Richards, John Francisco, II	1896
Doolittle Hall	USAFAcad	Doolittle, James Harold "Jimmy"	1896
Fairchild Hall	USAFAcad	Fairchild, Muir Stephen	1896c
Barksdale Air Force Base	USAF	Barksdale, Eugene Hoy	1897
Eglin Air Force Base	USAF	Eglin, Frederick Irving	1897
Eielson Air Force Base	USAF	Eielson, Carl Ben	1897
Luke Air Force Base	USAF	Luke, Frank, Jr.	1897
Wright-Patterson Air Force Base	USAF	Patterson, Frank Stewart	1897
Blaik Field	USMAcad	Blaik, Earl "Red" "Colonel"	1897
Buckley Air Force Base	USAF	Buckley, John Harold	1898c
Hamilton Air Force Base	USAF	Hamilton, Lloyd Andrew	1898c
Williams Air Force Base	USAF	Williams, Charles Linton	1898
Vandenberg Air Force Base	USAF	Vandenberg, Hoyt S.	1899
Vandenberg Hall	USAFAcad	Vandenberg, Hoyt S.	1899
Griffiss Air Force Base	USAF	Griffiss, Townsend E.	1900
Holloman Air Force Base	USAF	Holloman, George	1900c
Key Field	USAF	Key, Al & Fred	1900c
Mather Air Force Base	USAF	Mather, Carl Spencer	1900c
Leamy Hall	USCGAcad	Leamy, Frank	1900

Rickover Hall	USNAcad	Rickover, Hyman G.	1900
Rip Miller Field	USNAcad	Miller, Edgar E. "Rip"	1901
Howard Air Force Base	USAF	Howard, Charles H.	1903c
Seymour Johnson Air Force Base	USAF	Johnson, Seymour	1904
Travis Air Force Base	USAF	Travis, Robert F.	1904
Randolph Air Force Base	USAF	Randolph, Willaim Millican	1905c
Hanscom Air Force Base	USAF	Hanscom, Laurence G.	1906
Wurtsmith Air Force Base	USAF	Wurtsmith, Paul Bernard	1906
Bergstrom Air Force Base	USAF	Bergstrom, John August Earle	1907
Malmstrom Air Force Base	USAF	Malmstrom, Einar Axel	1907
Ricketts Hall	USNAcad	Ricketts, Claude Vernon	1907c
Castle Air Force Base	USAF	Castle, Frederick Walker	1908
Goldwater Visitor Center	USAFAcad	Goldwater, Barry Morris	1909
James K. Herbert Alumni Center	USMAcad	Herbert, James K.	1909
Moody Air Force Base	USAF	Moody, George Putnam	1910c
Schriever Air Force Base	USAF	Schriever, Bernard Adolph	1910
Ellsworth Air Force Base	USAF	Ellsworth, Richard E.	1911c
Laughlin Air Force Base	USAF	Laughlin, Jack T.	1914
Joe Foss Field (Sioux	Non-Mil	Foss, Joseph Jacob "Joe"	1915

Falls Regional Airport)

Otis Air National Guard Base	USAF	Otis, Frank "Jesse"	1915c
Carswell Air Force Base	USAF	Carswell, Horace Seaver	1916
Dyess Air Force Base	USAF	Dyess, William Edwin	1916
Nellis Air Force Base	USAF	Nellis, William Harell	1916
Vance Air Force Base	USAF	Vance, Leon Robert, Jr.	1916
Fort Gillem	Army	Gillem, Alvan C., II	1917
Lawson Army Air Field, Fort Benning, Georgia	Army Air	Lawson, Ted W.	1917
McEntire Air National Guard Station	USAF	McEntire, Barnie B.	1917c
Reese Air Force Base	USAF	Reese, Augustus Frank, Jr.	1917c
Edwards Air Force Base	USAF	Edwards, Glen	1918
Loring Air Force Base	USAF	Loring, Charles J.	1918
Seward Air Force Base	USAF	Seward, Alan J., Jr.	1918c
Kingsley Field	USAF	Kingsley, David	1919
Richards-Gebaur Air Force Base	USAF	Gebaur, Arthur William, Jr.	1919
Whiteman Air Force Base	USAF	Whiteman, George A.	1919
Munro Hall	USCGAcad	Munro, Douglas Albert	1919
Gillis Field House	USMAcad	Gillis, William G., Jr.	1919c
Tate Rink	USMAcad	Tate, Joseph S.	1919

Bakalar Air Force Base	USAF	Bakalar, John Edmund	1920
Dannelly Field (Montgomery Airport)	Non-Mil	Dannelly, Clarence Moore, Jr.	1920c
Forbes Air Force Base	USAF	Forbes, Daniel S.	1920
McConnell Air Force Base	USAF	McConnell, Fred & Thomas	1920c
McGuire Air Force Base	USAF	McGuire, Thomas B.	1920
Norton Air force Base	USAF	Norton, Leland Francis	1920
Peterson Air Force Base	USAF	Peterson, Edward J.	1920c
Tate Rink	USMAcad	Tate, Frederick H.S.	1920c
Dobbins Air Reserve Base	USAF	Dobbins, Charles M.	1921c
Cristl Arena	USMAcad	Cristl, Edward C., Jr.	1922c
Glenn Warner Soccer Center	USNAcad	Warner, Glenn	1922c
England Air Force Base	USAF	England, John B.	1923
Yeager Airport	Non-Mil	Yeager, Charles Elwood "Chuck"	1923
Volk Field Air National Guard Base	USAF	Volk, Jerome A.	1925
Grissom Air Reserve Base	USAF	Grissom, Virgil I. "Gus"	1926
Shea Stadium	USMAcad	Shea, Richard Thomas	1927
Wesley Brown Field House	USNAcad	Brown, Wesley	1927
Kincheloe Air Force Base	USAF	Kincheloe, Even C. Jr.	1928

Lichtenberg Tennis Center	USMAcad	Lichtenberg, Alan	1929c
Camp Elmore	USMC	Elmore, George W.	1931c
Armel-Leftwich Visitor Center	USNAcad	Armel, Lyle	1931
Armel-Leftwich Visitor Center	USNAcad	Leftwich, William Groom	1931
Lichtenberg Tennis Center	USMAcad	Lichtenberg, Herbert	1933c
Holleder Center	USMAcad	Holleder, Donald W.	1934
Robert Crown Sailing Center	USNAcad	Crown, Robert	1935c
Sijan Hall	USAFAcad	Sijan, Lance Peter	1942
Arvin Gym	USMAcad	Arvin, Robert	1943
Onizuka Air Force Station	USAF	Onizuka, Ellison Shoji	1946c

Appendix B
Names of Bases, Persons, Sorted by Type of Base, Then By Names, Alphabetically

Base, Hall or Monument Name	Base Type	Named For	Year Born
Camp Atterbury	Army	Atterbury, William W.	1866
Fort A. P. Hill	Army	Hill, Ambrose Powell	1825c
Fort Belvoir	Army	Location, Lord Fairfax	1693
Fort Benjamin Harrison	Army	Harrison, Benjamin	1833
Fort Benning	Army	Benning, Henry L.	1814
Camp Blanding / Fort Blanding	Army	Blanding, Albert H.	1876
Fort Bliss	Army	Bliss, William Wallace	1815
Fort Bragg	Army	Bragg, Braxton	1817
Fort Campbell	Army	Campbell, William Bowen	1807
Fort Carson	Army	Carson, Christopher "Kit"	1809
Fort Chaffee	Army	Chaffee, Adna R.	1842
Fort Crook	Army	Crook, George	1829
Fort Detrick	Army	Detrick, Frederick L.	1889
Fort Devens	Army	Devens, Charles A.	1820
Fort Dix	Army	Dix, John Adams	1798
Fort Douglas	Army	Douglas, Stephan A.	1813
Fort Drum	Army	Drum, Hugh A.	1879
Fort Eustis	Army	Eustis, Abraham	1786
Fitzsimons Army Hospital	Army	Fitzsimmons, William T.	1889
Fort George G. Meade	Army	Meade, George C.	1815
Fort Gillem	Army	Gillem, Alvan C.,II	1917
Fort Gordon	Army	Gordon, John B.	1832
Fort Hamilton, Ohio	Army	Hamilton, Alexander	1755c

Fort Hamilton, New York	Army	Hamilton, Alexander	1755c
Fort Hood	Army	Hood, John Bell	1831
Fort Hunter Liggett	Army	Liggett, Hunter	1857
Fort Irwin	Army	Irwin, George Leroy	1867c
Fort Jackson	Army	Jackson, Andrew	1767
Jefferson Barracks Military Post	Army	Jefferson, Thomas	1743
Fort Knox	Army	Knox, Henry	1750
Fort Lee, New Jersey	Army	Lee, Charles	1732
Fort Lee, Virginia	Army	Lee, Robert E.	1807
Fort Leonard Wood	Army	Wood, Leonard	1860
Fort Lesley J. McNair	Army	McNair, Lesley J.	1883
Fort Lewis	Army	Lewis, Meriwether	1774
Fort McClellan	Army	McClellan, George Brinton	1826
Camp McCoy	Army	McCoy, Bruce E.	1829
Fort McPherson	Army	McPherson, James Birdseye	1828
Fort Monroe	Army	Monroe, James	1758
Fort Myer	Army	Myer, Albert James	1828
Fort Ord	Army	Ord, Edward Otho Cresap	1818
Fort Pickett	Army	Pickett, George E.	1825
Fort Polk	Army	Polk, Leonidas	1806
Fort Ritchie	Army	Ritchie, Albert Cabell	1876
Fort Riley	Army	Riley, Bennett C.	1790
Camp Roberts	Army	Roberts, Harold W.	1895
Fort Rucker	Army	Rucker, Edmund	1815c
Fort Sam Houston	Army	Houston, Sam	1793
Schofield Barracks	Army	Schofield, John MacAllister	1831
Fort Sheridan	Army	Sheridan, Phillip Henry	1831
Fort Sill	Army	Sill, Joshua Woodrow	1831
Fort Stewart	Army	Stewart, Daniel	1761
Camp Wallace	Army	Wallace, Elmer J.	1883c
Andrews Air Force Base	USAF	Andrews, Frank Maxwell	1884

Arnold Air Force Base	USAF	Arnold, Henry Harlay	1886
Bakalar Air Force Base	USAF	Bakalar, John Edmund	1920
Barksdale Air Force Base	USAF	Barksdale, Eugene Hoy	1897
Beale Air Force Base	USAF	Beale, Edward Fitzgerald	1822
Bellows Air Force Station	USAF	Bellows, Franklin Barney	1896
(Bellows Field)			
Bergstrom Air Force Base	USAF	Bergstrom, John August Earle	1907
Bolling Air Force Base	USAF	Bolling, Raynal C.	1887
Brookley Field AFB	USAF	Brookley, Wendell H.	1896
Brooks Air Force Base	USAF	Brooks, Sidney Johnson, Jr.	1895
Buckley Air Force Base	USAF	Buckley, John Harold	1898c
Cannon Air Force Base	USAF	Cannon, John Kenneth	1892
Carswell Air Force Base	USAF	Carswell, Horace Seaver	1916
Castle Air Force Base	USAF	Castle, Frederick Walker	1908
Chanute Air Force Base	USAF	Chanute, Octave	1832
Dannelly Field	Non-Mil	Dannelly, Clarence Moore, Jr.	1920c
(Montgomery Airport)			
Davis-Monthan Air Force Base	USAF	Davis, Samuel H.	1885c
Davis-Monthan Air Force Base	USAF	Monthan, Oscar	1885
Davison Army Air Field	Army Air	Davison, Donald A.	1892
Dobbins Air Reserve Base	USAF	Dobbins, Charles M.	1921
Dover Air Force Base	USAF	Location	1683
Dyess Air Force Base	USAF	Dyess, William Edwin	1916
Eaker Air Force Base	USAF	Eaker, Ira Clarence	1896
Edwards Air Force Base	USAF	Edwards, Glen	1918
Eglin Air Force Base	USAF	Eglin, Frederick Irving	1897
Eielson Air Force Base	USAF	Eielson, Carl Ben	1897

Ellington Field	USAF	Ellington, Eric Lamar	1889
Ellsworth Air Force Base	USAF	Ellsworth, Richard E.	1911c
Elmendorf Air Force Base	USAF	Elmendorf, Hugh Merle	1895
England Air Force Base	USAF	England, John B.	1923
Fairchild Air Force Base	USAF	Fairchild, Muir S.	1894
Forbes Air Force Base	USAF	Forbes, Daniel S.	1920
Joe Foss Field (Sioux Falls Regional Airport)	Non-Mil	Foss, Joseph Jacob "Joe"	1915
George Air Force Base	USAF	George, Harold H.	1892
Goodfellow Air Force Base	USAF	Goodfellow, John J., Jr.	1891
Griffiss Air Force Base	USAF	Griffiss, Townsend E.	1900
Grissom Air Reserve Base	USAF	Grissom, Virgil I. "Gus"	1926
Gunter Air Force Base	USAF	Gunter, William	1880c
Hamilton Air Force Base	USAF	Hamilton, Lloyd Andrew	1898c
Hanscom Air Force Base	USAF	Hanscom, Laurence G.	1906
Hickam Air Force Base	USAF	Hickam, Horace Meek	1885
Hill Air Force Base	USAF	Hill, Ployer Peter	1894
Holloman Air Force Base	USAF	Holloman, George	1900c
Howard Air Force Base	USAF	Howard, Charles H.	1903c
Keesler Air Force Base	USAF	Keesler, Samuel Reeves, Jr.	1896
Kelly Air Force Base	USAF	Kelly, George E.M.	1878
Key Field	USAF	Key, Al & Fred	1900c
Kincheloe Air Force Base	USAF	Kincheloe, Even C. Jr.	1928
Kingsley Field	USAF	Kingsley, David	1919
Kirtland Air Force Base	USAF	Kirtland, Roy C.	1874

K.I. Sawyer Air Force Base	USAF	Sawyer, Kenneth Ingalls	1884
Lackland Air Force Base	USAF	Lackland, Frank	1885
Langley Air Force Base	USAF	Langley, Samuel Pierpont	1834
Laughlin Air Force Base	USAF	Laughlin, Jack T.	1914
Lawson Army Air Field, Fort Benning, Georgia	Army Air	Lawson, Walter Ralls	1893
Lawson Army Air Field, Fort Benning, Georgia	Army Air	Lawson, Ted W.	1917
Loring Air Force Base	USAF	Loring, Charles J.	1918
Lowry Air Force Base	USAF	Lowry, Francis	1894
Luke Air Force Base	USAF	Luke, Frank, Jr.	1897
MacDill Air Force Base	USAF	MacDill, Leslie	1889
Malmstrom Air Force Base	USAF	Malmstrom, Einar Axel	1907
March Air Reserve Base	USAF	March, Peyton C., Jr.	1896
Mather Air Force Base	USAF	Mather, Carl Spencer	1900c
Maxwell Air Force Base	USAF	Maxwell, William C.	1892
McChord Air Force Base	USAF	McChord, William C.	1881
McClellan Air Force Base	USAF	McClellan, Hezekiah	1894
McConnell Air Force Base	USAF	McConnell, Fred & Thomas	1920c
McEntire Air National Guard Station	USAF	McEntire, Barnie B.	1917c
McGuire Air Force Base	USAF	McGuire, Thomas B.	1920
General William Mitchell Airport	USAF	Mitchell, William	1879
Moody Air Force Base	USAF	Moody, George Putnam	1910c
Nellis Air Force Base	USAF	Nellis, William Harell	1916
Norton Air force Base	USAF	Norton, Leland Francis	1920
Offutt Air Force Base	USAF	Offutt, Jarvis	1894

Onizuka Air Force Station	USAF	Onizuka, Ellison Shoji	1946c
Otis Air National Guard Base	USAF	Otis, Frank "Jesse"	1915c
Patrick Air Force Base	USAF	Patrick, Mason Matthews	1863
Perrin Field	USAF	Perrin, lmer D.	1896
Peterson Air Force Base	USAF	Peterson, Edward J.	1920c
Pope Air Force Base	USAF	Pope, Harley Halbert	1879
Randolph Air Force Base	USAF	Randolph, William Millican	1905c
Reese Air Force Base	USAF	Reese, Augustus Frank, Jr.	1917c
Richards-Gebaur Air Force Base	USAF	Richards, John Francisco, II	1896
Richards-Gebaur Air Force Base	USAF	Gebaur, Arthur William, Jr.	1919
Rickenbacker International Airport	Non-Mil	Rickenbacker, Eddie	1890
Robins Air Force Base	USAF	Robins, Augustine Warner	1882
Schriever Air Force Base	USAF	Schriever, Bernard Adolph	1910
Scott Air Force Base	USAF	Scott, Frank E.	1884
Selfridge Air National Guard Base	USAF	Selfridge, Thomas	1882
Seymour Johnson Air Force Base	USAF	Johnson, Seymour	1904
Seward Air Force Base	USAF	Seward, Alan J., Jr.	1918c
Shaw Field Air Force Base	USAF	Shaw, Erwin David	1894
Shepherd Air Force Base	USAF	Shepherd, John Morris	1875
Tinker Air Force Base	USAF	Tinker, Clarence Leonard	1887
Travis Air Force Base	USAF	Travis, Robert F.	1904
Tyndall Air Force Base	USAF	Tyndall, Frank B.	1894
Vance Air Force Base	USAF	Vance, Leon Robert, Jr.	1916
Vandenberg Air Force Base	USAF	Vandenberg, Hoyt S.	1899

Volk Field Air National Guard Base	USAF	Volk, Jerome A.	1925
F.E. Warren Air Force Base	USAF	Warren, Francis E.	1844
Westover Air Reserve Base	USAF	Westover, Oscar	1883
Wheeler Field, Schofield Barracks	Army Air	Wheeler, Sheldon H.	1889
Whiteman Air Force Base	USAF	Whiteman, George A.	1919
Williams Air Force Base	USAF	Williams, Charles Linton	1898
Wright-Patterson Air Force Base	USAF	Wright, Orville	1871
Wright-Patterson Air Force Base	USAF	Wright, Wilber	1867
Wright-Patterson Air Force Base	USAF	Patterson, Frank Stewart	1897
Wurtsmith Air Force Base	USAF	Wurtsmith, Paul Bernard	1906
Yeager Airport	Non-Mil	Yeager, Charles Elwood "Chuck"	1923
Camp Smedley D. Butler Marine Corps Base	USMC	Butler, Smedley D.	1881
Cecil Field Naval Air Station	USNAS	Cecil, Henry Barton	1888c
Chase Field Naval Air Station	USNAS	Chase, Nathan Brown	1895c
Corry Station Naval Technical Training Center	USNAS	Corry, William M.	1888c
Earle Naval Weapons Station	USN	Earle, Ralph	1874
Camp Elmore	USMC	Elmore, George W.	1931c
Henderson Hall Marine Corps HQ	USMC	Henderson, Archibald	1783

Camp Lejeune Marine Corps Base	USMC	Lejeune, John A.	1867
Moffett Federal Airfield	USNAS	Moffett, William A.	1869
Camp Pendleton Marine Corps Base	USMC	Pendleton, Joseph Henry	1860
Saufley Field, NAS Pensacola	USNAS	Saufley, Richard C.	1884
The David Taylor Model Basin	USN	Taylor, David	1864
Whiting Field Naval Air Station	USNAS	Whiting, Kenneth	1881
Arnold Hall	USAFAcad	Arnold, Henry H. "Hap"	1886
Doolittle Hall	USAFAcad	Doolittle, James Harold "Jimmy"	1896
Fairchild Hall	USAFAcad	Fairchild, Muir Stephen	1896c
Goldwater Visitor Center	USAFAcad	Goldwater, Barry Morris	1909
Harman Hall	USAFAcad	Harman, Hubert R.	1892
Mitchell Hall	USAFAcad	Mitchell, William "Billy"	1879
Sijan Hall	USAFAcad	Sijan, Lance Peter	1942
Vandenberg Hall	USAFAcad	Vandenberg, Hoyt S.	1899
Chase Hall	USCGAcad	Chase, Salmon P.	1808
Dimick Hall	USCGAcad	Dimick, Chester E.	1875c
Hamilton Hall	USCGAcad	Hamilton, Alexander	1755c
Henriques Room	USCGAcad	Henriques, John A.	1826
Johnson Hall	USCGAcad	Johnson, Harvey F.	1882
Leamy Hall	USCGAcad	Leamy, Frank	1900
McAllister Hall	USCGAcad	McAllister, Charles Albert	1867
Michel Hall	USCGAcad	Michel, Carl	1890
Munro Hall	USCGAcad	Munro, Douglas Albert	1919
Satterlee Hall	USCGAcad	Satterlee, Charles	1875c
Smith Hall	USCGAcad	Smith, Edward H. "Iceberg"	1889
Waesche Hall	USCGAcad	Waesche, Russell R.	1886

Yeaton Hall	USCGAcad	Yeaton, Hopley	1739
Arvin Gym	USMAcad	Arvin, Robert	1943
Blaik Field	USMAcad	Blaik, Earl "Red" "Colonel"	1897
Cristl Arena	USMAcad	Cristl, Edward C., Jr.	1922c
Cullum Hall	USMAcad	Cullum, George Washington	1809
Doubleday Field	USMAcad	Doubleday, Abner	1819
Eisenhower Hall & Eisenhower Monument	USMAcad	Eisenhower, Dwight David	1890
Gillis Field House	USMAcad	Gillis, William G., Jr.	1919c
Grant Hall	USMAcad	Grant, Ulysses S.	1822
James K. Herbert Alumni Center	USMAcad	Herbert, James K.	1909
Holleder Center	USMAcad	Holleder, Donald W.	1934
Kosciuszko Monument	USMAcad	Kosciuszko, Thaddeus	1746
Lichtenberg Tennis Center	USMAcad	Lichtenberg, Alan	1929c
Lichtenberg Tennis Center	USMAcad	Lichtenberg, Herbert	1933c
MacArthur Monument	USMAcad	MacArthur, Douglas	1880
Michie Stadium	USMAcad	Michie, Dennis Mahan	1870c
Patton Monument	USMAcad	Patton, George Smith, Jr.	1885
Fort Putnam	USMAcad	Putnam, Rufus	1738
Sedgwick Monument	USMAcad	Sedgwick, John	1813
Shea Stadium	USMAcad	Shea, Richard Thomas	1927
Tate Rink	USMAcad	Tate, Joseph S.	1919c
Tate Rink	USMAcad	Tate, Frederick H.S.	1920c
Thayer Monument	USMAcad	Thayer, Sylvanus	1785
Washington Monument	USMAcad	Washington, George	1732
Armel-Leftwich Visitor Center	USNAcad	Armel, Lyle	1931
Armel-Leftwich Visitor Center	USNAcad	Leftwich, William Groom	1931
Bancroft Hall	USNAcad	Bancroft, George	1800

Wesley Brown Field House	USNAcad	Brown, Wesley	1927
Chauvenet Walk /Hall	USNAcad	Chauvenet, William	1815c
Robert Crown Sailing Center	USNAcad	Crown, Robert	1935c
Dahlgren Hall	USNAcad	Dahlgren, John Adolphus	1809
Dewey Basin & Dewey Field	USNAcad	Dewey, George	1837
Farragut Field	USNAcad	Farragut, David Glascow	1800c
Halligan Hall	USNAcad	Halligan, John, Jr.	1876
Halsey Field House	USNAcad	Halsey, William Frederick, Jr. "Bull"	1882
Herndon Monument	USNAcad	Herndon, William Louis	1813
Hubbard Hall	USNAcad	Hubbard, John	1848c
Ingram Field	USNAcad	Ingram, Jonas Howard	1886
Isherwood Hall	USNAcad	Isherwood, Benjamin Franklin	1822
King Hall	USNAcad	King, Ernest J.	1878
Lawrence Field	USNAcad	Lawrence, James	1781
Leahy Hall	USNAcad	Leahy, William Daniel	1875
Lejeune Hall	USNAcad	Lejeune, John A.	1867
Commodore Uriah P. Levy Center	USNAcad	Levy, Uriah P.	1792
Luce Hall	USNAcad	Luce, Stephen B.	1827
MacDonough Hall	USNAcad	MacDonough, Thomas	1783
Mahan Hall	USNAcad	Mahan, Alfred Thayer	1840
Maury Hall	USNAcad	Maury, Matthew Fontaine	1806
Melville Hall	USNAcad	Melville, George W.	1841
Michelson Hall	USNAcad	Michelson, Albert Abraham	1852
Rip Miller Field	USNAcad	Miller, Edgar E. "Rip"	1901
Mitscher Hall	USNAcad	Mitscher, Marc Andrew "Pete"	1877
Nimitz Library	USNAcad	Nimitz, Chester William	1885

Norman Scott Natatorium	USNAcad	Scott, Norman	1889c
Preble Hall	USNAcad	Preble, Edward	1761
Ricketts Hall	USNAcad	Ricketts, Claude Vernon	1907c
Rickover Hall	USNAcad	Rickover, Hyman G.	1900
Samson Hall	USNAcad	Samson, William	1840
Tecumseh Court	USNAcad	Techumseh	1785c
Thompson Stadium	USNAcad	Thompson, Robert Means	1849
Ward Hall	USNAcad	Ward, James H.	1806
Glenn Warner Soccer Center	USNAcad	Warner, Glenn	1922c
Wilson Park (Smoke Park)	USNAcad	Wilson, Henry Brad	1861
Worden Field	USNAcad	Worden, John Lorimer	1818

"c" indicates Best Guess